James Cox

My Native Land, The United States

It's Wonders, Beauties, And it's People

James Cox

My Native Land, The United States
It's Wonders, Beauties, And it's People

ISBN/EAN: 9783744708906

Printed in Europe, USA, Canada, Australia, Japan

Cover: Foto ©ninafisch / pixelio.de

More available books at **www.hansebooks.com**

Statue to Minute Man.

MY NATIVE LAND.

The United States: its Wonders, its Beauties, and its People;
with Descriptive Notes, Character Sketches, Folk
Lore, Traditions, Legends and History, for
the Amusement of the Old and the
Instruction of the Young.

... BY ...

JAMES COX,

Author of "Our Own Country," "Missouri at the World's Fair," "Old and New
St. Louis," "An Arkansas Eden," "Oklahoma Revisited," Etc.

*"Breathes there a man with soul so dead
Who never to himself has said,
This is my own, my native land."*

PROFUSELY ILLUSTRATED.

ST. LOUIS:
Published by The Blair Publishing Co.
1895.

CONTENTS.

CHAPTER I.

OUR NATION'S BIRTH.

The Story of Liberty Bell—Impartial Opinions on the Revolutionary War—The Shot that was Heard Around the World—The First Committee of Safety—A Defeat which Equaled a Victory—Washington's Earnestness—To Congress on Horseback—The First 4th of July Celebration.

CHAPTER II.

THE WITCH OF SALEM.

A Relic of Religious Bigotry—Parson Lawson's Tirade against Witchcraft—Extraordinary Court Records of Old Puritan Days—Alleged Supernatural Conjuring—A Man and his Wife both put to Death—Crushed for Refusing to Plead—A Romance of the Old Days of Witch Persecution.

CHAPTER III.

IN PICTURESQUE NEW YORK.

Some Local Errors Corrected—A Trip Down the Hudson River—The Last of the Mohicans—The Home of Rip Van Winkle—The Ladies of Vassar and their Home—West Point and its History—Sing Sing Prison—The Falls of Niagara—Indians in New York State.

CONTENTS.

CHAPTER IV.

IN THE CENTER OF THE COUNTRY.

The Geographical Center of the United States, and its Location West of the Mississippi River—The Center of Population—History of Fort Riley—The Gallant "Seventh"—Early Troubles of Kansas—Extermination of the Buffalo—But a Few Survivors out of Many Millions.

CHAPTER V.

THE MORMONS AND THEIR WIVES.

The Pilgrimage Across the Bad Lands to Utah—Incidents of the March—Success of the New Colony—Religious Persecutions—Murder of an Entire Family—The Curse of Polygamy—An Ideal City—Humors of Bathing in Great Salt Lake.

CHAPTER VI.

THE INVASION OF OKLAHOMA.

A History of the Indian Nation—Early Struggles of Oklahoma Boomers—Fight between Home-Seekers and Soldiers—Scenes at the Opening of Oklahoma Proper—A Miserable Night on the Prairie—A Race for Homes—Lawlessness in the Old Indian Territory.

CHAPTER VII.

COWBOYS—REAL AND IDEAL.

A Much Maligned Class—The Cowboy as he Is, and as he is Supposed to be—Prairie Fever and how it is Cured—

CONTENTS.

Life on the Ranch Thirty Years Ago and Now—Singular Fashions and Changes of Costume—Troubles Encountered by would-be Bad Men.

CHAPTER VIII.

WARDS OF OUR NATIVE LAND.

The Indians' Admirers and Critics—At School and After—Indian Courtship and Marriage—Extraordinary Dances—Gambling by Instinct—How "Cross-Eye" Lost his Pony—Pawning a Baby—Amusing and Degrading Scenes on Annuity Day.

CHAPTER IX.

CIVILIZATION—ACTUAL AND ALLEGED.

Tried in the Balances and Found Wanting—Indian Archers—Bow and Arrow Lore—Barbarous Customs that Die Slowly—"Great Wolf," the Indian Vanderbilt—How the Seri were Taught a Valuable Lesson—Playing with Rattlesnakes with Impunity.

CHAPTER X.

OLD TIME COMMUNISTS.

Houses on Rocks and Sand Hills—How Many Families Dwelt Together in Unity—Peculiarities of Costumes—Pueblo Architecture and Folk Lore—A Historic Struggle and how it Ended—Legends Concerning Montezuma—Curious Religious Ceremonies.

CONTENTS.

CHAPTER XI.

HOW CUSTER LIVED AND DIED.

"Remember Custer"—An Eye-Witness of the Massacre—Custer, Cody and Alexis—A Ride over the Scenes of the Unequal Conflict—Major Reno's Marked Failure—How "Sitting Bull" Ran Away and Lived to Fight Another Day—Why a Medicine Man did not Summon Rain.

CHAPTER XII.

AMONG THE CREOLES.

Meaning of the word "Creole"—An Old Aristocratic Relic—The Venice of America—Origin of the Creole Carnivals—Rex and his Annual Disguises—Creole Balls—The St. Louis Veiled Prophets—The French Market and other Landmarks in New Orleans—A Beautiful Ceremony and an Unfinished Monument.

CHAPTER XIII.

THE HEATHEN CHINEE IN HIS ELEMENT.

A Trip to Chinatown, San Francisco—A House with a History—Narrow Alleys and Secret Doors—Opium Smoking and its Effects—The Highbinders—Celestial Theatricals—Chinese Festivals—The Brighter Side of a Great City—A Mammoth Hotel and a Beautiful Park.

CHAPTER XIV.

BEFORE EMANCIPATION AND AFTER.

First Importation of Negro Slaves into America—The Original Abolitionists—A Colored Enthusiast and a Coward—Origin of the word "Secession"—John Brown's Fanati-

CONTENTS.

cism—Uncle Tom's Cabin—Faithful unto Death—George Augustus Sala on the Negro who Lingered too long in the Mill Pond.

CHAPTER XV.

OUR NATIONAL PARK.

A Delightful Rhapsody—Early History of Yellowstone Park—A Fish Story which Convulsed Congress—The First White Man to Visit the Park—A Race for Life—Philosophy of the Hot Springs—Mount Everts—From the Geysers to Elk Park—Some Old Friends and New Ones—Yellowstone Lake—The Angler's Paradise.

CHAPTER XVI.

THE HEROES OF THE IRON HORSE.

Honor to whom Honor is Due—A Class of Men Not Always Thoroughly Appreciated at their Worth—An Amateur's Ride on a Flying Locomotive—From Twelve Miles an Hour to Six Times that Speed—The Signal Tower and the Men who Work in it—Stealing a Train—A Race with Steam—Stories about Bewitched Locomotives and Providential Escapes.

CHAPTER XVII.

A RAILROAD TO THE CLOUDS.

Early History of Manitou—Zebulon Pike's Important Discovery—A Young Medicine Man's Peril and Final Triumph—A Health Resort in Years Gone By—The Garden of the Gods—The Railroad up Pike's Peak—Early Failures and Final Success—The Most Remarkable Road in the World—Riding Above the Clouds.

CONTENTS.

CHAPTER XVIII.

INTO THE BOWELS OF THE EARTH.

The Grand Cañon of the Colorado—Niagara Outdone—The Course of the Colorado River—A Survey Party Through the Cañon—Experiences of a Terrible Night—Wonderful Contrasts of Color in the Massive Rocks—A Natural Wall a Thousand Feet High—Hieroglyphics which have Never been Deciphered—Relics of a Superior Race—Conjecture as to the Origin of the Ancient Bearded White Men.

CHAPTER XIX.

OUR GREAT WATERWAYS.

Importance of Rivers to Commerce a Generation Ago—The Ideal River Man—The Great Mississippi River and its Importance to our Native Land—The Treacherous Missouri—A First Mate who Found a Cook's Disguise very Convenient—How a Second Mate got over the Inconvenience of Temporary Financial Embarrassment.

CHAPTER XX.

THROUGH THE GREAT NORTHWEST.

The Importance of Some of our Newest States—Romantic History of Montana—The Bad Lands and their Exact Opposite—Civilization Away Up in the Mountains—Indians who have Never Quarreled with White Men—Traditions Concerning Mount Tacoma—Wonderful Towns of the Extreme Northwest—A State Shaped like a Large Chair—The Falls of Shoshone.

CONTENTS.

CHAPTER XXI.

IN THE WARM SOUTHEAST.

Florida and its Appropriate Name—The First Portions of North America Discovered by White Men—Early Vicissitudes of its Explorers—An Enormous Coast Line—How Key West came to be a great Cigar Town—The Suwanee River—St. Augustine and its World-Renowned Hotel—Old Fort Marion.

LIST OF ILLUSTRATIONS.

Statue to Minute Man,	Frontispiece
Interior of Independence Hall, Philadelphia,	Page 17
Tomb of General Grant, Riverside Park,	" 35
A Memory of Rip Van Winkle,	" 53
The Exact Center of United States,	" 71
Brigham Young's Grave, Salt Lake City,	" 89
Chief Rain-in-the-Face and his Favorite Pony,	" 107
The Cowboy as He Is,	" 125
Civilized Indians,	" 143
An Uncivilized Savage,	" 161
The Belle of the Pueblo,	" 179
Custer Battlefield and Monument,	" 197
The Old French Market at New Orleans,	" 215
The Prettiest Chinese Woman in America,	" 233
Yellowstone Falls,	" 251
In and Around Yellowstone Park,	" 269
A Marvel of Magnificence,	" 287
Climbing Pike's Peak by Rail,	" 305
Hieroglyphic Memoirs of Past Ages,	" 323
A Fin de Siecle Pleasure Steamer,	" 341
Whaleback Steamer on the Lakes,	" 359
Two Views of Mount Tacoma,	" 377
A Restful Southern Home,	" 395

MY NATIVE LAND.

CHAPTER I.

OUR NATION'S BIRTH.

The Story of Liberty Bell — Impartial Opinions on the Revolutionary War — The Shot that was Heard Around the World — The First Committee of Safety — A Defeat which Equaled a Victory — Washington's Earnestness — To Congress on Horseback — The First 4th of July Celebration.

IT was not until April 19th, 1775, that the shot was fired which was "heard around the world." But the struggle for American Independence was really started nearly a quarter of a century earlier, when on the afternoon of August 27th, 1753, Liberty Bell was rung to call together the Assembly of the Province of Pennsylvania.

In the old days of town meetings, training days, town schools and Puritans, bells took a more prominent part in public affairs than they do to-day. It was usual to call the people together for purposes of deliberation by means of a village or town bell, and of these bells the one to which we refer was the most important and interesting. Liberty Bell is well named. It was ordered in the year 1751, and it was delivered a year later. Shortly afterwards, it cracked, and had to be recast, but in June, 1753, it was finally hung in the Pennsylvania State House at Philadelphia. It has never been removed from the building except on two occasions. The first of these was in 1777, when it was taken to Allentown for safety, and the second in 1885, when it was exhibited at New Orleans.

This bell, which sounded the death-blow to tyranny and oppression, was first rung to call together the Assembly, which immediately resolved to insist upon certain rights which had been denied the colonists by the British Crown. Eighteen months later, it was again rung to announce the meeting at which the rights of the colonists were sternly defined and insisted upon. In 1765, it convened the meeting of the Assembly at which it was resolved to be represented at the Congress of the Colonies in New York, and a month later it was muffled and tolled when the "Royal Charlotte" arrived, bearing the much-hated stamps, whose landing was not permitted. Again it rang muffled, when the Stamp Act went into operation, and when the people publicly burned stamp papers. In 1768, the Liberty Bell called a meeting of the men of Philadelphia, who protested once again against the oppression of government without representation. In 1771, it called the Assembly together to petition the King of England for the repeal of the duty on tea, and two years later it summoned together the largest crowd ever seen in Philadelphia up to that date. At that meeting it was resolved that the ship "Polly," loaded with tea, should not be allowed to land.

In 1774, the bell was muffled and tolled on the closing of the Port of Boston, and in the following year it convened the memorable meeting following the battle of Lexington. On this occasion 8,000 people assembled in the State House yard and unanimously agreed to associate for the purpose of defending, with arms, their lives, liberty and property against all attempts to deprive them of them.

In June, 1776, Liberty Bell announced the submission to Congress of the draft of the Declaration of Independence, and on July 4th of the same year, the same bell announced the signing of the Declaration. On July 8th of the same year, the bell was tolled vigorously for the great proclamation of America's Independence. The tolling was suspended while the Declaration was read, and was once more rung when that immortal document had been thus formally promulgated.

In April, 1783, Liberty Bell rang the proclamation of Peace, and on July 4th, 1826, it ushered in the year of Jubilee.

The last tolling of the bell was in July, 1835, when, while slowly tolling, and without any apparent reason, the bell, which had played such an important part in the War of Independence, and in the securing of liberty for the people of this great country, parted through its side, making a large rent, which can still be clearly seen. It was as though the bell realized that its great task was accomplished, and that it could leave to other and younger bells, the minor duties which remained to be performed.

This is not a history of the United States, but is rather a description of some of the most interesting and remarkable features to be found in various parts of it. It is difficult, however, to describe scenes and buildings without at least brief historical reference, and as we present an excellent illustration of the apartment in which the Declaration of Independence was signed, we are compelled to make a brief reference to the circumstances and events which preceded that most important event in the world's history.

As we have seen, the conflict between the home country and the colonies commenced long before there was any actual outbreak. As Mr. Thomas Wentworth Higginson so graphically expresses it, the surrender of Canada to England by France in 1763 suddenly opened men's eyes to the fact that British America had become a country so large as to make England seem ridiculously small. Even the cool-headed Dr. Franklin, writing that same year to Mary Stevenson in London, spoke of England as "that stone in a brook, scarce enough of it above water to keep one's shoes dry." A far-seeing French statesman of the period looked at the matter in the same way. Choiseul, the Prime Minister who ceded Canada, claimed afterwards that he had done it in order to destroy the British nation by creating for it a rival. This assertion was not made till ten years later, and may very likely have been an afterthought, but it was destined to be confirmed by the facts.

We have now to deal with the outbreak of a contest which was, according to the greatest of the English statesmen of the period, "a most accursed, wicked, barbarous, cruel, unnatural, unjust, and diabolical war." No American writer ever employed to describe it a combination of adjectives so vigorous as those brought together by the elder Pitt, afterwards Lord Chatham. The rights for which Americans fought seemed to him to be the common rights of Englishmen, and many Englishmen thought the same.

On the other hand, we are now able to do justice to those American Loyalists who honestly believed that the attempt at independence was a mad one, and who sacrificed all they had rather than rebel against their King. Massachusettensis, the well-known Tory pamphleteer, wrote that the annals of the world had not been deformed with a

Interior of Independence Hall, Philadelphia.

single instance of so unnatural, so causeless, so wanton, so wicked a rebellion.

These strong epithets used on both sides show how strangely opinions were divided as to the rebellion and its causes. Some of the first statesmen of England defended the colonists, and some of the best known men in the colonies defended England.

The City of Boston at this time had a population of about seventeen thousand, as compared with some half a million to-day. In its garrison there were three thousand British troops, and the laws of Parliament were enforced rigidly. The city suffered temporary commercial death in consequence, and there were the most vigorous efforts made to prevent an open outbreak of hostilities. In January, 1775, a conflict was barely averted at Marshfield, and in the following month the situation was so strained at Salem that nothing but great forbearance and presence of mind on the part of the colonists prevented bloodshed. The Boston massacre of less than five years before was still uppermost in men's thoughts, and it was determined that the responsibility of the first shot in the war, if war there must be, should rest with the Royal troops.

Accordingly, the colonists accepted insult and abuse until they were suspected by the British troops of cowardice. One officer wrote home telling his friends that there was no danger of war, because the colonists were bullies, but not fighters, adding that any two regiments ought to be decimated which could not beat the entire force arrayed against them. But the conflict could not be long delayed. It was on April 18th, 1775, that Paul Revere rode his famous ride. He had seen the two lights in a church steeple in Boston, which had been agreed upon as a signal that the British troops were about to seize the supplies of the patriots at Concord. Sergeant Monroe's caution against making unnecessary noise, was met by his rejoinder, "You will have noise enough here before long—the regulars are coming out."

Then he commenced his ride for life, or, rather, for the lives of others. We all know the result of his ride, and how church bells were tolled and signal shots fired to warn the people that the soldiers were coming. It was a night of tumult and horror, no one knowing what brutality they had to expect from the now enraged British soldiers. The women of the towns, warned by the pre-arranged signals, hurried their children from their homes, and fled to farm houses, and even barns in the vicinity. Before daybreak the British troops had reached Lexington Green. Here they found Captain Parker and 38 men standing up before twenty times that number of armed troops, indifferent as to their fate, but determined to protect their cause and their friends. The Captain's words have passed into history. They took the form of an order to the men:

"Don't fire unless you are fired on; but, if they want a war, let it begin here."

History tells us of few such unequal contests as this. The troops fired on the gallant little band, and seven of their number were killed. The fight at Concord followed, when 450 Americans met the British troops at the North Bridge, where

"Once the embattled farmers stood,
And fired the shot heard around the world."

The British detachment was beaten back in disorder, but the main body was too strong to be attacked. The minute men, however, made a most magnificent fight, and at the close of the day they had killed 273 British soldiers, only 93 of their own number being among the killed or missing.

Thus commenced the War of Independence, the event being described by Dr. Joseph Warren in a document of sufficient interest to warrant its reproduction in full.

"The barbarous murders committed on our innocent brethren," wrote the doctor, "have made it absolutely necessary that we immediately raise an army to defend our wives and our children from the butchering hands of an inhuman soldiery, who, incensed at the obstacles they met with in their bloody progress, and enraged at being repulsed from the field of slaughter, will, without the least doubt, take the first opportunity in their power to ravage this devoted country with fire and sword. We conjure you, therefore, by all that is dear, by all that is sacred, that you give all assistance possible in forming an army. Our all is at stake. Death and devastation are the instant consequences of delay. Every moment is infinitely precious. An hour lost may deluge our country in blood, and entail perpetual slavery upon the few of your posterity who may survive the carnage. We beg and entreat, as you will answer to your country, to your own consciences, and, above all, as you will answer to God himself, that you will hasten and encourage, by all possible means, the enlistment of men to form an army, and send them forward to headquarters at Cambridge, with that expedition which the vast importance and instant urgency of the affair demand."

Two days after the fight, the Massachusetts Committee of Safety resolved to enlist 8,000 men, an event which our old friend Liberty Bell celebrated by a vigorous tolling. All over the colonies a spirit of determination to resist spread like lightning, and the shot that was heard around the world was certainly heard very distinctly in every nook and corner of New England, and of the old Atlantic States. Naturally, there was at first a lack of concentration and even of discipline; but what was lacking in these features was more than made up for by bravery and determination. As John Adams wrote in 1818, the army at Cambridge at this time was not a National army, for there was no nation. It was not even an army of the United Colonies, because the Congress at Philadelphia had not adopted or acknowledged the army at Cambridge. It was not even the New England army, for each State had its separate armies, which had united to imprison the British army in Boston. There was not even the Commander-in-Chief of the allied armies.

These anomalies, of course, righted themselves rapidly. Gage's proclamation of martial law expedited the battle at Bunker Hill, which was brought about by the impatience of the British troops, and by the increased confidence among the colonists, resulting from the fights at Lexington and Concord. It is true, of course, that the untrained American troops failed to vanquish the British army at Bunker Hill, but the monument at that spot celebrates the fact that for two hours the attacks of the regulars were withstood. A prominent English newspaper described the battle as one of innumerable errors on the part of the British. As William Tudor wrote so graphically, "The Ministerial troops gained the hill, but were victorious losers. A few more such victories and they are undone." Many writers have been credited with the authorship of a similar sentiment, written from the American standpoint. "It is true that we were beaten, but it will not take many such defeats to accomplish a magnificent victory."

What began to be known as the great American army increased in strength. It was adopted by Congress, and George Washington placed in command. Under the historic elm tree at Cambridge, Mass., which was the scene of so many important councils in the first hours of the life of the United States, he assumed the authority bestowed upon him with this office, and a week later he held a council with his officers. He found some 17,000 men at his command, whom he described as a mixed multitude of people under very little discipline.

William Emerson, grandfather of the great poet, in a soliloquy on the strange turn events had taken, said "Who would have thought, twelve months past, that all Cambridge and Charleston would be covered over with American camps and cut up into forts and entrenchments, and all the lands, fields and orchards laid common, with horses and cattle feeding on the choicest mowing land, and large parks of well-regulated locusts cut down for firewood. This, I must say, looks a little melancholy. It is very diverting to walk among the camps. They are as different in their look as the owners are in their dress, and every tent is a portraiture of the temper and tastes of the persons who encamp in it. Some are made of boards and some of sailcloth; some partly of one and some partly of the other; again, others are made of stone and turf, brick or brush. Some are thrown up in a hurry, others curiously wrought with doors and windows, done with wreaths and withes, in the manner of a basket. Some are proper tents, looking like the regular camp of the enemy. In these are the Rhode Islanders, who are furnished with tent equipages and everything in the most exact English style. However, I think this great variety is rather a beauty than a blemish in the army."

As was to be expected, there was more or less of a lack of harmony and unity among the companies of men collected together to form an army to fight for liberty. History tells us that there was even a little jealousy between the four New England colonies. There was also a good deal of distrust of Washington. It was argued that at least one-third of the class from which he came had Tory and Royalist inclinations, and what guarantee had they that Washington was not one of their number? Washington himself found that those who styled themselves in old country parlance "The Gentry," were loyal to King George rather than to the colonies, and while his own men were inclined, at times, to doubt the sincerity of the Father of his Country, the very men with whom he was suspected of being in sympathy were denouncing him with vigor.

Washington, to his lasting credit be it said, was indifferent both to praise and censure. Seeing that discipline was the one thing needful, he commenced to enforce it with an iron hand. He declined any remuneration, and gave his services freely to the cause. He found himself short of ammunition, and several times he lost a number of his men. In the spring of 1776, Washington went to New York with his Continental army. Here he found new difficulties, and met with a series of mishaps. The failure of the advance into Canada during the winter had hurt materially, but the bravery of the troops in the Carolinas came as a grand encouragement.

We need not trace further the progress of the war, or note how, through many discouragements and difficulties, the cause of right was made to triumph over the cause of might. We will pass on to note a few of the interesting facts in connection with the signing of the Declaration of Independence. To-day, our Senators and Congressmen travel to the National Capital in Pullman cars, surrounded by every luxury that wealth and influence can bring them.

In the days of the Continental Congress it required a good deal more nerve to fulfill one's duty. The delegate had to journey to Congress on horseback. Sometimes he could find a little country inn at which he could sleep at night, but at others he had to camp in the open as best he could. Frequently a friendly warning would cause him to make a detour of several miles in order to escape some threatened danger, and, altogether, his march to the capital was far from being triumphant.

At this particular period the difficulties were more than usually great. The delegates arrived at Philadelphia jaded and tired. They found stable room for their horses, made the best toilet possible, and found their way at once to Independence Hall, where opinions were exchanged. On the 7th of June, Richard Henry Lee of Virginia submitted a series of resolutions, under the instructions of the Virginia Assembly—resolutions which, it may be stated, pledged the colonies to carry on the war until the English were entirely driven out of the country. Congress declared deliberately that the United States was absolved from all allegiance to the British Crown, and it then proceeded to burn its bridges, by declaring the expediency of taking effectual measures for forming foreign alliances. John

Adams seconded the resolutions, which were not passed without debate.

Delegates from New York, Pennsylvania and South Carolina opposed the proposition very vigorously, one member stating that it required the impudence of a New Englander for them, in their disjointed state, to propose a treaty to a nation now at peace; that no reason could be assigned for pressing this measure but the reason of every madman—a show of spirit. John Adams defended the resolutions, claiming that they proclaimed objects of the most stupendous magnitude, in which the lives and liberties of millions yet unborn were infinitely interested. Finally, the consideration was postponed, to be passed almost unanimously on July 2d. John Adams was most enthusiastic over this result, and, writing to his wife on the subject, he said:

"The 2d day of July, 1776, will be the most memorable epoch in the history of America. I am apt to believe that it will be celebrated by succeeding generations as the great anniversary festival. It ought to be commemorated as a day of deliverance, by solemn acts of devotion to God Almighty, from one end of the continent to the other, from this time forward, forevermore."

But although the day referred to by John Adams saw the thirteen colonies become independent States, it is July the 4th that the country celebrates. On that day the Declaration of Independence was promulgated. This marvelous document was prepared by Jefferson in a small brick house, which then stood out in the fields, but which is now known as the southwest corner of Market and Seventh Streets, Philadelphia. It is situated within about four hundred yards of Independence Square. In his little room in this house, on a very small writing desk, which is still in existence, Jefferson drafted the title deed of our liberties. He wrote without reference of any kind, merely placing upon paper the succession of thoughts which had been paramount in his mind for years. In the original document, as submitted by Jefferson, there appeared a stern condemnation of the "piratical warfare against human nature itself," as slavery was described. This was stricken out by Congress, and finally the document, as amended, was adopted by the vote of twelve colonies, New York declining to vote.

We give an illustration of the Interior of Independence Hall. Here it was that the Declaration was signed. According to some authorities the signing did not take place on July 4th, while according to others it did. Some records seem to show that fifty-four of the fifty-six names were attached to the parchment on August 2d. Jefferson frequently stated that the signing of the Declaration was hastened by a very trivial circumstance. Near the Hall there was a large stable, where flies abounded. All the delegates wore silk stockings, and were thus in a condition to be easily annoyed by flies. The heat was intolerable, and a tremendous invasion by the little pests, who were not retarded by fly screens or mosquito bars, drove the legislators almost frantic, and caused them to append their signatures to the document with almost indecent haste.

However this may be, the Declaration was finally signed, and Liberty Bell proclaimed the fact to all within hearing. John Hancock, we are told, referred to his almost schoolboy signature with a smile, saying that John Bull could read his name without spectacles. Franklin is said to have remarked that they must all hang together, or else most assuredly they would all hang separately—a play upon words showing that the patriot's sense of humor was too admirably developed to be dimmed even by an event of this magnitude.

There were rejoicings on every hand that the great act had been accomplished. A very pleasing story tells of how an aged bell-ringer waited breathlessly to announce to waking thousands the vote of Congress. This story has since been denied, and it seems evident that the vote was not announced until the following day, when circulars were issued to the people. On July 6th, the Declaration was printed in a Philadelphia newspaper, and on the 8th, John Nixon read the Declaration in the yard of Independence Hall. On the same day, the Royal Arms over the door of the Supreme Court Room were torn down, and the trophies thus secured burned.

The first 4th of July celebration of which we have any record, took place two years after the signing. General Howe had left the city shortly before, and every one was feeling bright and happy. In the diary of one of the old patriots who took part in this unique celebration, appears the following quaint, and even picturesque, description of the events of the day:

"On the glorious 4th of July (1778), I celebrated in the City Tavern, with my brother delegates of Congress and a number of other gentlemen, amounting, in whole, to about eighty, the anniversary of Independency. The entertainment was elegant and well conducted. There were four tables spread; two of them extended the whole length of the room; the other two crossed them at right angles. At the end of the room, opposite the upper table, was erected an Orchestra. At the head of the upper table, and at the

President's right hand, stood a large baked pudding, in the center of which was planted a staff, on which was displayed a crimson flag, in the midst of which was this emblematic device: An eye, denoting Providence; a label, on which was inscribed, 'An appeal to Heaven;' a man with a drawn sword in his hand, and in the other the Declaration of Independence, and at his feet a scroll inscribed, 'The declaratory acts.' As soon as the dinner began, the music, consisting of clarionets, hautboys, French horns, violins and bass-viols, opened and continued, making proper pauses, until it was finished. Then the toasts, followed by a discharge of field-pieces, were drank, and so the afternoon ended. On the evening there was a cold collation and a brilliant exhibition of fireworks. The street was crowded with people during the exhibition.

"What a strange vicissitude in human affairs! These, but a few years since colonies of Great Britain, are now free, sovereign, and independent States, and now celebrate the anniversary of their independence in the very city where, but a day or two before, General Howe exhibited his ridiculous Champhaitre."

Independence Hall remains to-day in a marvelous state of preservation. At the great Centennial Exposition, held to celebrate the hundredth anniversary of the events to which we have alluded in this chapter, tens of thousands of people passed through the room in which the Declaration of Independence was signed, and gazed with mingled feelings upon the historical bell, which, although it had long outlived its usefulness, had in days gone by done such grand proclaiming of noble truth, sentiment and action. Up to quite a recent date, justice was administered in the old building, but most of the courts have now been moved to the stately structure modern Philadelphia is now erecting at the cost of some $16,000,000.

Independence Hall and Independence Square are lovingly cared for, and visitors from all nations are careful to include them both in their tour of sight-seeing while in this country. Within the Hall they find old parchments and Eighteenth Century curiosities almost without number, and antiquarians find sufficient to interest and amuse them for several days in succession. Every lover of his native land, no matter what that land may be, raises his hat in reverence when in this ancient and memory-inspiring building, and he must be thoughtless, indeed, who can pass through it without paying at least a mental tribute of respect to the memories of the men who were present at the birth of the greatest nation the world has ever seen, and who secured for the people of the United States absolute liberty.

The illustration of the interior of Independence Hall on page 17, was furnished for use in this work by the National Company of St. Louis, publishers of "Our Own Country," a large work descriptive of a tour throughout the most picturesque sections of the United States. The letter-press in "Our Own Country" was written by the author of this work, and it is one of the finest tributes to the picturesqueness of America that has ever been published. Other illustrations in this work were also kindly supplied by the same publishing house.

CHAPTER II.

THE WITCHES OF SALEM.

A Relic of Religious Bigotry — Parson Lawson's Tirade Against Witchcraft—Extraordinary Court Records of Old Puritan Days—Alleged Supernatural Conjuring—A Man and his Wife both put to Death—Crushed for Refusing to Plead—A Romance of the Old Days of Witch Persecution.

AMONG the curiosities of New England shown to tourists and visitors, is the original site of some of the extraordinary trials and executions for witchcraft in the town of Salem, now known as Danvers, Mass. Looking back upon the events of two hundred years ago, the prosecution of the alleged witches appears to us to have been persecution of the most infamous type. The only justification for the stern Puritans is the fact that they inherited their ideas of witchcraft and its evils from their forefathers, and from the country whence most of them came.

One of the earliest precepts of religious bigotry was, "Thou shalt not allow a witch to live," and from time immemorial witchcraft appears to have been a capital offense. It is on record that thousands of people have, from time to time, been legally murdered for alleged intercourse and leaguing with the Evil One. The superstition seems to have gained force rather than lost it by the spread of early Christianity. As a rule, the victims of the craze were women, and the percentage of aged and infirm women was always very large. One of the greatest jurists of

England, during the Seventeenth Century, condemned two young girls to the gallows for no other offense than the alleged crime of having exerted a baneful influence over certain victims, and having, what would be called in certain districts, "hoodooed" them.

In Scotland the craze was carried to still further lengths. To be accused of witchcraft was to be condemned as a matter of course, and the terrible death of burning at the stake was the invariable sentence. Most of the victims made imaginary confessions, preferring to die at once than to be tortured indefinitely. In the year 1716, a wealthy lady and her nine-year-old daughter were hanged for witchcraft, and even thirty or forty years later the records of Great Britain are sullied by another similar case of persecution.

These unsavory records are given in order to correct a misapprehension as to the part the old Puritans took in the persecutions. Many people seriously believed that the idea of witchcraft, as a capital offense, originated in Salem, and attribute to the original witch-house the reputation of having really given birth to a new superstition and a new persecution. As we have seen, this is entirely erroneous. The fact that the Puritans copied a bad example, instead of setting a new one, should, at least, be remembered in palliation of the unfortunate blot upon their otherwise clean escutcheon.

In the year 1704, one Deodat Lawson, minister at Salem during the last sixteen or seventeen years of the Seventeenth Century, published a remarkable work, entitled "Christ's Fidelity, the only Shield against Satan's Malignity." In this work appears a record of the so-called calamity at Salem, which the author tells us was afflicted, about the year 1692, "with a very sore and grievous infliction, in which they had reason to believe that the Sovereign and Holy God was pleased to permit Satan and his instruments to affright and afflict those poor mortals in such an astonishing and unusual manner."

The record of Parson Lawson is so realistic and emblematic of the times in which he lived, that we reproduce some of his own expressions. Thus, he says, "Now, I having for some time before attended the work of the Ministry in Salem Village, the report of those great afflictions came quickly to my notice, the more so, because the first person afflicted was in the minister's family, who succeeded me after I was removed from them. In pity, therefore, to my Christian friends and former acquaintance there, I was much concerned about them, frequently consulted with them, and (by Divine assistance) prayed for them; but especially my concern was augmented when it was reported at an examination of a person suspected for witchcraft, that my wife and daughter, who died three years before, were sent out of the world under the malicious operations of the infernal powers, as is more fully represented in the following remarks. I did then desire, and was also desired by some concerned in the court, to be there present that I might hear what was alleged in that respect, observing, therefore, when I was amongst them, that the case of the afflicted was very amazing and deplorable, and the charges brought against the accused such as were grounds of suspicion, yet very intricate and difficult to draw up right conclusions about them. They affirmed that they saw the ghosts of several departed persons, who, at their appearing, did instigate them to discover such as (they said) were instruments to hasten their death, threatening sorely to afflict them if they did not make it known to the magistrates.

"They did affirm at the examination, and again at the trial of an accused person, that they saw the ghosts of his two wives (to whom he had acted very ill in their lives, as was proved by several testimonies), and also that they saw the ghosts of my wife and daughter (who died above three years before), and they did affirm that when the very ghosts looked on the prisoner at the bar they looked red, as if the blood would fly out of their faces with indignation at him. The manner of it was thus: Several afflicted being before the prisoner at the bar, on a sudden they fixed all their eyes together on a certain place on the floor before the prisoner, neither moving their eyes nor bodies for some few minutes, nor answering to any question which was asked them. So soon as that trance was over, some being out of sight and hearing, they were all, one after another, asked what they saw, and they did all agree that they saw those ghosts above mentioned. I was present and heard and saw the whole of what passed upon that account during the trial of that person who was accused to be the instrument of Satan's malice therein.

"Sundry pins have been taken out the wrists and arms of the afflicted, and one, in time of examination of a suspected person, had a pin run through both her upper and lower lip when she was called to speak, yet no apparent festering followed thereupon after it was taken out. Some of the afflicted, as they were striving in their fits in open court, have (by invisible means) had their wrists bound together with a real cord, so as it could hardly be taken off without cutting. Some afflicted have been found with their arms tied and hanged upon a hook, from whence

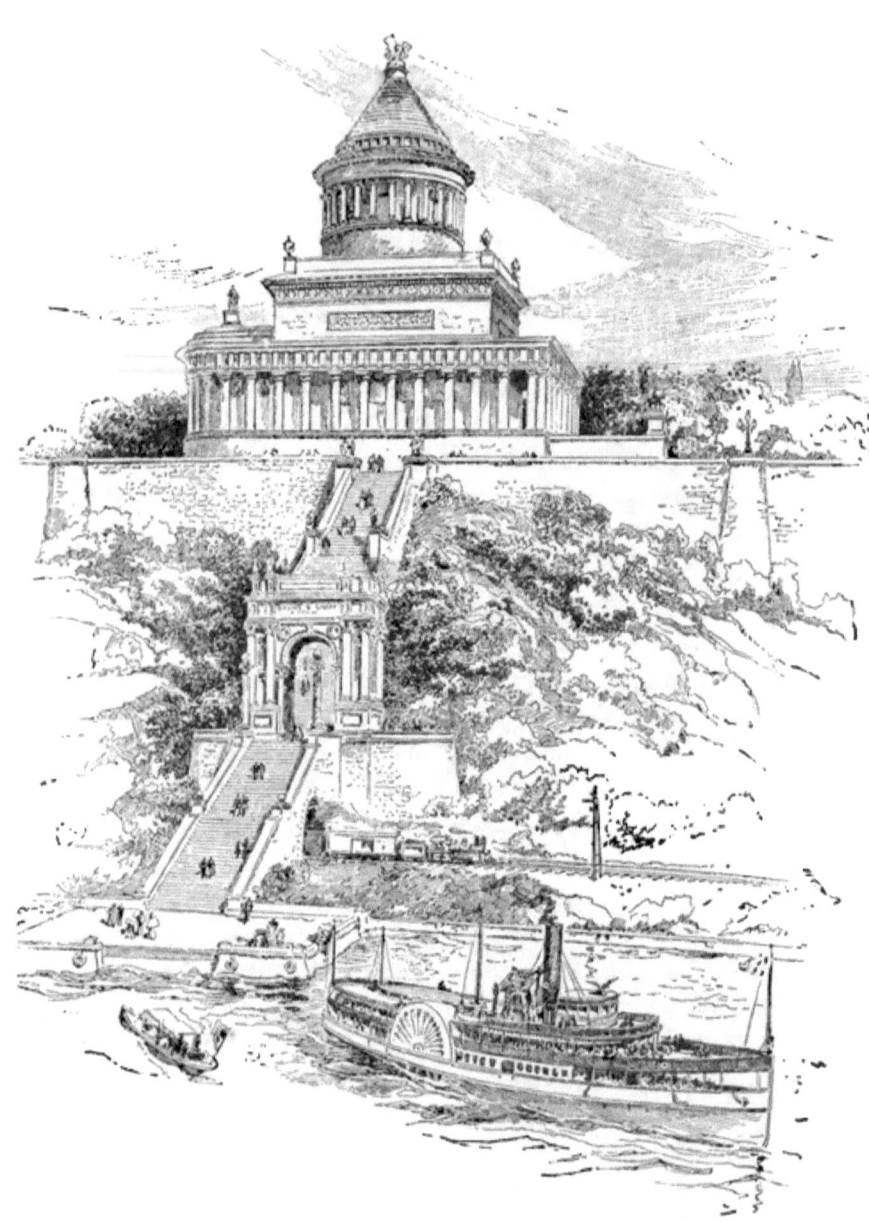

Tomb of General Grant, Riverside Park, New York.

others have been forced to take them down, that they might not expire in that posture. Some afflicted have been drawn under tables and beds by undiscerned force, so as they could hardly be pulled out. And one was drawn half way over the side of a well, and with much difficulty recovered back again. When they were most grievously afflicted, if they were brought to the accused, and the suspected person's hand but laid upon them, they were immediately relieved out of their tortures; but if the accused did but look on them, they were immediately struck down again. Wherefore, they used to cover the face of the accused while they laid their hands on the afflicted, and then it obtained the desired issue. For it hath been experienced (both in examinations and trials) that so soon as the afflicted came in sight of the accused, they were immediately cast into their fits. Yea, though the accused were among the crowd of people, unknown to the sufferers, yet on the first view they were struck down; which was observed in a child of four or five years of age, when it was apprehended that so many as she would look upon, either directly or by turning her head, were immediately struck into their fits.

"An iron spindle of a woolen wheel, being taken very strangely out of an house at Salem Village, was used by a spectre as an instrument of torture to a sufferer, not being discernible to the standers by until it was by the said sufferer snatched out of the spectre's hand, and then it did immediately appear to the persons present to be really the same iron spindle.

"Sometimes, in their fits, they have had their tongues drawn out of their mouths to a fearful length, their heads turned very much over their shoulders, and while they have been so strained in their fits, and had their arms and legs, etc., wrested as if they were quite dislocated, the blood hath gushed plentifully out of their mouths for a considerable time together; which some, that they might be satisfied that it was real blood, took upon their finger and rubbed on their other hand. I saw several together thus violently strained and bleeding in their fits, to my very great astonishment that my fellow mortals should be so grievously distressed by the invisible powers of darkness. For certainly all considerate persons who beheld these things must needs be convinced their motions in their fits were preternatural and involuntary, both as to the manner, which was so strange, as a well person could not (at least without great pain) screw their bodies into; and as to the violence, also, they were preternatural motions, being much beyond the ordinary force of the same persons when they were in their right minds. So that, being such grievous sufferers, it would seem very hard and unjust to censure them of consenting to or holding any voluntary converse or familiarity with the devil.

"Some of them were asked how it came to pass that they were not affrighted when they saw the Black-man. They said they were at first, but not so much afterwards. Some of them affirmed they saw the Black-man sit on the gallows, and that he whispered in the ears of some of the condemned persons when they were just ready to be turned off—even while they were making their last speech.

"Some of them have sundry times seen a White-man appearing among the spectres, and as soon as he appeared, the Black-Witches vanished; they said this White-man had often foretold them what respite they should have from their fits; as, sometimes, a day or two or more, which fell out accordingly. One of the afflicted said she saw him in her fit, and was with him in a glorious place, which had no candle or sun, yet was full of light and brightness, where there was a multitude in 'white, glittering robes,' and they sang the song in Rev. v, 9. She was loth to leave that place and said: 'How long shall I stay here? Let me be along with you.' She was grieved she could stay no longer in that place and company.

"A young woman that was afflicted at a fearful rate had a spectre appear to her with a white sheet wrapped about it, not visible to the standers by, until this sufferer (violently striving in her fit) snatched at, took hold and tore off the corner of that sheet. Her father, being by her, endeavored to lay hold of it with her, that she might retain what she had gotten; but at the passing away of the spectre, he had such a violent twitch of his hand as it would have been torn off. Immediately thereupon appeared in the sufferer's hand the corner of a sheet, a real cloth, visible to the spectators, which (as it is said) remains still to be seen."

It was proved, the records of the time continue, by substantial evidences against one person accused, that he had such an unusual strength (though a very little man) that he could hold out a gun with one hand, behind the lock, which was near seven foot in the barrel, being such as a lusty man could command with both hands, after the usual manner of shooting. It was also proved that he lifted barrels of metal and barrels of molasses out of a canoe alone; and that, putting his fingers into a barrel of molasses, full within a finger's length, according to custom, he carried it several paces. And that he put his finger into the muzzle of a gun which was more than five foot in

the barrel, and lifted up the butt end thereof, lock, stock
and all, without any visible help to raise it. It was also
testified that, being abroad with his wife and his wife's
brother, he occasionally stayed behind, letting his wife and
her brother walk forward; but, suddenly coming up with
them, he was angry with his wife for what discourse had
passed betwixt her and her brother. They wondering how
he should know it, he said: "I know your thoughts," at
which expression they, being amazed, asked him how he
could do that, he said: "My God whom I serve makes
known your thoughts to me."

Some affirmed that there were some hundreds of the
society of witches, considerable companies of whom were
affirmed to muster in arms by beat of drum. In time of
examinations and trials, they declared that such a man was
wont to call them together from all quarters to witch-
meetings, with the sound of a diabolical trumpet.

Being brought to see the prisoners at the bar, upon their
trials, they swore, in open court, that they had oftentimes
seen them at witch meetings, "where was feasting, dancing and jollity, as also at devil sacraments, and particularly
that they saw such a man amongst the accursed crew,
and affirming that he did minister the sacrament of Satan
to them, encouraging them to go on in their way, and that
they should certainly prevail. They said, also, that such a
woman was a deacon and served in distributing the diabolical element. They affirmed that there were great numbers
of the witches."

With such sentiments as these prevailing, it is not at
all remarkable that the alleged witches were treated with
continual and conspicuous brutality. One old lady of
sixty, named Sarah Osburn, was hounded to death for

being a witch. The poor old lady, who was in fairly good circumstances, and appears to have been of good character, was put upon her trial for witchcraft. For three days, more or less ridiculous testimony was given against her, and a number of little children, who had evidently been carefully coached, stated upon the stand that Mrs. Osburn had bewitched them. She was called upon by the court to confess, which she declined to do, stating that she was rather a victim than a criminal. She was sent to jail, and treated with so much brutality that she died before it was possible to execute her in the regulation manner.

Bridget Bishop was another of the numerous victims. The usual charges were brought against her, and she was speedily condemned to death. Before the sentence was executed, the custom of taking council with the local clergy was followed. These good men, while they counseled caution in accepting testimony, humbly recommended the government to the speedy and vigorous prosecution of such as "had rendered themselves obnoxious by infringing the wholesome statutes of the English Nation for the detection of witchcraft." Following this recommendation, double and treble hangings took place, and there was enough brutality to appease the appetite of the most vindictive and malicious.

Perhaps the most extraordinary record of witchcraft persecution at the end of the Seventeenth Century was that of Giles Corey and his wife Martha. The singular feature of the case is, that the husband had been one of the most enthusiastic declaimers against the unholy crime of witchcraft, while his good wife had been rather disposed to ridicule the idea, and to condemn the prosecutions as persecutions. She did her best to prevent Giles from attending trials, and one of the most serious charges against her was that on one occasion she hid the family saddle, so as to prevent her lord and master from riding to one of the examinations.

This attempt to assert woman's rights two hundred years ago was resented very bitterly, and two enthusiastic witch-hunters were sent to her house to entrap her into a confession. On the way they made inquiries, which resulted in their being able to patch up a charge against the woman for walking in ghostly attire during the night. When the detectives called at the house she told them she knew the object of their visit, but that she was no witch, and did not believe there was such a thing. The mere fact of her knowing the object of their visit was regarded as conclusive evidence against her, although a fair-minded person would naturally suggest that, in view of local sentiment, her guess was a very easy one. The poor woman was immediately arrested and placed on trial. Several little children were examined, and these shouted out in the witness-stand, that when the afflicted woman bit her lip in her grief, they were seized with bodily pains, which continued until she loosened her teeth. The chronicles of the court tell us, with much solemnity, that when the woman's hands were tied her victims did not suffer, but the moment the cords were removed they had fits.

Even her husband was called as a witness against her. His evidence does not appear to have been very important or relevant. But another witness, a Mrs. Pope, who appears to have been an expert in these matters, and to have been called at nearly every trial, took off her shoe in court and threw it at the prisoner's head, an act of indecorum which was condoned on the ground of the evident sincerity of the culprit. The poor woman was condemned, as a matter of course, and when she was removed to jail, a deputation from the church of which she was a member called upon her and excommunicated her. She mounted the ladder which led to the gallows with much dignity, and died without any attempt to prolong her life by a confession.

The fate of her husband was still more terrible. Notwithstanding his zeal, and the fact that he had given evidence against his own wife, he was arrested, charged with a similar offense. Whether hypnotic influences were exerted, or whether the examining justices merely imagined things against the prisoner, cannot be known at this time. The court records, however, state that while the witnesses were on the stand, they were so badly afflicted with fits and hurts, that the prisoner's hands had to be tied before they could continue their testimony. Unlike his wife, the poor man did not deny the existence of witchcraft, and merely whined out, in reply to the magistrate's censure, that he was a poor creature and could not help it. The evidence against him was very slight, indeed, and he was remanded to jail, where he lay unmolested, and apparently forgotten, for five or six months.

He was then excommunicated by his church, and brought before the court again. Sojourn in jail seems to have made the old man stubborn, for when he was once more confronted by his persecutors he declined to plead, on the ground that there was no charge against him. An old obsolete English law was revived against him, and the terrible sentence was pronounced that for standing mute he be remanded to the prison from whence he came and put into a low, dark chamber. There he was to be laid on his back, on the bare floor, without clothing. As great a weight of iron as he could bear was to be placed upon his body, and there to remain. The first day he was to have three morsels of bread, and on the second day three draughts of water, to be selected from the nearest pool that could be found. Thus was the diet to be alternated, day by day, until he either answered his accusation or died.

On September 19th, 1692, death came as a happy relief to the miserable man, who had begged the sheriff to add greater weights so as to expedite the end. This is the only case on record of a man having been "pressed to death" in New England for refusing to plead, or for any other offense. There are a few cases on record where this inhuman law was enforced previously in England, but it was always regarded as a relic of mediaeval barbarity, and the fact that it was revived in the witch persecutions is a very significant one. After his death, an attempt was made to justify the act by the statement that Corey himself had pressed a man to death. This justification appears feeble, and to be without any corroborative testimony.

Another very remarkable witch story has about it a tinge of romance, although the main facts actually occurred as stated. A sailor named Orcutt, left his sweetheart on one of his regular voyages, promising to return at an early date to claim his bride. The girl he left behind him, whose name was Margaret, appears to have been a very attractive, innocent young lady, who suffered considerably from the jealousy of a rival. Soon after the departure of her lover, the witch difficulty arose, and the young girl was much worried and grieved at what happened. On one occasion she happened to say to a friend that she was sorry for the unfortunate witches who were to be hanged on the following day. The friend appears to have been an enemy in disguise, and, turning to Margaret, told her that if she talked that way she would herself be tried as a witch. As an evidence of how vindictive justice was at this time, the poor girl was arrested by the sheriff on the following day, in the name of the King and Queen, on a charge of witchcraft. The young girl was led through the streets and jeered at by the crowd. Arrived at the court, her alleged friend gave a variety of testimony against her. The usual stories about aches and pains were of course told. Some other details were added. Thus, Margaret by looking at a number of hens had killed them. She had also been seen running around at night in spectral attire. The poor girl fainted in the dock, and this was regarded as a chastisement from above, and as direct evidence of her guilt. She was removed to the jail, where she had to lie on a hard bench, only to be dragged back into court the following day, to be asked a number of outrageous questions.

With sobs she protested her innocence, but as she did so, the witnesses against her called out that they were in torment, and that the very motion of the girl's lips caused them terrible pain. She was sentenced to be hanged with eight other alleged witches two days later, and was carried back, fainting, to her cell. In a few minutes the girl was delirious, and began to talk about her lover, and of her future prospects. Even her sister was not allowed to remain with her during the night, and the frail young creature was left to the tender mercies of heartless jailors.

A few hours before the time set for execution, young Orcutt sailed into the harbor, and before daybreak he was at the house. Here he learned for the first time the awful calamity which had befallen his sweetheart in his absence. At 7 o'clock he was allowed to enter the jail, with the convicted girl's sister. At the prison door they were informed that the wicked girl had died during the night. Knowing that there was no hope under any circumstances of the sentence being remitted, the bereaved ones regarded the news as good, and although they broke down with grief at the shipwreck of their lives, they both realized that, to use the devout words of the victim's sister, "The Lord had delivered her from the hands of her enemies."

The record of brutality in connection with the witch agitation might be continued almost without limit, for the number of victims was very great. Visitors to Danvers to-day are often shown by local guides where some of the tragedies of the persecution were committed. The superstition was finally driven away by educational enlightenment, and it seems astounding that it lasted as long as it did. Two hundred years have nearly elapsed since the craze died out, and it is but charitable to admit, that although many of the witnesses must have been corrupt and perjured, the majority of those connected with the cases were thoroughly in earnest, and that although they rejoiced at the undoing of the ungodly, they regretted very much being made the instruments of that undoing.

CHAPTER III.

IN PICTURESQUE NEW YORK.

Some Local Errors Corrected—A Trip Down the Hudson River—The Last of the Mohicans—The Home of Rip Van Winkle—The Ladies of Vassar and their Home—West Point and its History—Sing Sing Prison—The Falls of Niagara—Indians in New York State.

RESIDENTS in the older States of the East are frequently twitted with their ignorance concerning the newer States of the West, and of the habits and customs of those who, having taken Horace Greeley's advice at various times, turned their faces toward the setting sun, determined to take advantage of the fertility of the soil, and grow up with the country of which they knew but little.

It needs but a few days' sojourn in an Eastern city by a Western man to realize how sublimely ignorant the New Englander is concerning at least three-fourths of his native land. The writer was, on a recent occasion, asked, in an Eastern city, how he managed to get along without any of the comforts of civilization, and whether he did not find it necessary to order all of his clothing and comforts by mail from the East. When he replied that in the larger cities, at any rate, of the West, there were retail emporiums fully up to date in all matters of fashion and improvement, and caterers who could supply the latest delicacies in season at reasonable prices, an incredulous smile was the result, and regret was expressed that local prejudice and pride should so blind a man to the actual truth.

Yet there was no exaggeration whatever in the reply, as the experienced traveler knows well. Neither Chicago nor St. Louis are really in the West, so far as points of the compass are concerned, both of these cities being hundreds of miles east of the geographical center of the United States. But they are both spoken of as "out West," and are included in the territory in which the extreme Eastern man is apt to think people live on the coarsest fare, and clothe themselves in the roughest possible manner. Yet the impartial and disinterested New York or Boston man who visits either of these cities speedily admits that he frequently finds it difficult to believe that he is not in his own much loved city, so close is the resemblance in many respects between the business houses and the method of doing business. Denver is looked upon by the average Easterner almost in the light of a frontier city, away out in the Rockies, surrounded by awe-inspiring scenery, no doubt, but also by grizzly bears and ferocious Indians. San Francisco is too far away to be thought of very intelligently, but a great many people regard that home of wealth and elegance as another extreme Western die-in-your-boots, rough-and-tumble city.

This ignorance, for it is ignorance rather than prejudice, results from the mania for European travel, which was formerly a characteristic of the Atlantic States, but which of recent years has, like civilization, traveled West. The Eastern man who has made money is much more likely to take his family on a European tour than on a trip through his native country. He incurs more expense by crossing the Atlantic, and although he adds to his store of knowledge by traveling, he does not learn matter of equal importance to him as if he had crossed the American continent and enlightened himself as to the men and manners in its different sections and States.

Nor is this sectional ignorance confined, by any means, to the East. People in the West are apt to form an entirely erroneous impression of Eastern States. The word, "East," to them conveys an impression of dense population, overcrowding, and manufacturing activity. That there are thousands and thousands of acres of scenic grandeur, as well as farm lands, in some of the most crowded States, is not realized, and that this is the case will be news to many. Last year a party of Western people were traveling to New York, and, on their way, ran through Pennsylvania, around the picturesque Horse Shoe Curve in the Alleghenies, and along the banks of the romantic and historic Susquehanna. A member of the party was seen to be wrapped in thought for a long time. He was finally asked what was worrying him.

"I was thinking," was his reply, "how singular it is that the Republican party ran up a majority of something like a hundred thousand at the election, and I was wondering where all the folks came from who did the voting. I haven't seen a dozen houses in the last hour."

Our friend was only putting into expression the thought which was indulged in pretty generally by the entire crowd. Those who were making the transcontinental trip for the first time marveled at the expanse of open country, and the exquisite scenery through which they passed; and they were wondering how they ever came to think that the noise of the hammer and the smoke of the factory chimney were part and parcel of the East, where they knew the money, as well as the "wise men," came from. The object of this book being to present some of the prominent features of all sections of the United States, it is necessary to remove, as far as possible, this false impression; and in order to do so, we propose to give a brief description of the romantic and historic River Hudson. This river runs through the great State of New York, concerning which the greatest ignorance prevails. The State itself is dwarfed, in common estimation, by the magnitude of its metropolis, and if the Greater New York project is carried into execution, and the limits of New York City extended so as to take in Brooklyn and other adjoining cities, this feeling will be intensified, rather than otherwise.

But "above the Harlem," to use an expression so commonly used when a political contest is on, there are thousands of square miles of what may be called "country," including picturesque mountains, pine lands which are not susceptible of cultivation, and are preserved for recreation and pleasure purposes, and fertile valleys, divided up into homesteads and farms.

It is through country such as this that the River Hudson flows. It rises in the Adirondack Mountains, some 300 miles from the sea, and more than 4,000 feet above its level. It acts as a feeder and outlet for numerous larger and smaller lakes. At first it is a pretty little brook, almost dry in summer, but noisy and turbulent in the rainy seasons. From Schroon Lake, near Saratoga, it receives such a large quantity of water that it begins to put on airs. It ceases to be a country brook and becomes a small river. A little farther down, the bed of the river falls suddenly, producing falls of much beauty, which vary in intensity and volume with the seasons.

At Glens Falls the upper Hudson passes through a long defile, over a precipice some hundred feet long. It was here that Cooper received much of his inspiration, and one of the most startling incidents in his "The Last of the Mohicans" is supposed to have been enacted at the falls. When Troy is reached, the river takes upon itself quite another aspect, and runs with singular straightness almost direct to New York harbor. Tourists delight to sail up the Hudson, and they find an immense quantity of scenery of the most delightful character, with fresh discoveries at every trip. Millionaires regard the banks of the Hudson as the most suitable spots upon which to build country mansions and rural retreats. Many of these mansions are surrounded by exquisitely kept grounds and beautiful parterres, which are in themselves well worth a long journey to see.

Beacon Island, a few miles below Albany, is pointed out to the traveler as particularly interesting, because four counties corner upon the river just across from it. The island has a history of more than ordinary interest. It used to be presided over by a patroon, who levied toll on all passing vessels. Right in the neighborhood are original Dutch settlements, and the descendants of the original immigrants hold themselves quite aloof from the English-speaking public. They retain the language, as well as the manners and customs, of Holland, and the tourist who strays among them finds himself, for the moment, distinctly a stranger in a strange land. The country abounds with legends and romances, and is literally honeycombed with historic memories.

The town of Hudson, a little farther down the river, is interesting because it was near here that Henry Hudson landed in September, 1609. He was immediately surrounded by Indians, who gave him an immense amount of information, and added to his store of experiences quite a number of novel ones. Here is the mouth of the Catskill River, with the wonderful Catskill Mountains in the rear. It will be news, indeed, to many of our readers that in these wild (only partially explored) mountains there are forests where bears, wild cats and snakes abound in large numbers.

Many people of comparative affluence reside in the hills, where there are hotels and pleasure resorts of the most costly character. During the storms of winter these lovers of the picturesque find themselves snowed in for several days at the time, and have a little experience in the way of frontier and exploration life.

The sunrises in the Catskills are rendered uniquely beautiful by the peculiar formation of the ground, and from the same reason the thunder storms are often thrilling in character and awful in their magnificence. Waterfalls of all sizes and kinds, brooks, with scenery along the banks of every description, forests, meadows, and lofty peaks make monotony impossible, and give to the Catskill region an air of majesty which is not easy to describe on paper.

Every visitor asks to be shown the immortalized bridge at Sleepy Hollow, and as he gazes upon it he thinks of Washington Irving's unrivaled description of this country. He speedily agrees with Irving that every change of weather, and indeed every hour of the day, produces some change in the magical hues and shapes of these mountains,

A Memory of Rip Van Winkle.

and they are regarded by all the good wives far and near as perfect barometers. When the weather is fair and settled they are clothed in blue and purple, and print their bold outlines on the clear evening sky, but, sometimes, when the rear of the landscape is clear and cloudless, they will gather a hood of gray vapors which, in the last rays of the setting sun, will grow up like a crown of glory.

Here it was that Rip Van Winkle is supposed to have lived and slept, and astonished his old friends and neighbors, and their descendants. The path along which Rip Van Winkle marched up the mountain, prior to his prolonged sleep, is shown to the tourist, who hears at his hotel, in the conveyance he hires for the day, and among the very mountains themselves, countless local legends as to Rip Van Winkle, and as to the percentage of fact and fiction in Washington Irving's masterly production.

If he is antiquarian enough to desire it, he can be shown the very spot upon which Rip Van Winkle laid himself down to sleep. Local opinion differs as to the exact spot, but there is so much faith displayed by the people that no one can doubt that they are genuine in their beliefs and sincere in their convictions. The tourist can also be shown the site of the old country inn, upon the bench in front of which Rip Van Winkle sat and astonished the natives by his extraordinary conversation, and his refusal to believe that a generation had elapsed since he was in the town last.

The chair upon which Dame Van Winkle is supposed to have sat, while she was berating her idle and incorrigible lord and master, is also shown to the visitor, and the more credulous ones gaze with interest upon a flagon which they are assured is the very one out of which Rip Van Winkle drank. The only thing needed to complete the illusion is the appearance of the old dog, which the man who had so grievously overslept himself was sure would have recognized him, had he put in his appearance.

It is almost impossible to outlive one's welcome in the Catskill Mountains, or to wear one's self out with sight seeing, so many are the novelties which greet the gaze. The Catskills are abounding with traditions quite as interesting and extraordinary as the Rip Van Winkle story. They were known originally as the "Mountains of the Sky," a name given them by the Indians, who for so many generations held them in undisputed possession. Hyde Peak, the loftiest point in the Catskills, was regarded by the Indians as the throne of the Great Spirit, and the Dutch settlers who crowded out the Indians seem to have been almost as generous in their superstitions and legends. These settlers dropped the name, "Mountains of the Sky," and adopted the, to them, more euphonic one of the Katzberg Mountains, from which the more modern name has been adopted.

The village of Catskill deserves more than a passing notice. It is the home of a large number of well-known people, including the widows of many men whose names are famous in history. The old Livingston Manor was located near the village, and a little farther down is Barrytown, where the wealthy Astors have a palatial summer resort. A little farther down the river are two towns with a distinctly ancient and Dutch aspect. They were settled by the Dutch over two hundred years ago, and there are many houses still standing which were built last century, so strongly did our forefathers construct their homes, and make them veritable castles and impregnable fortresses.

Another very old town on the Hudson is the celebrated seat of learning, Poughkeepsie. Of this, it has been said that there is more tuition to the square inch than in any other town in the world. The most celebrated of the educational institutions at this point is the Vassar College, the first ladies' seminary in the world, and the butt of so many jokes and sarcasms. Poughkeepsie is not quite as old as the hills above it, but it is exceedingly ancient. Here was held the celebrated State convention for the ratification of the Federal Constitution, in which Alexander Hamilton, Governor Clinton, and John Jay, and other men of immortal names took part.

It is only comparatively recently that the first stone building erected in this town was torn down, to make room for improvements, after it had weathered storm and time in the most perfect manner for more than a century and a quarter. At Newburgh, a few miles farther south, an old gray mansion is pointed out to the visitor as Washington's headquarters on several occasions during the Revolution. Fortunately, the State has secured possession of the house and protects it from the hands of the vandal.

This wonderful old house was built just a century and a half ago. A hundred and twelve years ago Washington's army finally disbanded from this point, and the visitor can see within the well-preserved walls of this house the historical room, with its seven doors, within which Washington and his generals held their numerous conferences, and in which there are still to be found almost countless relics of the Revolutionary War.

While sailing on the Hudson, a glimpse is obtained of West Point, the great military school from which so many of America's celebrated generals have graduated. West

Point commands one of the finest river passes in the country. The fort and chain stretched across the river were captured by the British in 1777 (two years after it was decided that West Point should be established a military post), but were abandoned after Burgoyne's surrender. The Continental forces then substituted stronger works. West Point thus has a history running right back to the Revolutionary War, and the ruins of Forts Clinton and Montgomery, which were erected in 1775, are in the immediate vicinity.

There are 176 rooms in the cadet barrack. There is no attempt at ornamentation, and the quarters are almost rigid in their simplicity and lack of home comfort. Not only are the embryo warriors taught the rudiments of drill and warfare, but they are also given stern lessons in camp life. Each young man acts as his own chambermaid, and has to keep his little room absolutely neat and free from litter and dirt of any kind.

The West Point Chapel is of interest on account of the number of tablets to be found in it, immortalizing many of the Revolutionary heroes. A winding road leads up to the cemetery, where are resting the remains of many other celebrated generals, including Winfield Scott. The State Camp meets annually at Peekskill, another very ancient town, replete with Revolutionary War reminiscences. It was settled in the year 1764 by a Dutch navigator, from whom it takes its name. Another house used by General Washington for headquarters is to be found near the town, as well as St. Peter's Church, in which the Father of his Country worshiped.

Tarrytown is another of the famous spots on the Hudson. Near here Washington Irving lived, and on the old Sleepy Hollow road is to be found the oldest religious structure in New York State. The church was built by the Dutch settlers in the year 1699, and close to it is the cemetery in which Washington Irving was interred. Sunnyside, Irving's home, is a most interesting stone structure, whose numerous gables are covered with ivy, the immense mass of which has grown from a few slips presented to Irving by Sir Walter Scott.

A sadder sight to the tourist on the Hudson, but one which is of necessity full of interest, is the Sing Sing Prison, just below Croton Point. In this great State jail an army of convicts are kept busy manufacturing various articles of domestic use. The prison itself takes its name from the Indian word "Ossining," which means "stone upon stone." The village of Sing Sing, strange to say, contains many charming residences, and the proximity of the State's prison does not seem to have any particular effect on the spirits and the ideas of those living in it.

Still further down the Hudson is Riverside Park, New York, the scene of General Grant's tomb, which overlooks the lower section of the river, concerning which we have endeavored to impart some little information of an interesting character. Of the tomb, we present a very accurate illustration.

While in New York State, the tourist, whether he be American or European, is careful to pay a visit to the Niagara Falls, which have been viewed by a greater number of people than any other scene or wonder on the American continent. This fact is due, in part, to the admirable railroad facilities which bring Niagara within easy riding distance of the great cities of the East. It is also due, very largely, to the extraordinary nature of the falls themselves, and to the grandeur of the scene which greets the eye of the spectator.

The River Niagara is a little more than thirty-three miles long. In its short course it takes care of the overflow of Lakes Superior, Michigan, Huron and Erie, and as it discharges the waters of these lakes into Lake Ontario, it falls 334 feet, or more than ten feet to the mile.

The rapids start some sixteen miles from Lake Erie. As the river channel suddenly narrows, the velocity of the current increases with great abruptness. The rapids are but a third of a mile in length, during which distance there is a fall of fifty-two feet. The boat caught in these rapids stands but a poor chance, as at the end of the torrent the water dashes down a cataract over 150 feet deep. The Canadian Fall passes over a rocky ledge of immense area, and in the descent leaves a space with a watery roof, the space being known as the "Cave of the Winds," with an entrance from the Canadian side. The Canadian Fall has a sweep of 1,100 feet and is considerably deeper than the other.

It is little more than a waste of words to endeavor to convey an impression of the grandeur and magnificence of Niagara. People have visited it from all parts of the world. Monarchs and princes have acknowledged that it exceeded their wildest expectation, and every one who has gazed upon it agrees that it is almost impossible to exaggerate its grandeur, or to say too much concerning its magnitude. Even after the water has dashed wildly 150 feet downwards, the descent continues. The river bed contracts in width gradually, for seven miles below the falls, where the whirlpool rapids are to be seen. After the second fall, the river seems to have exhausted its vehemence, and runs more deliberately, cutting its channel deeper into the rocky bed, and dropping its sensational habits.

Some writers have hazarded an opinion that, as time changes all things, so the day may come when Niagara Falls shall cease to exist. Improbable as this idea naturally sounds, it has some foundation in fact, for there have been marvelous changes in the falls during the last few generations. About two hundred and fifty years ago a sketch was taken of Niagara, and a hundred years later another artist made a careful and apparently accurate picture. These two differ from one another materially, and they also differ greatly from the appearance of the falls at the present time. Both of the old pictures show a third fall on the Canadian side. It is known that about a hundred years ago several immense fragments of rock were broken off the rocky ledge on the American side, and, more recently, an earthquake affected the appearance of the Canadian Fall. Certain it is, that the immense corrosive action of the water, and the gradual eating away of the rock on both the ledge and basin, has had the effect of changing the location of the falls, and forcing up the river in the direction of Lake Erie. Time alone can decide the momentous question as to whether the falls will eventually be so changed in appearance as to be beyond recognition. The lover of the beautiful and grand, and more especially the antiquarian, sincerely trusts that no such calamity will ever take place.

The history of the Indians in New York State is a very interesting one. Prior to the discovery of America by Columbus, the section of country including a majority of New York State and the northern portion of Pennsylvania, was occupied by the Iroquois, Mohawks, Oneidas, Onondagas, Cayugas and Senecas. These formed the historical Five Nations, of whom writers of the last century tell us so much that is of lasting importance. These tribes were self-governed, their rulers being selected on the hereditary plan. There was a federal union between them for purposes of offense and defense, and they called themselves, collectively, the "People of the Long House." This imaginary house had an eastern door at the mouth of the Mohawk River, and a western door at the Falls of Niagara.

Bashfulness was not a characteristic of these old-time red men, who had a special name of many letters for themselves, which, being interpreted, meant "Men surpassing all others." They trace their origin from the serpent-haired God, Atotarhon, and other traditions attribute their powers of confederation and alliance to the legendary Hiawatha. They built frame cabins and defended their homes with much skill. Their dress was chiefly made out of deer and elk hide, and relics still in existence show that they had good ideas of agriculture, tanning, pottery, and even carving. They were about 12,000 strong, and they appear to have been the most powerful Indian combination prior to the arrival of the white man.

They were powerful in war as well as comparatively sensible in peace. Their religion was, at least, consistent, and included a firm belief in immortality. They maintained what may be termed civilized family relations, and treated their women with proper respect. Their conduct towards the white men was much more friendly than might have been expected, and almost from the first they displayed a conciliatory attitude, and entered into alliances with the newcomers. They fought side by side with the New

Englanders against the French, and the hostile Indians who allied with them, and in the year 1710, five of their sachems or legislators crossed the Atlantic, and were received with honors by the Queen of England. In diplomacy they did not prove themselves in the long run as skillful as the newcomers, who by degrees secured from them the land over which they had previously exercised sovereign rights.

The survivors of these Indians have not sunk to as low a level as many other tribes have done. It is not generally known in the West that there are on the New York reservations, at the present time, more than 5,000 Indians, including about 2,700 survivors of the once great Seneca tribe.

The State of New York is about the same size as the Kingdom of England. It is the nineteenth State in the Union in point of size, possessing area of more than 49,000 square miles, of which 1,500 square miles is covered by water, forming portions of the lakes. Its lake coast line extends 200 miles on Lake Ontario and 75 miles on Lake Erie. Lake Champlain flows along the eastern frontier for more than 100 miles, receiving the waters of Lake George, which has been described as the Como of America. The lake has a singular history. It was originally called by the French Canadians who discovered it, the "Lake of the Holy Sacrament," and it was the scene of battles and conflicts for over a hundred years.

The capital of the Empire State, with its population of such magnitude that it exceeds that of more than twenty important foreign nations, is Albany, which was founded by the Dutch in 1623, and which has since earned for itself the title of the "Edinburgh of America." Compared with

New York City it is dwarfed in point of population and commercial importance.

Of the actual metropolis of the great Empire State it is impossible to speak at any length in the limited space at one's command. Of New York itself, Mr. Chauncey Depew said recently, in his forcible manner, "To-day, in the sisterhood of States, she is an empire in all that constitutes a great commonwealth. An industrious, intelligent, and prosperous population of 5,000,000 of people live within her borders. In the value of her farms and farm products, and in her manufacturing industries, she is the first State in the Union. She sustains over 1,000 newspapers and periodicals, has $80,000,000 invested in church property, and spends $12,000,000 a year on popular education. Upward of 300 academies and colleges fit her youth for special professions, and furnish opportunities for liberal learning and the highest culture, and stately edifices all over the State, dedicated to humane and benevolent objects, exhibit the permanence and extent of her organized charities. There are $600,000,000 in her savings banks, $300,000,000 in her insurance companies, and $700,000,000 in the capital and loans of her State and National banks. Six thousand miles of railroads, costing $600,000,000, have penetrated and developed every accessible corner of the State, and maintain, against all rivalry and competition, her commercial prestige."

CHAPTER IV.

IN THE CENTER OF THE COUNTRY.

The Geographical Center of the United States and its Location West of the Mississippi River—The Center of Population—History of Fort Riley—The Gallant "Seventh"—Early Troubles of Kansas—Extermination of the Buffalo—But a Few Survivors out of Many Millions.

KANSAS is included by most people in the list of Western States; by many it is regarded as in the extreme West. If the Pilgrim Fathers had been told that the haven of refuge they had selected would, within two or three hundred years, be part of a great English-speaking nation with some 70,000,000 of inhabitants, and with its center some 1,500 miles westward, they would have listened to the story with pardonable incredulity, and would have felt like invoking condemnation upon the head of the reckless prophet who was addressing them.

Yet Kansas is to-day in the very center of the United States. This is not a printer's error, nor a play upon words, much as the New Englander may suspect the one or the other. There was a time when the word "West" was used to apply to any section of the country a day's journey on horseback from the Atlantic Coast. For years, and even generations, everything west of the Allegheny Mountains or of the Ohio River was "Out West." Even to-day it is probable that a majority of the residents in the strictly Eastern States regard anything west of the Mississippi River as strictly Western.

There is no doubt that when Horace Greeley told the young men of the country to "Go West and grow up with the country," he used the term in its common and not its strictly geographical sense, and many thousand youths, who took the advice of the philosopher and statesman, stopped close to the banks of the Mississippi River, and have grown rich in their new homes. It cannot be too generally realized, however, that the Mississippi River slowly wends its way down to the Gulf of Mexico well within the eastern half of the greatest nation in the world. At several points in the circuitous course of the Father of Waters, the distance between the river and the Atlantic Ocean is about 1,000 miles. In an equal number of points the distance to the Pacific Ocean is 2,000 miles, showing that whatever may be said of the tributaries of the Mississippi River, and especially of its gigantic tributary the Missouri, the Mississippi is an Eastern and not a Western river.

We give an illustration of the point which competent surveyors and engineers tell us is the exact geographical center of the United States proper. The monument standing in the center of this great country is surrounded by an iron railing, and is visited again and again by tourists, who find it difficult to believe the fact that a point apparently so far western is really central. The center of the United States has gone west with the absorption of territory, and the Louisiana purchase, the centenary of which we shall shortly celebrate, had a great effect on the location.

The center of population has moved less spasmodically, but with great regularity. A hundred years ago the City of Baltimore was the center of population, and it was not until the middle of the century that Ohio boasted of owning the population center. For some twenty years it remained near Cincinnati, but during the '80s it went as far as Columbus, Indiana, where it was at the last Government census. At the present time it is probably twenty or thirty miles west of Columbus, and in the near future Fort Riley will be the population, as well as the geographical, center.

Fort Riley is an interesting spot for civilian and soldier alike. Having been selected by the Government as the permanent training school for the two mounted branches of the service—the cavalry and light artillery—its 21,000 acres have been improved at lavish expense. It seems really remarkable that so metropolitan a bit of ground could be found out on the plains, where, though civilization is making rapid strides, and the luxuries of wealth are being acquired by the advancing population, it is unusual to find macadamized streets and buildings that can harbor a regiment and still not be crowded. Yet such are some of the characteristics of Fort Riley Reservation, and the newness of it all is the best evidence of the interest the War Department has taken in its development. Many of the recently erected buildings would grace the capital itself. Nearly $1,000,000 have been expended in the past four years in new structures, all of magnesia limestone, and built along the lines of the most approved modern architecture, and of a character which insures scores of years of usefulness.

The fort is situated on the left bank of the Kansas River, near the junction of the Republican and Smoky Hill Forks. It was first laid out in 1852, and has ever since been one of the leading Western posts. Located, though it is, far out on the Kansas prairies, it has, particularly in late years, been fully in touch with the social life of the East, through the addition of new officers and the interchange of post courtesies.

The post, as it stands to-day, consists of officers' quarters, artillery and cavalry barracks, administration buildings, sheds, hospital, dispensary, etc., scattered over 150 acres of ground. The Kansas River is formed just southwest of it by the union of the Smoky Hill and Republican Forks, and the topography for practice and sightseeing could not be surpassed in the State. Five miles of macadamized streets, 150,000 feet of stone and gravel walks, six miles of sewers, four miles of water and steam heating pipes, leading to every room of each of the sixty buildings, make up the equipment, which is, of course, of the highest quality throughout. All the stone is quarried on the reservation, and is of lasting variety, and makes buildings which bear a truly substantial appearance. The Government has an idea toward permanency in its improvements.

The history of Fort Riley has been one of vicissitudes. When it was laid out in 1852, it was at first called Camp Center, but was changed to its present name by order of the War Department in honor of General B. C. Riley. In 1855, the fort suffered from Asiatic cholera, and Major E. A. Ogden, one of the original commissioners who laid out the reservation, who was staying there, nursed the soldiers with a heroic attachment to duty, and himself fell a victim to the disease. A handsome monument marks his resting place. He was a true soldier hero, and his name is still spoken in reverence by the attaches of the post.

Another notable feature of the reservation is the dismantled rock wall to the east of the fort, which is all that now remains of the once ambitious capitol building of the State of Kansas. It has a strange history, being the "Pawnee House," in which the Territorial Legislature met in the early ante-bellum days, confident of protection by the soldiers from the roaming Indian bands infesting the prairies.

A famous dweller at the fort for two decades was old Comanche, the only living creature to escape from the Custer massacre on the side of the Government. He was the horse ridden by an officer in that memorable fight, and by miracle escaped, after having seven balls fired into him. He was found roaming over the prairie, after the massacre, and was ordered put on the retired list, and stationed at Fort Riley, where for twenty years he was petted and cared for, but never ridden. His only service was to be led in processions of ceremony, draped in mourning. Now that he is dead, his body has been preserved with the taxidermist's best skill, and is one of the State's most noted relics.

The fort has been of unusual interest of late. In addition to the maneuvers of the school for mounted service, in which the soldiers have been regularly drilled, engaging in sham battles, throwing up mimic fortifications, fording the rivers, etc., the War Signal Service has been conducting some interesting experiments. The Signal Service has had its huge balloon, which was exhibited at the World's Fair, at the post, and its ascensions and the operations put in practice have proved very attractive and instructive.

The new riding hall, or cavalry practice building, makes it possible for the training school to go on the year round, regardless of the weather. It has an open floor space 300 feet long and 100 feet wide, making it an admirable room for the purpose.

The Fort Riley troops are always called on when there is trouble in the West. They have put down a dozen Indian uprisings on the plains, and only a few months ago were sent for to keep order in Chicago during the railway strikes. From this trip, four old members of the post were brought back dead, having met their fate in the bursting of a caisson, while marching along a paved street.

The fort is the great pleasure resort of Kansas. The late commanding officer, Colonel Forsyth, now General Forsyth, is much given to hospitality, and the people of the State take great pride in the post's advancement and its victories. During the summer, on several occasions, the national holidays especially, the soldiers "receive," and excursion trains bring hundreds of visitors from every direction, who are delighted to feast their eyes on real cannon, uniforms and shoulder straps. They are entertained royally. Drills, salutes, sham battles and parades, occupy every hour of the day, and in the evening the drill floor becomes a dancing place for all who enjoy the delights of a military ball.

The history of the fort has been, in a measure, that of the Seventh Cavalry, which for nearly two decades has had its residence there, and become identified with the spot. The Seventh Cavalry dates its glory from before the days of the intrepid Custer, whose memory it cherishes. It has taken part in scores of Indian battles—indeed, there has not, for years, been an uprising in the West in which it has not done duty. Its last considerable encounter was at Wounded Knee and Drexel Mission, where the Custer massacre was in a degree avenged. Here

Near Fort Riley, Kan., the Exact Center of the United States.

it lost twenty-four of its members, and a magnificent granite monument has been erected at the fort to their memory. It bears the names of those who fell, and tells briefly the story of their bravery.

In the Wounded Knee battle, on the plains of Dakota, during the closing days of 1891, the four troops of the regiment were treacherously surprised by the Sioux, and because, after the attack, Colonel Forsyth ordered a charge, resulting in the killing of many of the savages, he was suspended by his superior officer, General Miles, for disobedience of orders, which were not to fire on the enemy. An investigation, however, amply justified his action, and he was reinstated in charge of his post as before. Early in November, 1894, on the promotion of General McCook to be Major General, Colonel Forsyth stepped up to the Brigadier Generalship, and his place at Fort Riley will be taken by Colonel Sumner. There is a rumor, however, in army circles, that the old Seventh will be stationed in the far Northwest, and the Fifth Cavalry will succeed it as resident regiment here. The post has become so closely identified with the fortunes of the former regiment that it will seem strange to have any other troops call it home.

There are usually at the fort three squadrons of cavalry, of four troops each, and five batteries of light artillery, engaged in the maneuvers of the school for mounted service, which has its headquarters for the entire army here. The principal object of this school is instruction in the combined operations of the cavalry and light artillery, and this object is kept steadily in view. The troops of each arm form a sub-school, and are instructed nine months in the year in their own arm, preparatory to the three months of combined operations. Thus the batteries are frequently practiced in road marching in rapid gaits; the Kansas River is often forded; rough hills are climbed at "double quick," and guns are brought to action on all sorts of difficult ground, with the result that, when the combined operations begin, the batteries may be maneuvered over all kinds of obstacles.

Among the plans of the future is one, which was a favorite with General Sheridan, of making Fort Riley the horse-furnishing headquarters for the entire army. The location being so central, it insures the nearest approach to perfect acclimation of animals sent to any part of the Union. Two plans are being contemplated for the accomplishment of this object. One is to make it a breeding station; the other is to simply make it a purchasing station, which shall buy of the farmers of the West the horses needed by the army, and train the animals for regular use before sending them to the various posts.

Present plans also include an increase in the number of soldiers stationed at Fort Riley to 3,000. If the proposed increase in the standing army is carried out, there may be more than that. The Government evidently has faith in the location of the fort. While it has abandoned and consolidated other stations, it has all the time been increasing its expenditures here, and the estimates for the next year aggregate expenditures of over $500,000, provided the Appropriation Committee does its duty. There are plans of still further beautifying the grounds, and the addition of more turnpikes and macadamized roads.

The State of Kansas, and especially Geary and Riley Counties, in which the fort is situated, reap a considerable benefit from its location. The perishable produce of the commissary department comes from the country around.

Hundreds of horses are bought at round prices, while the soldier trade has sent Junction City, four miles west, ahead of all competitors in Central Kansas for volume of business and population. Naturally, Kansas is glad to see Fort Riley a permanency, and hopes that it may be made the Government's chief Western post.

Kansas has been spoken of as the most wonderful State in the Union, and in many respects it is fully entitled to its reputation in this respect. It has had enough discouragements and drawbacks to ruin half a dozen States, and nothing but the phenomenal fertility of the soil, and the push and go of the pioneers who claim the State as their own, has enabled Kansas to withstand difficulties and to sail buoyantly through waves of danger into harbors of refuge. In its early days, border warfare hindered development and drove many most desirable settlers to more peaceful spots. Since then the prefix "Bleeding" has again been used repeatedly in connection with the State, because of the succession of droughts and plagues of grasshoppers and chinch bugs, which have imperiled its credit and fair name. But Kansas remains to-day a great State, with a magnificent future before it. The fertility of the soil is more than phenomenal. Kansas corn is known throughout the world for its excellency, and at the World's Fair in 1893 it took highest awards for both the white and yellow varieties. In addition to this, it secured the gold medal for the best corn in the world, as well as the highest awards for red winter wheat flour, sorghum sugar and apples. Indeed, Kansas soil produces almost anything to perfection, and the State, thanks largely to works of irrigation in the extreme western section, is producing larger quantities of indispensable agricultural products every year.

The very motto of the State indicates the early troubles through which it went, the literal interpretation being "To the stars (and stripes) through difficulties." The State is generally known now as the "Sunflower State," and for many years the sword has given place to the plowshare. But the very existence of Fort Riley shows that this was not always the condition of affairs. Early in the Eighteenth Century, French fur-traders crossed over into Kansas, and, later on, Spanish explorers were struck with the possibilities of the fertile plains. Local Indian tribes were then at war, but a sense of common danger caused the antagonistic red men to unite, and the white immigrants were massacred in a body. After the famous Missouri Compromise of 1820, and the Kansas-Nebraska Act of thirty years later, the slave issue became a very live one in Kansas, and for some time the State was in a condition bordering upon civil war. The convention of 1859, at Wyandotte, settled this difficulty, and placed Kansas in the list of anti-slavery States.

Some ten years ago, after Kansas had enjoyed a period of the most unique prosperity, from an agricultural standpoint, the general impression began to prevail that the State was destined to become almost immediately the greatest in the nation. Corn fields were platted out into town sites, and additions to existing cities were arranged in every direction. For a time it appeared as though there was little exaggeration in the extravagant forecast of future greatness. Town lots sold in a most remarkable manner, many valuable corners increasing in value ten and twenty-fold in a single night. The era of railroad building was coincident with the town boom craze, and Eastern people were so anxious to obtain a share of the enormous profits to be made by speculating in Kansas town lots, that money was telegraphed to agents and banks all over the State, and options on real estate were sold very much on the plan adopted by traders in stocks and bonds in Wall Street.

The greed of some, if not most, of the speculators, soon killed the goose which laid the golden egg. The boom burst in a most pronounced manner. People who had lost their heads found them again, and many a farmer who had abandoned agriculture in order to get rich by trading in lots, went back to his plow and his chores, a sadder and wiser, although generally poorer, man. Many hundreds of thousands of dollars changed hands during the boom. Exactly who "beat the game," to use the gambler's expression, has never been known. Certain it is, that for every man in Kansas who admits that he made money out of the excitement and inflation, there are at least fifty who say that the boom well-nigh ruined them.

Kansas is as large as Great Britain, larger than the whole of New England combined, and a veritable empire in itself. It is a State of magnificent proportions, and of the most unique and delightful history. Three and a half centuries ago, Coronado, the great pioneer prospector and adventurer, hunted Kansas from end to end in search of the precious metals which he had been told could be found there in abundance. He wandered over the immense stretch of prairies and searched along the creek bottoms without finding what he sought. He speaks in his records of "mighty plains and sandy heaths, smooth and wearisome and bare of wood. All the way the plains are as full of crooked-back oxen as the mountain Serena in Spain is of sheep."

These crooked-back oxen were of course buffaloes, or, more correctly speaking, species of the American bison. No other continent was ever blessed with a more magnificent and varied selection of beasts and birds in forests and prairies than was North America. Kansas in particular was fortunate in the possession of thousands of herds of buffaloes. Now it has none, except a few in a domesticated state, with their old regal glory departed forever. When we read the reports of travelers and trappers, written little more than half a century ago, and treating of the enormous buffalo herds that covered the prairies as far as the eye could reach, we wonder whether these descriptions can be real, or whether they are not more in the line of fables and the outgrowth of a too vivid imagination.

If, thirty years ago, some wiseacre had come forward and predicted that it would become necessary to devise means for the protection of this enormous amount of game, he would have been laughed out of countenance. Yet this extraordinary condition of affairs has actually come to pass. Entire species of animals which belonged to the magnificent fauna of North America are already extinct or are rapidly becoming so. The sea-cow is one of these animals: the last specimens of which were seen in 1767 and 1768. The Californian sea-elephant and the sea-dog of the West Indies have shared a like fate. Not a trace of these animals has been found for a long time. The extinction of the Labrador duck and the great auk have often been deplored. Both of these birds may be regarded as practically extinct. The last skeleton of the great auk was sold for $600, the last skin for $650, and the last egg brought the fabulous sum of $1,500.

Last, not least, the American bison is a thing of the past!

It has been historically proven that at the time of the discovery of America, the buffalo herds covered the entire enormous territory from Pennsylvania to Oregon and Nevada, and down to Mexico, and thirty years ago the large emigrant caravans which traveled from the Eastern States across the Mississippi to the gold fields of California, met with herds of buffaloes, not numbering thousands, but hundreds of thousands. The construction trains of the first Pacific Railroad were frequently interrupted and delayed by wandering buffalo herds.

To-day the United States may be traversed from end to end, and not a single buffalo will be seen, and nothing remains to even indicate their presence but the deep, well-trodden paths which they made years ago. Rain has not been able to wash away these traces, and they are counted among the "features" of the prairies, where the bisons once roamed in undisturbed glory. It was a difficult task for the Government to gather the last remnants, about 150 to 200 head, to stock Yellowstone Park with them, and to prevent their complete extinction.

Undoubtedly, the buffalo was the most stupid animal of the prairies. In small flocks, he eluded the hunter well enough; but in herds of thousands, he cared not a whit for the shooting at the flanks of his army. Any Indian or trapper, stationed behind some shrubs or earth hill, could kill dozens of buffalo without disturbing the herd by the swish of the arrow, the report of the rifle, or the dying groans of the wounded animals. A general stampede ensued at times, which often led the herd into morasses, or the quick-sand of the rivers, where they perished miserably. The destruction was still greater when the leader of the herd came upon some yawning abyss. Those behind drove him down into the deep, and the entire herd followed blindly, only to be dashed to death.

The very stupidity of the bison helped to exterminate the race, where human agency would have seemed well nigh inadequate.

Among the large game of the continent, the bison was the most important, and furnished the numerous Indian tribes not only with abundant food, but other things as well. They covered their tents with the thick skins, and made saddles, boats, lassoes and shoes from them. Folded up, they used them as beds, and wore them around their shoulders as a protection against the winter's cold. Spoons and other utensils for the household could be made from their hoofs and horns, and their bones were shaped into all kinds of arms and weapons. The life and existence of the prairie Indian depended almost entirely upon that of the buffalo. There is no doubt that the Indians killed many buffaloes, but while the damage may have been great, there was not much of a reduction noticeable in their numbers, for the buffalo cow is an enormous breeder.

Conditions were changed, however, when the white man arrived with his rifle, settled down on the shores of the Atlantic Ocean, and began to drive the aborigines of the American continent further and further West. With this crowding back of the Indians began that also of the buffalo, and the destruction of the latter was far more rapid than that of the former.

It was about the middle of the Seventeenth Century when the first English colonists climbed the summits of the Allegheny Mountains. Enormous herds of buffalo grazed then in Western Pennsylvania, Ohio, Indiana, Illinois, Tennessee, and in the famous blue grass regions of

Kentucky. How fast the buffaloes became exterminated may best be illustrated by the fact that, at the beginning of the present century, the bison had entirely disappeared from the eastern banks of the Mississippi. A few isolated herds could be found in Kentucky in 1792. In 1814 the animal had disappeared in Indiana and Illinois. When the white settlers crossed the Mississippi, to seek connection with the territories on the Pacific coast, the buffalo dominion, once so vast, decreased from year to year, and finally it was split in two and divided into a northern and southern strip. The cause of this division was the California overland emigration, the route of which followed the Kansas and Platte Rivers, cutting through the center of the buffalo regions. These emigrants killed hundreds of thousands of animals, and the division became still greater after the completion of the Union Pacific line and the settlement of the adjacent districts.

The buffaloes of the southern strip were the first to be exterminated, particularly when the building of the Atchison, Topeka & Santa Fe Railroad facilitated entrance to the southern range.

Aside from the pleasure and excitement from a buffalo hunt, the yield was a rich one, and troops of hunters swarmed over the Western prairies; buffalo hunting became an industry which gave employment to thousands of people. But human avarice knew no bounds, and massacred senselessly the finest game with which this continent was stocked. The dimensions to which this industry grew may best be guessed when it is stated that in 1872 more than 100,000 buffaloes were killed near Fort Dodge in three months. During the summer of 1874, an expedition composed of sixteen hunters killed 2,800 buffaloes, and during that same season one young trapper boasted of having killed 3,000 animals. The sight of such a slaughter scene was gruesome to behold. Colonel Dodge writes of it: "During the fall of 1873 I rode across the prairie, where a year ago I had hunted several herds. At the time we enjoyed the aspect of a myriad of buffaloes, which were grazing peacefully over the prairies. Now we rode past myriads of decaying cadavers and skeletons, which filled the air with an insufferable stench. The broad plain which, a year ago, had teemed with animals, was nothing more than a dead, foul desert."

Mr. Blackmore, another traveler, who went through Kansas at about the same time, says that he counted, on four acres of ground, no less than sixty-seven buffalo carcasses. As was to be expected, this wholesale and, indeed, wanton slaughter brought its own reward and condemnation. The price of buffalo skins dropped to 50 cents, although as much as $3.00 had been paid regularly for them. Moreover, as the number of animals killed was greater than could be removed, the decaying carcasses attracted wolves, and even worse foes, to the farmyard, and terrible damage to cattle resulted.

The Indians also were disturbed. "Poor Lo" complained of the wanton and senseless killing of the principal means of his sustenance, and when the white man with a laugh ignored these complaints, the Indians got on the war-path, attacked settlements, killed cattle and stole provisions, thus giving rise to conflicts, which devoured not only enormous sums of money, but cost the lives of thousands of people. When the locust plague swept over the fields of Kansas and destroyed the entire crop, the settlers themselves hungered for the buffalo meat of which they had robbed themselves, and vengeance came in more ways than one.

The extermination of the buffalo of the southern range was completed about 1875; to the bisons of the northern range were given a few years' grace. But the same scenes which were enacted in the South, repeated themselves in the North, and the white barbarians were not satisfied until they had killed the last of the noble game in 1885. When the massacre was nearly over, a few isolated herds were collected and transported to Yellowstone Park, where they have increased to about 400 during the last few years, protected by the hunting laws, which are strictly enforced. With the exception of a very few specimens, tenderly nursed by some cattle raisers in Kansas and Texas, and in some remote parts of British America, these are the last animals of a species, which two decades ago wandered in millions over the vast prairies of the West.

CHAPTER V.

THE MORMONS AND THEIR WIVES.

The Pilgrimage Across the Bad Lands to Utah — Incidents of the March — Success of the New Colony — Religious Persecutions — Murder of an Entire Family — The Curse of Polygamy — An Ideal City — Humors of Bathing in Great Salt Lake.

ABOUT half a century ago one of the most remarkable pilgrimages of modern times took place. Across what was then, not inaptly, described by writers as an arid and repulsive desert, there advanced a procession of the most unique and awe-inspiring character. History tells us of bands of crusaders who tramped across Europe in order to rescue the Holy Land from tyrants and invaders. On that occasion, all sorts and conditions of men were represented, from the religious enthusiast, to the ignorant bigot, and from the rich man who was sacrificing his all in the cause that he believed to be right, to the tramp and ne'er-do-well, who had allied himself with that cause for revenue only.

But the distance traversed by the crusaders six or seven hundred years ago was insignificant compared with the distance traversed by the pilgrims to whom we are referring. In addition to this, the country to be crossed presented difficulties of a far more startling and threatening character. There was before them a promised land in the extreme distance, but there intervened a tract of land which seemed as impassable a barrier as the much talked-of, but seldom inspected, Chinese Wall of old. There was a region of desolation and death, extending from the Sierra Nevadas to the border lines of Nebraska, and from the Yellowstone to the Colorado Rivers. A profane writer once suggested that the same Creator could hardly have brought into existence this arid, barren and inhospitable region and the fertile plains and beautiful mountains which surrounded it on all sides.

Civilization and irrigation have destroyed the most awful characteristics of this region, but at the time to which we are referring, it was about as bad from the standpoint of humanity and human needs as could well be imagined. Here and there, there were lofty mountains and deep cañons, as there are now, but the immense plains, which occupy the bulk of the land, were unwatered and uncared for, giving forth volumes of a penetrating alkali dust, almost as injurious to human flesh as to human attire. Here and there, there were, of course, little oases of comparative verdure, which were regarded by unfortunate travelers not only as havens of refuge, but as little heavens in the midst of a sea of despair. The trail across the desert, naturally, ran through as many as possible of these successful efforts of nature to resist decay, and along the trail there were to be found skeletons and ghastly remains of men whose courage had exceeded their ability, and who had succumbed to hunger and thirst in this great, lonesome desert.

That no one lived in this region it would seem superfluous to state. Occasionally a band of Indians would traverse it in search of hunting grounds beyond, though, as a general rule, the red man left the country severely alone, and made no effort to dispute the rights of the coyotes and buzzards to sole possession.

Along the trail mentioned, there advanced at the period to which we have referred, a procession which we have likened, in some respects, to the advance of the crusaders in mediæval days. Those who happened to see it pass described this cavalcade as almost beyond conception. The first impression from a distance was that an immense herd of buffalo were advancing and creating the cloud of dust, which seemed to rise from the bare ground and mount to the clouds. As it came nearer, and the figures became more discernible, it was seen that the caravan was headed by a band of armed horsemen. The animals were jaded and fatigued, and walked with their heads low down and their knees bent out of shape and form. Their riders seemed as exhausted as the animals themselves, and they carried their dust-begrimed guns in anything but military fashion. Behind them came hundreds, nay, thousands, of wagons, of all shapes and builds, some of them entirely open and exposed, and others protected more or less by canvas tilts. These wagons seemed to stretch back indefinitely into space, and even when there was no undulation of the surface to obstruct the view, the naked eye could not determine to any degree the length of the procession. Near the front of the great cavalcade was a wagon different in build and appearance to any of the others. It was handsomely and even gaudily decorated, and it was covered in so carefully that its occupants could sleep and rest as secure from annoyance by the dust as though they were in bed at home.

Instead of two broken-down horses, six well-fed and well-watered steeds were attached to the wagon, and it was evident that no matter how short had been the supply of food and water, the horses and occupants of this particular conveyance had had everything they desired. The occupant of this wagon was a man who did not look to be more than thirty years of age, but whose face and manner indicated that he was in the habit of being obeyed rather than obeying. A great portion of his time was occupied in reading from a large vellum-bound book, but from time to time he laid it on one side to settle disputes which had arisen among some of his ten thousand followers, or to issue orders of the most emphatic and dogmatic character.

This man was Brigham Young, the successor of Joseph Smith, and the chosen Prophet of the Mormons, who were marching across the desert in search of the promised land, which they were informed had been set aside for their purpose by the Ruler of the Universe.

We need not follow the fortunes and misfortunes of the zealous, if misguided, men and families who followed their leader across the great unwatered and almost unexplored desert. No one knows how many fell by the wayside and succumbed to hunger, exhaustion or disease. The bulk of the column, however, persevered in the march, and, through much sadness and tribulation, finally arrived at a country which, while it was not then by any means up to expectation or representation, at least presented facilities and opportunities for living. When the great valleys of Utah were reached, men who a few months before had been strong and hardy, but who now were lank and lean, fell on their knees and offered up thanksgiving for their deliverance, while the exhausted women and children sought repose and rest, which had been denied them for so many long, wearisome days.

But there was no time to be wasted in rejoicings over achievements, or regrets over losses. The virgin acres before them were theirs for the asking, or rather taking, and the Mormon colony set to work at once to parcel out the land and to commence the building of homes. Whatever may be said against the religious ideas of these pilgrims, too much credit cannot be given them for the business-like energy which characterized their every movement. A site was selected for what is now known as Salt Lake City. Broad streets were laid out, building plans and rules adopted, and every arrangement made for the construction of a handsome and symmetrical city. Houses, streets and squares appeared almost by magic, and in a very few weeks quite a healthy town was built up. Those who in more Eastern regions had learned different trades were set to work at callings of their choice, and for those who were agriculturally disposed, farms were mapped out and reserved.

Fortunately for the newcomers, industry was a watchword among them, and a country which had been up to that time a stranger to the plow and shovel was drained and ditched, and very speedily planted to corn and wheat. So fertile did this so-called arid ground prove to be, that one year's crop threw aside all fears of further poverty, and prosperity began to reign supreme. Had the Mormons confined themselves to work, and had abandoned extreme religious and social ideas, impossible in an enlightened age and country, they would have risen long before this into an impregnable position in every respect.

But polygamy, hitherto restrained and checked by laws of Eastern States and Territories, was now indulged in indiscriminately. The more wives a member of the Mormon church possessed, the greater was his standing in the community. The man who had but two or three wives

Brigham Young's Grave, Salt Lake City.

was censured for his want of enthusiasm, and he was frequently fined heavily by the church, which was not above levying fines, and thus licensing alleged irregularities. Some of the elders had more than a hundred wives each, and these were maintained under relations of a most peculiar character.

At first the polygamous tenents of the church did not cause much comment on the outside, because the Mormons were so shut off from civilization that they seemed to occupy a little world of their own, and no one claimed the right to censure or interfere with them. Gradually, however, there became a shortage of marriageable women, and this resulted in mysterious raids being made on neighboring settlements. Wanderers upon the mountains spoke with horror of mysterious tribes of men who wandered around engaged in acts of plunder, and from time to time strange women appeared in the towns and settlements.

Like so many other bands of persecuted men who had fled from their oppressors in search of liberty, the early Mormons soon adopted the tactics of which they had complained so bitterly. The man who refused to obey the orders of the church, or who was in any way rebellious, was apt to disappear from his home without warning or explanation. He was not arrested or tried; he was simply spirited away, and no mark or sign proclaimed his last resting place. The Danite Band, or the Avenging Angels, came into existence, and some of their terrible deeds have contributed dark pages to the history of our native land.

It is not to be supposed that acts such as these were approved indiscriminately by the newcomers. Occasionally a mild protest would be uttered, but it seemed as though the very walls had ears, for even if a man in the bosom of his family criticised the conduct of the church, his doom appeared to be sealed, and he generally disappeared within a few days. Occasionally a family would attempt to escape from Utah, in order to avoid compliance with laws and orders which they believed to be criminal in character, as well as contrary to their preconceived notions of domestic happiness and right. To make an attempt of this character was to invite death. In the first place, it was almost impossible to traverse the surrounding mountains and deserts, and even if these natural obstacles were overcome, the hand of the avenger was constantly uplifted against the fugitives, who were blotted off the face of the earth, on the theory that dead men tell no tales.

On one occasion, a man left his home in Utah in the way described, because he declined to bring home a second wife. Brigham Young, in the course of his pastoral calls, entered the comfortable house occupied by the family, and called upon the man to introduce to him his wives. He was one of the few men who, while in every other respect a zealous Mormon, had declined to break up his family relations by bringing a young wife into his home. The mother of his children informed the Prophet with much vehemence of this fact, and in words more noble than discreet assured him that no effort of his could disturb the domestic relations of the house, or make her husband untrue to vows he had taken twenty years before.

The Prophet was too astounded to lose his temper, but turning to the happy husband and father, he told him in stentorian tones that unless within one month he complied with the orders of the church, it would have been better for him had he never been born, or had he died while on the terrible march across the Bad Lands and the alkali desert. That the Prophet was in earnest was evidenced by the arrival the following day of some of his minions, who brought with them more explicit directions, as well as the names of certain young women to whom the man must be "sealed" or "married" within the time mentioned by Young.

No idea of complying with this order ever occurred to the head of the house. He knew that his wife would far rather die than be dishonored, and he himself was perfectly willing to sacrifice his life rather than his honor. But for the sake of his four children he determined to make an attempt to escape, and accordingly, a few days later, the family, having collected together all their available and easily transported assets, hitched up their wagon and drove away in the dead of night. Their departure in this manner was not expected, and was not discovered for nearly forty-eight hours, during which time the refugees had made considerable progress over the surrounding mountains. They maintained their march for nearly a week, without incident, and were congratulating themselves upon their escape, when the disaster which they had feared overtook them.

They were camped by the side of a little stream in a fertile valley, and all were sleeping peacefully but the elder boy, who was acting as sentinel. His attention was first called to danger by the uneasiness displayed by the horses, which, by their restless manner and sudden anxiety, showed that instinct warned them of an approaching party. Without wasting a moment's time, the young man hastily aroused the sleepers, who prepared to abandon their camp and seek refuge in the adjoining timber. They had barely reached cover when a party of mounted armed men rode up.

Finding a deserted camp, they separated, and commenced to scour the surrounding country. One of the number soon came upon the retreating family, but before he could cover them with his rifle he had been shot dead by the infuriated father, who was determined to resist to the uttermost the horrible fate which now stared them in the face.

The noise was taken by the other searchers as a signal to them that the hunted family had been found, and knowing that this would be so, the man and his sons hurried the woman and younger children to a secluded spot at a little distance, and seeking convenient cover determined to make a desperate effort to protect those for whose safety they were responsible. Unfortunately for the successful carrying out of this plan, the helpless section of the party was discovered first. The avenging party then divided up into two sections, one of which dragged away the woman and her young children, and the others went in search of the man and his two sons. They speedily found them, and in the fight which followed two lives were lost on both sides.

The oldest son of the escaping party was wounded and left for dead. Several hours later consciousness returned to him, and the first sight that met his gaze was the dead bodies of his father and brother. A chance was offered him to escape, but weak as he was from loss of blood, he determined to follow up the kidnaping party, forming the desperate resolve that if he could not rescue his mother and sisters, he would at least save them from the horrible fate that he knew awaited them. This resolve involved his death, for he was no match for the men he was contending against. No grave was ever dug for his remains, and no headstone tells the story of his noble resolution and his intrepid effort to carry it into execution.

There were hundreds, and probably thousands, of similar incidents, and Mormonism proved a sad drawback to the happiness of a people who otherwise had before them prospects of a most delightful character. Brigham Young proved a marvelous success as a ruler. He had eighteen wives and an indefinite number of children, estimates concerning the number of which vary so much that it is best not to give any of them. It is generally stated and understood that the so-called revelation calling upon the chosen people to practice polygamy, was an invention on the part of Young, designed to cover up his own immorality, and to obtain religious sanction for improper relationships he had already built up. However this may be, it is certain that polygamy had a serious blow dealt at it by the death of its ardent champion. Since then stern federal legislation has resulted in the practical suppression of the crime, and in recent years the present head of the church has officially declared the practice to be improper, and the habit dead.

Brigham Young's grave, of which we give an illustration, has been visited from time to time by countless pleasure and sight-seekers. Like the man, it is unique in every respect. It is situated in the Prophet's private burial ground, which was surveyed and laid out by him with special care. He even went so far as to select the last resting place for each of his eighteen wives, and so careful was he over these details that the honor of resting near him was given to each wife in order of the date of her being "sealed" to him, in accordance with the rites and laws of the church. Most of the Mrs. Youngs have been buried according to arrangements made, but all of the remarkable aggregation of wives has not yet been disposed of in the manner desired. The Prophet's favorite wife, concerning whose relationship to Mrs. Grover Cleveland there has been so much controversy, was named Amelia Folsom. For her special comfort the Prophet built the Amelia Palace, one of the most unique features of Salt Lake City. Here the lady lived for several years.

Let us leave the unpleasant side of Mormon history and see what the zealous, if misguided, people have succeeded in accomplishing. Salt Lake City, which was originally settled by Brigham Young and his followers in July, 1847, is perhaps the most uniform city in the world so far as its plans are concerned. The original settlers laid out the city in squares ten acres large. Instead of streets sixty and eighty feet wide, as are too common in all our crowded cities, a uniform width of 130 feet was adopted, with more satisfactory results. In the original portion of the city these wide streets are a permanent memorial to the forethought of the early Mormons. The shade trees they planted are now magnificent in their proportions, and along each side of the street there runs a stream of water of exquisite clearness. There is very little crowding in the way of house-building. Each house in the city is surrounded by a green lawn, a garden and an orchard, so that poverty and squalor of the slum type is practically unknown. The communistic idea of homes in common, which has received so much attention of late years, was not adopted by the founders of this city, who, however, took excellent precautions to stamp out loafing, begging and other accompaniments of what may be described as professional pauperism.

Within thirty years of the building of the first house in Salt Lake City, which, by the way, is still standing, the number of inhabitants ran up to 20,000. It is now probably more than 50,000, and the city stands thirty-first in the order of those whose clearing-house returns are reported and compared weekly. Hotels abound on every side, and benevolent institutions and parks are common. Churches, of course, there are without number, and now that the Government has interfered in the protection of so-called Gentiles, almost all religious sects are represented.

No description of the Mormon Temple can convey a reasonable idea of its grandeur. Six years after the arrival of the pilgrims at Salt Lake City, or in 1853, work was commenced on this immense structure, upon which at least $7,000,000 have been expended. Its length is 200 feet, its width 100 feet, and its height the same. At each corner there is a tower 220 feet high. The thickness of the walls is 10 feet, and these are built of snow-white granite. So conspicuous and massive is this building, that it can be seen from the mountains fifty and even a hundred miles away.

The Tabernacle, which is in the same square as the Temple, and just west of it, is aptly described by Mr. P. Donan as one of the architectural curios of the world. It looks like a vast terrapin back, or half of a prodigious egg-shell cut in two lengthwise, and is built wholly of iron, glass and stone. It is 250 feet long, 150 feet wide, and 100 feet high in the center of the roof, which is a single mighty arch, unsupported by pillar or post, and is said to have but one counterpart on the globe. The walls are 12 feet thick, and there are 20 huge double doors for entrance and exit. The Tabernacle seats 13,462 people, and its acoustic properties are so marvelously perfect that a whisper or the dropping of a pin can be heard all over it. The organ is one of the largest and grandest toned in existence, and was built of native woods, by Mormon workmen and artists, at a cost of $100,000. It is 58 feet high, has 57 stops, and contains 2,648 pipes, some of them nearly as large as the chimneys of a Mississippi River steamer.

The choir consists of from 200 to 500 trained voices, and the music is glorious beyond description. Much of it is in minor keys, and a strain of plaintiveness mingles with all its majesty and power. All the seats are free, and tourists from all parts of the world are to be found among the vast multitudes that assemble at every service. Think of seeing the Holy Communion broken bread, and water from the Jordan River, instead of wine, administered to from 6,000 to 8,000 communicants at one time! One can just fancy the old-time Mormon elders marching in, each followed by his five or twenty-five wives and his fifty or a hundred children.

Close by is Assembly Hall, also of white granite, and of Gothic architecture. It has seats for 2,500 people, and is most remarkable for the costly fresco work on the ceiling, which illustrates scenes from Mormon history, including the alleged discovery of the golden plates and their delivery to Prophet Smith by the Angel Moroni.

All around this remarkable city are sights of surpassing beauty. Great Salt Lake itself ought to be regarded as one of the wonders of the world. Although an inland sea, with an immense area intervening between it and the nearest ocean, its waters are much more brackish and salty than those of either the Atlantic or the Pacific, and its specific gravity is far greater. Experts tell us that the percentage of salt and soda is six times as great as in the waters of the Atlantic, and one great advantage of living in its vicinity is the abundance of good, pure salt, which is produced by natural evaporation on its banks. It would be interesting, if it were possible, to explain why it is that the water is so salty. Various reasons have been advanced from time to time for this phenomenon, but none of them are sufficiently practical or tangible to be of great interest to the unscientific reader.

It is just possible that this wonderful lake may in course of time disappear entirely. Some years ago its width was over 40 miles on an average, and its length was very much greater. Now it barely measures 100 miles from end to end and the width varies from 10 to 60 miles. In the depth the gradual curtailment has been more apparent. At one time the average depth was many hundred feet, and several soundings of 1,000 feet were taken, with the result reported, in sailors' parlance, of "No bottom." At the present time the depth varies from 40 to 100 feet, and appears to be lessening steadily, presumably because of the extraordinary deposit of solid matter from the very dense waters with which it is filled.

The lake is a bathers' paradise, and the arrangements for bathing from Garfield Beach are like everything else in the land of the Mormons, extraordinary to a degree. In one year there were nearly half a million bathers accommodated at the four principal resorts, and so rapidly are these bathing resorts and establishments multiplied, that the day is not distant when every available site on the eastern shore of the lake will be appropriated for the purpose. As a gentleman who has bathed in this lake again and again says, it seems preposterous to speak of the finest sea-bathing on earth a thousand miles from the ocean, although the bathing in Great Salt Lake infinitely surpasses anything of the kind on either the Atlantic or Pacific coasts.

The water contains many times more salt, and much more soda, sulphur, magnesia, chlorine, bromine and potassium than any ocean water on the globe. It is powerful in medicinal virtues, curing or benefiting many forms of rheumatism, rheumatic gout, dyspepsia, nervous disorders and cutaneous diseases, and it acts like magic on the hair of those unfortunates whose tendencies are to baldheadedness. It is a prompt and potent tonic and invigorant of body and mind, and then there is no end of fun in getting acquainted with its peculiarities. A first bath in it is always as good as a circus, the bather being his or her own trick mule. The specific gravity is but a trifle less than that of the Holy Land Dead Sea.

The human body will not and cannot sink in it. You can walk out in it where it is fifty feet deep, and your body will stick up out of it like a fishing-cork from the shoulders upward. You can sit down in it perfectly secure where it is fathoms deep. Men lie on top of it with their arms under their heads and smoking cigars. Its buoyancy is indescribable and unimaginable. Any one can float upon it at the first trial; there is nothing to do but lie down gently upon it and float.

But swimming is an entirely different matter. The moment you begin to "paddle your own canoe," lively and —to the lookers-on—mirth-provoking exercises ensue. When you stick your hand under to make a stroke your feet decline to stay anywhere but on top; and when, after an exciting tussle with your refractory pedal extremities, you again get them beneath the surface, your hands fly out with the splash and splutter of a half-dozen flutter wheels. If, on account of your brains being heavier than your heels, you chance to turn a somersault, and your head goes under, your heels will pop up like a pair of frisky, dapper ducks.

You cannot keep more than one end of yourself under water at once, but you soon learn how to wrestle with its novelties, and then it becomes a thing of beauty and a joy for any summer day. The water is delightful to the skin, every sensation is exhilarating, and one cannot help feeling in it like a gilded cork adrift in a jewel-rimmed bowl of champagne punch. In the sense of luxurious ease with which it envelops the bather, it is unrivaled on earth. The only approximation to it is in the phosphorescent waters of the Mosquito Indian coast.

The water does not freeze until the thermometric mercury tumbles down to eighteen degrees above zero, or fourteen below the ordinary freezing point. It is clear as crystal, with a bottom of snow-white sand, and small objects can be distinctly seen at a depth of twenty feet. There is not a fish or any other living thing in all the 2,500 to 3,000 square miles of beautiful and mysterious waters, except the yearly increasing swarms of summer bathers. Not a shark, or a stingaree, to scare the timid swimmer or floater; not a minnow, or a frog, a tadpole, or a pollywog —nothing that lives, moves, swims, crawls or wiggles. It is the ideal sea-bathing place of the world.

CHAPTER VI.

THE INVASION OF OKLAHOMA.

A History of the Indian Nation—Early Struggles of Oklahoma Boomers—Fight between Home-Seekers and Soldiers—Scenes at the Opening of Oklahoma Proper—A Miserable Night on the Prairie—A Race for Homes—Lawlessness in the Old Indian Territory.

OKLAHOMA, the youngest of our Territories, is in many respects also the most interesting. Many people confound Oklahoma Territory with the Indian Territory, but the two are separate and distinct, the former enjoying Territorial Government, while the latter, unfortunately, is in a very anomalous condition, so far as the making and enforcing of laws is concerned.

Up to within a few years Oklahoma was a part of what was then the "Indian Territory." Now it has been separated from what may be described as its original parent, and is entirely distinct. It contains nearly 40,000 square miles, and has a population of about a quarter of a million, exclusive of about 18,000 Indians. It contains more than twice as many people to the square mile as many of the Western States and Territories, and is in a condition of thriving prosperity, which is extraordinary, when its extreme youth as a Territory is considered.

In 1888, Oklahoma was the largest single body of unimproved land capable of cultivation in the Southwest. It was nominally farmed by Indian tribes, but the natural productiveness of the soil, and the immense amount of land at their disposal, cultivated habits of indolence, and there was a grievous and even sinful waste of fertility. To the south was Texas, and on the north, Kansas, both rich, powerful and wealthy States. The Indian possessions lying between disturbed the natural growth and trend of empire.

Seen from car windows only, the country appeared inviting to the eye. It was known, from reports of traders, to have all the elements of agricultural wealth.

And this made the land-hungry man hungrier.

The era of the "boomer" began; and the "boomer" did not stop until he had inserted an opening wedge, in the shape of the purchase and opening to settlement of a vast area right in the heart of the prairie wilderness. When the first opening took place it seemed as though the supply would be in excess of the demand. Not so. Every acre— good, bad, or indifferent—was gobbled up, and, like as from an army of Oliver Twists, the cry went up for more. Then the Iowa and Pottawatomie reservations were placed on the market. They lasted a day only, and the still unsatisfied crowd began another agitation. Resultant of this, a third bargain-counter sale took place. The big Cheyenne and Arapahoe country was opened for settlement. Immigrants poured in, and now every quarter-section that is tillable there has its individual occupant and owner.

But still on the south border of Kansas there camped a landless and homeless multitude. They looked longingly over the fertile prairies of the Cherokee Strip country, stirred the camp-fire embers emphatically, and sent another dispatch to Washington asking for a chance to get in. Congress heard at last, and in the fall of 1893 the congestion was relieved.

The scenes attending the wild scramble from all sides of the Strip are a matter of history and do not require repetition. Five million acres were quickly taken by 30,000 farmers.

The old proverb or adage, which states that the man who makes two blades of grass grow where one grew before is a public benefactor, would seem to proclaim that Oklahoma is peopled with philanthropists, for the sturdy pioneers who braved hardship and ridicule in order to obtain a foothold in this promised land, have, in five or six years, completely changed the appearance of the country. A larger proportion of ground in this youthful Territory shows that it is a sturdy infant, and it is doubtful whether in any part of the United States there has been more economy in land, or a more rapid use made of opportunities so bountifully provided by nature.

Truth is often much stranger than fiction, and the story of the invasion of Oklahoma reads like one long romance. Many men lost their lives in the attempt, some few dying by violence, and many others succumbing to disease brought about by hardship. Many of the men who started the agitation to have Oklahoma opened for settlement by white citizens are still alive, and some of them have had their heart's desire fulfilled, and now occupy little homes they have built in some favorite nook and corner of their much loved, and at one time grievously coveted, country.

Oklahoma came into the possession of the Seminole Indians by the ordinary process, and remained their alleged home until about thirty years ago. In 1866, the country was ceded to the United States Government for a consideration, and in 1873, it was surveyed by Federal officers, and section lines established according to law.

It was the natural presumption that this expense was incurred with a view to the immediate opening of the Territory for settlement. For various reasons, more or less valid, and more or less the result of influence and possible corruption, the actual opening of the country was deferred for more than twenty years after its cession to the United States Government, and in the meantime it occupied a peculiar condition. Immense herds of cattle were pastured on it, and bad men and outlaws from various sections of the country awoke reminiscences of biblical stories about cities of refuge by squatting upon it, making a living by hunting and indifferent agriculture, and resting secure from molestation from officers of the law.

To remedy this anomaly, and to secure homes for themselves and families in what was reported to be one of the most fertile tracts in the world, Captain Payne and a number of determined men organized themselves into colonies. There has always been a mania for new land, and many people are never happy unless they are keeping pace with the invasion of civilization into hitherto unknown and unopened countries. Many who joined the Payne movement were doubtless roving spirits of this character, but the majority of them were bona fide home-seekers, who believed as citizens of this country they had a right to quarter-sections in the promised land, and who were determined to enforce those rights.

No matter, however, what were the motives of the "boomers," as they were called from the first, it is certain that they went to work in a business-like manner, planned a regular invasion, and formed a number of colonies or small armies for the purpose.

We will follow the fortune of one of these colonies in

order to show what extraordinary difficulties they went through, and how much more there is in heaven and earth than is dreamt of in our humdrum philosophy. The town of Caldwell, on the southern line of Kansas, was the camp from which the first colonists started. It consisted of about forty men, and about 100 women and children. Each family provided itself with such equipment and conveniences as the scanty means at disposal made possible. A prairie schooner, or a wagon with a covering to protect the inmates from the weather and secure a certain amount of privacy for the women and children, was an indispensable item. When the advance was made, there were forty such covered wagons, each drawn by a pair of horses or mules, and each containing such furniture as the family possessed. The more fortunate ones also had in the wagons certain material to be used in building the little hut, which was to be their home until they could earn enough to build a more pretentious residence.

Eye witnesses describe the starting of the colony as one of the most remarkable sights ever witnessed. The wagons advanced in single file, and some few of the men rode on horseback in order to act as advance guides to seek suitable camping grounds, and to protect the occupants of the wagons from attack. In some cases one or two cows were attached by halters to the rear of the wagons, and there were several dogs which evidently entered heartily into the spirit of the affair. The utmost confidence prevailed, and hearty cheers were given as the cavalcade crossed the Kansas State line and commenced its long and dreary march through the rich blue grass of the Cherokee Strip.

The journey before the home-seekers was about 100 miles, and at the slow rate of progress they were compelled

Chief "Rain-in-the-Face" and his Favorite Pony.

to make, it was necessarily a long and arduous task. Some few of the women were a little nervous, but the majority had thoroughly fallen in with the general feeling and were enthusiastic in the extreme. The food they had with them was sufficient for immediate needs, and when they camped for the night, the younger members of the party generally succeeded in adding to the larder by hunting and fishing.

We have all heard of invading armies being allowed to proceed on their march unmolested only to be treated with additional severity on arriving at the enemies' camp. So it was with the colonists. They got through with very little difficulty, and no one took the trouble to interfere with their progress. Men who had been in the promised land for the purpose, had located a suitable spot for the formation of the proposed colony, and here the people were directed. One of the party had some knowledge of land laws, and after a long hunt he succeeded in locating one of the section corners established by the recent Government survey. This being done, quarter-sections were selected by each of the newcomers, and work commenced with a will. Tents and huts were put up as rapidly as possible, and before a week had passed the newcomers were fairly well settled. They even selected a town site and built castles in the air of a most remarkable character.

That they were monarchs of all they surveyed seemed to be obvious, and for some weeks their right there was none to dispute. Then by degrees the cowboys who were herding cattle in the neighborhood began to drop hints of possible interference, and while these suggestions were being discussed a company of United States troops suddenly appeared. With very little explanation they arrested every man in the colony for treason and conspiracy, and proceeded to drive the colonists out of the country. The men were compelled to hitch up their horses, and, succumbing to force of numbers, the colonists sadly and wearily advanced to Fort Reno, where they were turned over to the authorities. After being kept in confinement for five days they were released, and told to get back into Kansas as rapidly as possible. Government officials saw that the order was carried out, and then left the colonists to themselves.

The men lost no time in making up their minds to organize a second attempt to establish homes for their families, and once more they made the march. A bitter disappointment awaited them, for they found that their cabins had all been destroyed and they had to commence work over again. This they did, and they had scarcely got themselves comfortable when another small detachment of troops arrived to turn them out. The men were tied by means of ropes to the tail-ends of wagons, and driven like cattle across the prairie to the military fort. For a third time they conducted an invasion, and for the third time they were attacked by Government troops.

A spirit of determination had, however, come over the men in the interval, and an attempt was made to resist the onslaught of the soldiers. The Lieutenant in charge was astonished at the attitude assumed, and did not care to assume the responsibility of ordering his men to fire, as many of the colonists were well armed and were undoubtedly crack shots. He, accordingly, adopted more diplomatic measures, and, by establishing somewhat friendly relations, got into close quarters with the settlers. A rough and tumble fight with fists soon afterwards resulted, and the hard fists and brawny arms of the settlers proved too much for the regulars, who were for the time being driven off.

The result of the boomers' victory was the sending of 600 soldiers to dislodge them, and it being impossible to resist such a force as this, the colonists yielded with the best grace they could and sadly deserted the homes they had tried so hard to build up. Some of the men were actually imprisoned for the action they had taken, and the colony for a time was completely broken up. The example set was followed by several others, and for some years a conflict, not particularly creditable to the Government, went on. No law was discovered to punish the boomers and thus put a final end to the invasions. All that could be done was to drive the families out as fast as they went in, a course of action far more calculated to excite disorder than to quell it. Sometimes the soldiers displayed a great deal of forbearance, and even went out of their way to help the women and children and reduce their sufferings to the smallest possible point. Again, they were sometimes unduly harsh, and more than one infant lost its life from the exposure the evictions brought about. The soldiers by no means relished the work given them, and many of them complained bitterly that it was no part of their duty to fight women and babies. Still they were compelled to obey orders and ask no questions.

While the original colonists, or boomers, gained little or nothing for themselves by the hardships they insisted on encountering, they really brought about the opening for settlement of Oklahoma. About the year 1885 it began to be generally understood that the necessary proclamation would be issued, and from all parts of the country home-hunters began to set out on a journey, varying in length from a few hundreds to several thousand miles. The Kansas border towns on the south were made the headquarters for the home-seekers, and as they arrived at different points they were astonished to find that others had got there before them. In the neighborhood of Arkansas City, particularly, there were large settlements of boomers, who from time to time made efforts to enter the promised land in advance of the proclamation, only to be turned back by the soldiers who were guarding every trail. The majority of the newcomers thought it better to obey the law, and these settled down, with their wagons for their homes, and sought work with which to maintain their families until the proclamation was issued and the country opened to them.

It was a long and dreary wait. The children were sent to school, the men obtained such employment as was possible, and life went on peacefully in some of the most peculiar settlements ever seen in this country. Finally the Springer Bill was passed and the speedy opening of at least a portion of Oklahoma assured. The news was telegraphed to the four winds of heaven, and where there had been one boomer before there were soon fifty or a hundred. In the winter of 1888, various estimates were made as to the number of people awaiting the President's proclamation, and the total could not have been less than 50,000 or 60,000. Finally the long-looked-for document appeared, and Easter Monday, 1889, was named as the date on which the section of Oklahoma included in the bill was to be declared open. There was a special proviso that any one entering the promised and mysterious land prior to noon on the day named, would be forever disqualified from holding land in it, and accordingly the opening resolved itself into a race, to commence promptly at high noon on the day named.

Seldom has such a remarkable race been witnessed in any part of the world. The principal town sites were on the line of the Sante Fe Railroad, and those who were seeking town lots crowded the trains, which were not allowed to enter Oklahoma until noon. All available rolling stock was brought into requisition for the occasion, and provision was made for hauling thousands of home-seekers to the towns of Guthrie and Oklahoma City, as well as to intervening points. Before daylight on the morning of the opening, the approaches of the railway station at Arkansas City were blocked with masses of humanity, and every train was thronged with town boomers, or with people in search of free land or town lots.

The author was fortunate in securing a seat on the first train which crossed the Oklahoma border, and which arrived at Guthrie before 1 o'clock on the day of the opening. It was presumed that the law had been enforced, and that we should find nothing but a land-office and a few officials on the town site.

But such was far from being the case. Hundreds of people were already on the ground. The town had been platted out, streets located, and the best corners seized in advance of the law and of the regulations of the proclamation.

There was no time to argue with points of law or order. Those who got in in advance of the law were of a determined character, and their number was so great that they relied on the confusion to evade detection. One of their number told an interesting story to the writer, concerning the experience he had gone through. He had slipped into Oklahoma prior to the opening, carrying with him enough food to last him for a few days. He found a hiding place in the creek bank, and there laid until a few minutes before noon on the opening day. When his watch and the sun both told him that it lacked but a few minutes of noon, he emerged from his hiding place, with a view to leisurely locating one of the best corner lots in the town. To his chagrin he saw men advancing from every direction, and he was made aware of the fact that he had no patent on his idea, which had been adopted simultaneously by several hundred others. He secured a good lot for himself, and sold it before his disqualification on account of being too "previous" in his entry was discovered.

As each train unloaded its immense throngs of passengers, the scene was one that must always baffle description. The town site was on rising ground, and men, and even women, sprang from the moving trains, falling headlong over each other, and then rushing up hill as fast as their legs would carry them, in the mad fight for town lots free of charge. The town site was entirely occupied within half an hour, and the surrounding country in every direction was appropriated for additions to the main "city." Before night there were at least 10,000 people on the ground, many estimates placing the number as high as 20,000.

Some few had brought with them blankets and provisions, and these passed a comparatively comfortable night. Thousands, however, had no alternative but to sleep on the open prairie, hungry, as well as thirsty. The water in the creek was scarcely fit to drink, and the railroad company had to protect its water tank by force from the thirsty adventurers and speculators.

The night brought additional terrors. There was no danger of wild animals or of snakes, for the stampede of the previous day had probably driven every living thing miles away, with the solitary exception of ants, which, in armies ten thousand strong, attacked the trespassers. By morning several houses had been erected, and the arrival of freight trains loaded with provisions not only enabled thoughtful caterers to make small fortunes, but also relieved the newcomers of much of the distress they had been suffering. Within a week the streets were well defined, and houses were being built in every direction, and within six months there were several brick buildings erected and occupied for business and banking purposes.

The process of building up was one of the quickest on record, and Guthrie, like its neighbor on the south, Oklahoma City, is to-day a large, substantial business and financial center. Those of our readers who crossed Oklahoma by rail, even as lately as the winter of 1888, will remember that they saw nothing but open prairie, with occasional belts of timber. There was not so much as a post to mark the location of either of these two large cities, nor was there a plow line to define their limits.

In no other country in the world could results such as these have been accomplished. The amount of courage required to invest time and money in a prospective town in a country hitherto closed against white citizens is enormous, and it takes an American, born and bred, to make the venture. The Oklahoma cities are not boom towns, laid out on paper and advertised as future railroad and business centers; from the first moment of their existence they have been practical, useful trading centers, and every particle of growth they have made has been of a permanent and lasting character.

But if the race to the Oklahoma town sites was interesting, the race to the homesteads was sensational and bewildering. All around the coveted land, anxious, determined men were waiting for the word "Go," in order to rush forward and select a future home. In some instances the race was made in the wagons, but in many cases a solitary horseman acted as pioneer and galloped ahead, in order to secure prior claim to a coveted, well-watered quarter-section. Shortly before the hour of noon, a number of boomers on the northern frontier made an effort to advance in spite of the protests of the soldiers on guard. These latter were outnumbered ten to one, and could not attempt to hold back the home-seekers by force. Seeing this fact, the young Lieutenant in charge addressed a few pointed sentences to the would-be violators of the law. He knew most of the men personally, and was aware that several of them were old soldiers. Addressing these especially, he appealed to their patriotism, and asked whether it was logical for men who had borne arms for their country to combine to break the laws, which they themselves had risked their lives to uphold. This appeal to the loyalty of the veterans had the desired effect, and what threatened to be a dangerous conflict resulted in a series of hearty hand-shakes.

A mighty shout went up at noon, and the deer, rabbits and birds, which for years had held undisputed possession of the promised land, were treated to a surprise of the first water. Horses which had never been asked to run before, were now compelled to assume a gait hitherto unknown to them. Wagons were upset, horses thrown down, and all sorts of accidents happened. One man, who had set his heart on locating on the Canadian River near the Old Payne Colony, rode his horse in that direction, and urged the beast on to further exertions, until it could scarcely keep on its feet. Finally he reached one of the creeks running into the river. The jaded animal just managed to drag its rider up the steep bank of the creek, and it then fell dead. Its rider had no time for regrets. He had still four or five miles to cover, and he commenced to run as fast as his legs would carry him. His over-estimate of his horse's powers of endurance, and his under-estimate of the distance to be covered, lost him his coveted home; for when he arrived a large colony had got in ahead of him from the western border, and there were two or three claimants to every homestead.

In other cases there were neck and neck races for favored locations, and sometimes it would have puzzled an experienced referee to have determined which was really the winner of the race. Compromises were occasionally agreed to, and although there was a good deal of bad temper and recrimination, there was very little violence, and the men whose patience had been sorely taxed, behaved themselves admirably, earning the respect of the soldiers who were on guard to preserve order. The excitement and uproar was kept up long after night-fall. In their feverish anxiety to retain possession of the homes for which they had waited and raced, hundreds of men stayed up all night to continue the work of hut building, knowing that nothing would help them so much in pressing their claims for a title as evidence of work on bona fide improvements. They kept on day after day, and, late in the season as it was, many of the newcomers raised a good crop that year.

The opening of other sections of the old Indian Territory, now included in Oklahoma, took place two or three years later, when the scenes we have briefly described were repeated. To-day, Oklahoma extends right up to the southern Kansas line, and the Cherokee Strip, on whose rich blue grass hundreds of thousands of cattle have been fattened, is now a settled country, with at least four families to every square mile, and with a number of thriving towns and even large cities. At the present time the question of Statehood for the youngest of our Territories is being actively debated. No one disputes the fact that the population and wealth is large enough to justify the step, and the only question at issue is whether the whole of the Indian Territory should be included in the new State, or whether the lands of the so-called civilized tribes should be excluded.

The lawlessness which has prevailed in some portions of the Indian Territory is held to be a strong argument in favor of opening up all the lands for settlement. At present the Indians own immense tracts of land under very peculiar conditions. A large number of white men, many of them respectable citizens, and many of them outlaws and refugees from justice, have married fair Cherokee, Choctaw and Creek girls, and these men, while not recognized by the heads of the tribes, are able to draw from the Government, in the names of their wives, the large sums of money from time to time distributed. Advocates of Statehood favor the allotment to each Indian of his share of the land, and the purchase by the Government of the immense residue, which could then be opened for settlement.

Until this question is settled, the anomaly will continue of civilization and the reverse existing side by side. Some of the Indians have assumed the manners, dress, virtues and vices of their white neighbors, in which case they have generally dropped their old names and assumed something reasonable in their place. But many of the red men who adhere to tradition, and who object to innovation, still stick to the names given them in their boyhood. Thus, in traveling across the Indian Territory, Indians with such names as "Hears-Something-Everywhere," "Knows-Where-He-Walks," "Bear-in-the-Cloud," "Goose-Over-the-Hill," "Shell-on-the-Neck," "Sorrel Horse," "White Fox," "Strikes-on-the-Top-of-the-Head," and other equally far-fetched and ridiculous terms and cognomens.

Every one has heard of Chief "Rain-in-the-Face," a characteristic Indian, whose virtues and vices have both been greatly exaggerated from time to time. A picture is given of this representative of a rapidly decaying race, and of the favorite pony upon which he has ridden thousands of miles, and which in its early years possessed powers of endurance far beyond what any one who has resided in countries removed from Indian settlements can have any idea or conception of.

CHAPTER VII.

COWBOYS—REAL AND IDEAL.

A Much Maligned Class—The Cowboy as he Is, and as he is Supposed to be—Prairie Fever and how it is Cured—Life on the Ranch Thirty Years Ago and Now—Singular Fashions and Changes of Costume—Troubles Encountered by would-be Bad Men.

AMONG the thoroughly American types of humanity, none is more striking or unique than the cowboy. This master of horsemanship and subduer of wild and even dangerous cattle, has been described in so many ways that a great difference of opinion exists as to what he was, and what he is. We give a picture of a cowboy of to-day, and will endeavor to show in what important respects he differs from the cowboy of fiction, and even of history.

Sensational writers have described the cowboy as a thoroughly bad man, and, moreover, as one who delights in the word "bad," and regards it as a sort of diploma or qualification. Travelers over the region in which the cowboy used to be predominant give him a very different character, and speak of him as a hard-working, honest citizen, generous to a fault, courteous to women and aged or infirm men, but inclined to be humorous at the expense of those who are strong and big enough to return a joke, or resent it, if they so prefer.

We have spoken of the cowboy in two tenses: the present and the past. Strictly speaking, we should, perhaps, have only used one, for many of the best judges say that there is no such thing as a cowboy in this day and generation. He flourished in all his glory in the days of immense ranges, when there was an abundance of elbow room for both man and beast, and when such modern interferences with the cattle business as the barb-wire fence did not exist. The work of cattle herding and feeding to-day certainly differs in a most remarkable manner from that of thirty and even twenty years ago, and the man has naturally changed with his work. Now, the cowboy is, to all intents and purposes, a farm hand. He feeds the stock, drives it to water when necessary, and goes to the nearest market town to dispose of surplus products, with all the system and method of a thoroughly domesticated man. Formerly he had charge of hundreds, and perhaps thousands, of branded cattle, which ranged at will over boundless prairies, and the day's work was frequently varied by a set-to with some unfriendly Indians or some exceptionally daring cattle thieves.

The very nature of his work used to make the cowboy somewhat desperate in his habits, and apt to be suspicious of newcomers. He was never such a terrible individual as has been frequently stated in print. His work confined him to a few frontier States and Territories, and hence he was a very convenient person to ridicule and decry. The man who met the average cowboy face to face, generally learned to respect him, and speedily appreciated the fact that it paid to be at least civil. Writers who never went within 500 miles of the nearest cattle ranch or cowboy's home, treated him with less courtesy and described him in all sorts of terms.

Dime literature, with its yellow covers and sensational pictures of stage robberies and the like, has always libeled the American cowboy to a most outrageous extent. As a result of the misapprehensions thus created, what is known as cowboy or prairie fever is quite a common disease among youths who are trying to raise a mustache for a first time. The feats of recklessness, the absolute disregard of conventionality and the general defiance attributed to the man who herds cattle on the prairie, seem to create a longing on the part of sensationally inclined youths, and many of these have cut their teeth and learned their lesson in a very different manner from what was expected.

Let us imagine for a moment the experiences of the young man from the East, who has convinced himself, by careful reasoning and reading, that nature intended him to shine in the West. It is probable that he came to this most important conclusion many years before, and it is not unlikely that his first cowboy enthusiasm was fed by attacks upon the cat, with the nearest approach he could obtain to a rawhide whip. From this primitive experience, sensational literature, and five and ten-cent illustrated descriptions of the adventures of "Bill, the Plunger," and "Jack, the Indian Slayer," completed the education, until the boy, or young man, as the case may be, determines that the hour has arrived for him to cast away childish things and become a genuine bad man of the West.

Just how he gets half way across the continent is a matter of detail. Sometimes the misguided youth is too proud to beg and too honest to steal, in which case he probably saves up his pocket money and buys a cheap ticket. The more romantic and strictly correct course to adopt is to start out without a dollar, and to beat one's way across the continent, so as to be thoroughly entitled to recognition on the prairie. Many a young man who has commenced the pilgrimage towards glorified badness, has had the fever knocked out of him before advancing 100 miles, but others have succeeded in getting through, and have arrived in Texas, Wyoming or Montana, as the case may have been, thoroughly convinced of their own ability to hold their own in all company.

The disappointment that awaits the adventurous one is almost too great to be expressed in words. If the cowboys were one-half as bad as they are painted, they would proceed to demonstrate their right to an evil reputation by murdering the newcomer, and stealing his wearing apparel and any money he might happen to have with him. Instead of doing this, the cowboy generally looks with amusement on the individual who has come so many miles to join him. The greeting is not of the exuberant character expected, and frequently the heart of the newcomer is broken by being told to go back to his mammy and spend a few years more in the nursery. A runaway tenderfoot just fresh from school is not wanted on the cattle ranch, and although Western farmers are too good-natured to resent very severely the liberty taken, they never flatter the newcomer by holding out any inducements or making any prophecies as to his future.

The writer met a runaway enthusiast of this character a few years ago. His destination was the extreme West. As he did not know himself the State to which he was bound, he presumed that no one else did. When found, he had got as far as Kansas City, and hunger and lack of a place where he could sleep in comfort had cooled his ardor and inaugurated a vigorous attack of home-sickness.

As the ideal cowboy life does not provide for feather beds or meals served in courses, it was suggested to the lad that possibly he was having a good experience in advance, and getting himself accustomed to the privations of the life he had decided to adopt.

This logic did not commend itself at all to the runaway, whose sole ambition now was to borrow enough money to telegraph a message of penitence to his father. A small sum necessary for the purpose was given him, and the dispatch sent. Within an hour an answer was received and money transmitted by wire to supply the lad with a ticket for his home, where it is exceedingly probable what little cowboy fever he had left in him was speedily removed in old-fashioned and regulation manner.

The cowboy must not be confounded with the cattle baron. Ten or twelve years ago, when a great deal of money was made out of raising cattle, there was an invasion of the prairie States by men who knew nothing whatever about cattle raising, but who had made up their minds to secure a fortune by raising steers. They took with them as inconsistent ideas as did the youth in search of adventure. Often they carried large sums of money, which they invested very lavishly in business, and they also took with them ridiculously fine clothes, patent leather boots, velveteen jackets, and other evidences of luxury, which made them very unpopular and very ridiculous in their new homes. Nine-tenths of these called themselves "cattle barons," and about the same proportion obtained a great deal of experience but very little money, while trying to revolutionize the cattle business.

It is not necessary to own cattle at all to be a cowboy, although many members of this interesting profession own

The Cowboy as He Is.

a few beasts of their own and are allowed to have them graze with the other stock on the ranch. Generally speaking, the term used to be applied to all those who were engaged in handling the cattle, and in getting them together on the occasion of the annual round-ups. The old-time cowboy did not have a very high reputation, nor was he always looked upon quite as leniently as his surroundings demanded. About twenty years ago, a well-known cattleman wrote the following description of the cowboy and the life he led:

"If any one imagines that the life of a cowboy or ranchman is one of ease and luxury, or his diet a feast of fat things, a brief trial will dispel the illusion, as is mist by the sunshine. True, his life is one of more or less excitement or adventures, and much of it is spent in the saddle, yet it is a hard life, and his daily fare will never give the gout. Corn bread, mast-fed bacon, and coffee, constitute nine-tenths of their diet; occasionally they have fresh beef, and less often they have vegetables of any description. They do their own cooking in the rudest and fewest possible vessels, often not having a single plate or knife and fork, other than their pocket knife, but gather around the camp-kettle in true Indian style, and with a piece of bread in one hand, proceed to fish up a piece of 'sow belly,' and dine sumptuously, not forgetting to stow away one or more quarts of the strongest coffee imaginable, without sugar or cream. Indeed, you would hesitate, if judging it from appearance, whether to call it coffee or ink. Of all the vegetables, onions and potatoes are the most desired and the oftenest used, when anything more than the 'old regulation' is had. Instead of an oven, fireplace or cooking stove, a rude hole is dug in the ground and a fire made therein, and the coffee pot, the camp kettle and the skillet are his only culinary articles used.

"The life of the cowboy is one of considerable daily danger and excitement. It is hard and full of exposure, but is wild and free, and the young man who has long been a cowboy has but little taste for any other occupation. He lives hard, works hard, has but few comforts, and fewer necessities. He has but little, if any, taste for reading. He enjoys a coarse practical joke, or a smutty story; loves danger, but abhors labor of the common kind; never tires of riding, never wants to walk, no matter how short the distance he desires to go. He would rather fight with pistols than pray; loves tobacco, liquor and woman better than any other trinity. His life borders nearly upon that of an Indian. If he reads anything, it is in most cases a blood and thunder story of the sensational style. He enjoys his pipe, and relishes a practical joke on his comrades, or a tale where abounds animal propensity.

"His clothes are few and substantial, scarce in number and often of a gaudy pattern. The 'sombrero' and large spurs are inevitable accompaniments. Every house has the appearance of lack of convenience and comfort, but the most rude and primitive modes of life seem to be satisfactory to the cowboy. His wages range from $15.00 to $20.00 a month in specie. Mexicans can be employed for about $12.00 per month. The cowboy has few wants and fewer necessities, the principal one being a full supply of tobacco.

"We will here say for the benefit of our Northern readers, that the term 'ranch' is used in the Southwest instead of 'farm,' the ordinary laborer is termed a 'cowboy,' the horse used a 'cow horse,' and the herd of horses a 'cavvie yard.'

"The fame of Texas as a stock-growing country went abroad in the land, and soon after her admission to the Union, unto her were turned the eyes of many young men born and reared in the older Southern States, who were poor in this world's goods, but were ambitious to make for themselves a home and a fortune. Many of this class went to Texas, then a new and comparatively thin and unsettled country, and began in humblest manner, perhaps for nominal wages, to lay the foundation for future wealth and success."

This is a very severe description, and relates to a class of men who were found in the wildest parts of Texas shortly after the war. It certainly does not adequately describe the cowboy of the last twenty years. Another writer, who was himself for more than a quarter of a century engaged in the work of herding cattle, gives a much fairer description of the cowboy. He divides those entitled to this name into three classes, and argues that there is something noble about the name. He also claims that in view of the peculiar associations, privations, surroundings and temptations of the cowboy, he is entitled to much credit for the way in which he has retained the best characteristics of human nature, in spite of his absence from the refining influences of civilization.

According to this authority, the first class of cowboys include the genuine, honest worker on the prairie, the man who has due respect for the rights of all. He is scrupulously honest, but yet charitable enough to look leniently on the falling away from grace of his less scrupulous brothers, and he is loyal to a remarkable extent to every one who has a right to claim his friendship. In the second class is placed the less careful cowboy, who is not quite so strict in his moral views, although no one would like to class him as a thief. The story is told of the Irishman who found a blanket bearing upon it the Government mark "U. S." Paddy examined the blanket carefully and on finding the mark shouted out: "U. for Patrick and S. for McCarty. Och, but I'm glad I've found me blanket. Me fayther told me that eddication was a good thing, and now I know it; but for an eddication I never would have found the blanket."

Reasoning of this kind is quite common among this second class or division of the cowboy. It is not suggested that he is exactly a thief, because he would scorn the acts of the city light-fingered gentleman, who asks you the time of day, and then, by a little sleight-of-hand, succeeds in introducing your watch to a too obliging and careless pawnbroker at the next corner. But he is a little reckless in his ideas of what lawyers call the rights of individuals, and he is a little too much inclined, at times, to think that trifles that are not his own ought to be so.

The writer, to whom we are referring, includes in class three the typical cowboy, and the man used by the fiction writer as a basis for his exaggerations and romances. Into this class drifts the cowboy who is absolutely indifferent as to the future, and who is perfectly happy if he has enough money to enable him to buy a fancy bridle or a magnificent saddle. These are about the beginning and the end of his ideas of luxury; although he enjoys a good time, he looks upon it rather as incidental and essential to pleasure. A steady position at a small salary, a reasonable amount to do, and fairly good quarters, constitute all he looks for or expects. He is perfectly honest with all his indifference. He is often whole-souled and big-hearted, constantly allows himself to be imposed upon, but has an inconvenient habit of occasionally standing up for his rights and resenting too much oppression. He is exceedingly good-natured, and will often drive some stray cattle several miles for the convenience of a perfect stranger, and a man to whom he owes no obligation whatever.

It is said that such a thing as distress among the relatives or descendants of cowboys was impossible, because of the delightful tenderheartedness of men with rough exterior and whose daily life makes them appear hardened. The working cowboy is seldom rich, even in the most generous acceptation of the term. The small wages he earns are expended almost entirely on decorations for his horse or himself. Even when he succeeds in saving a few dollars, the money seems to burn a hole in his pocket, and he generally lends it to some one in greater need than himself. But every man working on a ranch has something to spare for the widow or children of a deceased brother, especially if he was killed in the course of his duties. An instance of this generous-hearted disposition might well be given, but it is sufficient to say that the rule is invariable, and that a promise made to a dying man in this respect is never forgotten.

Leaving for a moment the personal characteristics of the much-maligned cowboy, who has been described as everything from a stage-robber to a cutthroat, we may with profit devote a little space to a consideration of his attire as it was, and as it is. In the picture of a cowboy in this work the modern dress is shown very accurately. It will be seen that the man is dressed conveniently for his work, and that he has none of the extraordinary handicaps to progress, in the way of grotesque decorations, which he had been thought to believe were, at least, part and parcel of the cowboy's wardrobe and get up. Certainly at the present time men engaged in feeding and raising cattle are almost indifferent as to their attire, wearing anything suitable for their purpose, and making their selections rather with a view to the durability, than the handsomeness, of the clothing.

But in years gone by, there was almost as much fashion changing among the men on the prairie as among the woman in the drawing-room. At the close of the war the first of the arbitrary dictates of fashion went out. A special form of stirrup was introduced. It was very narrow and exceedingly inconvenient, but it was considered the right thing, and so everybody used it. Rawhide was used in place of lines, and homespun garments were uniform. Calfskin leggings, made on the prairie, with the hair on the outside, were first worn, and large umbrella-like straw hats came into use. A little later it was decided the straw hat was not durable enough for the purpose. When excited a cowboy frequently starts his horse with his hat, and when he is wearing a straw, four or five sharp blows knock out of the hat any semblance it may ever have had to respectability and symmetry. The wide brim woolen hat was declared to be the correct thing, and every one was glad of the change. The narrow stirrup gave place to a wider one, and the stirrup leather was shortened so as to compel the rider to keep his knees bent the whole time. The most important change in fashion twenty years ago, was the introduction of tanned leather leggings and of handsome bridles. Many a man now pays two or three months' wages for his bridle, and since the fashion came in, it is probable that many thousand dollars have been invested in ornamental headgear for prairie horses and ponies. A new saddle, as well as bow and tassel decorations, also came in at this period, and it is to be admitted that for a time exaggeration in clothing became general. It is an old joke on the prairie that the average man's hat costs him more than his clothes.

Many a cowboy earning $30.00 a month has spent three times that sum on his saddle alone. More than one man earning $25.00 a month has invested every cent of his salary in silver buckles for his strange looking hat. Equally extravagant is the average man as to his saddle, bridle, and even spurs and bit. Those who talk so much about the bad habits of these people, will hardly credit the fact that many a cowboy abstains from liquor and tobacco for an entire year at a stretch, simply because he wants to purchase some article of attire, which he thinks will make him the envy of the entire ranch.

The cow pony is worthy of as much attention and thought as the cowboy. It is often said that the latter is hard and cruel, and that he uses his pony roughly. This is far from being correct. Between the cowboy and his pet pony there is generally a bond of sympathy and a thorough understanding, without which the marvelous feats of horsemanship which are performed daily would be impossible. Perhaps in the preliminary breaking in of the pony there is more roughness than is quite necessary. At the same time, it should be remembered that to subdue an animal which was born on the prairie and has run wild to its heart's content, is not a very simple matter. The habit of bucking, which a Texas pony seems to inherit from its ancestors, is a very inconvenient one, and an expert rider from the East is perfectly helpless upon the back of a bucking pony. The way in which he mounts assures the animal at once that he is a stranger in those parts. A natural desire to unseat the daring stranger becomes paramount, and the pony proceeds to carry out the idea.

At first it moves quietly and the rider congratulates himself on having convinced the animal that resistance will be in vain. But just as he begins to do this the animal gets down its head, arches up its back, something after the manner of an angry cat, leaps into the air and comes down on the ground with its four legs drawn together under it, perfectly stiff and straight. The rider seldom knows how it happened. He only knows that it felt as though a cannon ball had struck him, and that he fell off most ungracefully.

A pony never bucks viciously when a cowboy is riding it. It has learned by long experience that the process is distinctly unprofitable. Breaking in a pony and convincing it that the way of the transgressor is hard, is one of the difficulties of prairie life. When, however, it is once accomplished, an almost invaluable assistant has been secured. The staying powers of the cow pony are almost without limit. He will carry his master 100 miles in a day, apparently with very little fatigue. In point of speed he may not be able to compete with his better bred Eastern cousin, but in point of distance covered he entirely outclasses him. Assuming an easy gait within its powers of endurance, a pony of the prairie will keep it up almost indefinitely. At the end of a very long ride, the man is generally more fatigued than his steed. The latter, after being relieved of its saddle and bridle, rolls vigorously to get rid of the stiffness, and, after an hour or two, is apparently in as good condition as ever.

The charm connected with cowboy life is found in the disregard of strict rules of etiquette and ceremony, and in the amount of fun which is considered to be in place around the prairie fire. We have already seen that the wages paid to cowboys are, and always have been, very small. The hours that have to be worked, and the hardships that have to be encountered, seem to combine together to deter men from leading the life at all. We know that it does neither, and that it is seldom there is really any dearth of help on the prairie or among the cattle herds. The greatest delight is derived from jokes played at the expense of smart tenderfeet, who approach the camp with too much confidence in themselves. The commonest way of convincing the newcomer that he has made a mistake is to persuade him to ride an exceptionally fractious pony. The task is generally approached with much confidence, and almost invariably ends in grief. If the stranger can retain his seat and thus upset the rehearsed programme, the delight of the onlookers is even greater than their disappointment, and the newcomer is admitted at once into the good fellowship of the crowd.

Nothing aggravates a cowboy so much, or makes him more desperate in his selection of tricks, as the affectation of badness on the part of a newcomer. A year or two ago a young man, who had been saving up his money for years in order to emulate the deeds of some of the heroes described in the cheap books he had been reading, arrived in the Southwest, and proceeded to introduce himself to a number of employes of a cattle ranch who, a few years ago, would have been known as regulation cowboys. The unlimited impudence and the astounding mendacity of the youth amused the cowboys very much, and they allowed him to narrate a whole list of terrible acts he had committed in the East. Before he had been in his new company an hour, he had talked of thefts and even killings with the nonchalance of a man who had served a dozen years in jail. His listeners enjoyed the absurdity of the situation, and allowed him to talk at random without interruption.

The story telling was brought to an end in a very sensational manner indeed. One of the listeners knew that a deputy sheriff was in the neighborhood looking out for a dangerous character. Skipping out from the party, he hunted up the deputy, and told him that one of the hunted man's confederates was in the camp. The deputy, who was new to the business and anxious to make a reputation for himself, rushed to the camp and arrested the story-teller in spite of his protests. The young man, who had been so brave a few minutes before, wept bitterly, and begged that some one would telegraph his mother so as to have his character established and his liberty assured. The joke was kept up so long that the young man was actually placed in safe keeping all night. The following morning he was released, as there was nothing whatever against him except artistic lying. The speed that he managed to attain while hurrying to the nearest railroad station showed that with proper training he might have made a good athlete.

He waited around the station until the next train went East, and no passenger was more delighted when the conductor said "All aboard," than was the youth who was going back home very much discouraged, but very considerably enlightened.

On another occasion a typical cowboy was traveling on the cars, and as is quite common with members of his profession, had been approached by a sickly looking youth, who asked him dozens of questions and evinced a great anxiety to embark upon prairie life. There was very little to interest the cattle-worker, and after awhile he determined to get rid of his not overwelcome, self-introduced friend. He accordingly pointed out a rough-looking man at the far end of the car, and told the questioner that he was the leader of a dangerous band of train robbers. The individual was probably some hard-working man of perfectly honest habits, but the would-be brave young man, who a few moments before had been a candidate for a life of danger and hardship, was so horrified at the bare idea, that he decided in a moment to emulate the Irishman who said he had left his future behind him, and jumped from the moving train, preferring a succession of knocks and bruises to actual contact with a man of the character he had schooled himself into admiring.

Every man who creates a disturbance, defies the law, and discharges fire-arms at random is spoken of as a cowboy, although in a majority of instances he has never done a day's work to justify the name. The tough man from the East who goes West to play the bad cowboy, is liable to find that he has been borrowing trouble. He finds out that an altercation is likely to bring him up facing the muzzle of a pistol in the hands of a man much more ready to pull the trigger off-hand than to waste time in preliminary talk. He soon learns the lesson of circumspection and, if he survives the process, his behavior is usually modified to fit his new surroundings. A tragic illustration of the results that may come from a tenderfoot's attempt to masquerade as a bad man west of the Mississippi River, took place in the winter of 1881-82 in New Mexico, on a southward-bound Atchison train. One of the strangers was terrorizing the others. He was a tough-looking fellow from some Eastern city; he had been drinking, and he paraded the cars talking loudly and profanely, trying to pick quarrels with passengers and frequently flourishing a revolver. The train hands did not seem inclined to interfere with him, and among the people aboard whom he directly insulted, he did not happen to hit upon any one who had the sand or the disposition to call him down.

Toward the members of a theatrical company, traveling in one of the coaches, he particularly directed his violence and insults. His conduct with them at last became unbearable, and when, after threatening two actors with his revolver and frightening the women to the verge of hysterics, he passed onward into another car, a hurried council of war was held in the coach he had just vacated, and every man who had a pistol got it in readiness, with the understanding that if he returned, he was to be shot down at the first aggressive movement. But that phase of trouble was averted, for, as it happened, he remained in the car ahead until, at dusk, the train rolled into Albuquerque.

Here the proprietor of the Armijo House was at the station with his hackman awaiting the train's arrival. He called out the name of his house at the door of one car, and then turning to the hackman said: "You take care of the passengers in this car, and I will go to the next."

These inoffensive words caught the ear of the tough man from the East, who was pushing his way to the car platform. He drew his pistol and started for the nearest man on the station platform, shouting:

"You'll take care of us, will you? I'll show you smart fellows out here that you are not able to take care of me."

He flourished his revolver as he spoke and, just as his feet struck the second step of the car, he fired, the ball passing over the head of the man on the station platform. The sound of his pistol was quickly followed by two loud reports, and the tough man fell forward upon the platform dead. The man at whom he had apparently fired had drawn his revolver and shot him twice through the heart.

A crowd gathered as the train rolled on, leaving the tough man where he had fallen. Of course the man who killed him, a gambler of the town, was fully exonerated at the inquest, and was never even indicted for the killing.

CHAPTER VIII.

WARDS OF OUR NATIVE LAND.

The Indians' Admirers and Critics—At School and After—Indian Courtship and Marriage—Extraordinary Dances—Gambling by Instinct—How "Cross-Eye" Lost his Pony—Pawning a Baby—Amusing and Degrading Scenes on Annuity Day.

OPINIONS differ materially as to the rights and wrongs, privileges and grievances, and worthiness and worthlessness of the North American Indian. Some people think that the red man has been shamefully treated and betrayed by the white man, and that the catalogue of his grievances is as long as the tale of woe the former is apt to tell, whenever he can make himself understood by a sympathetic listener.

Holders of this opinion live for the most part in districts where there are no Indians located.

There are others who think that the Indian has been absurdly pampered by the Government, and that it would be as sensible to try to change the arrangement of seasons as to attempt to prevent the survival of the fittest, or, in other words, to interfere with the gradual, but in their opinion inevitable, extermination of the Indian.

Those holding this extreme view are for the most part those who live near Indian reservations, and who have had opportunities of studying the red man's character.

Both views are of course unduly severe. As a useful citizen the Indian varies considerably, and it is rather as an interesting study that we approach the subject.

Civilization has a very peculiar effect upon the American Indian. The schools for Indian children are well managed, and the education imparted should be sufficient to prevent the possibility of a relapse into the unsatisfactory habits and the traditional uncleanliness of the different tribes. Sometimes the effect of education is excellent. There are many Indians to be found who have adopted civilized modes of living, and who have built up homes and amassed little fortunes by farming, raising cattle and trading. Some of the Indians, notably those of the five civilized tribes or nations in Indian Territory, resemble white men in appearance very much. They will sometimes work side by side with swarthy Caucasians, whose skin has been tanned by exposure to the sun, and except for the exceptionally high cheek bone and the peculiarly straight hair, there is little to distinguish the Indian from the white man.

But these cases are exceptions to the general rule, which is that education is looked upon by Indians as a degradation rather than otherwise. Great difficulty is often experienced in persuading parents to allow their children to be taken to the training schools at all, and so much compulsion is often necessary that an appearance of kidnaping is imparted. The first thing that is done with an Indian boy or girl admitted to one of these schools, is to wash the newcomer with considerable vigor from head to foot, and to cut off the superfluous, and, generally speaking, thickly matted hair.

The comfort of short hair, neatly combed and brushed, seldom impresses itself upon the youthful brave. For obvious reasons this is, however, insisted upon, and while the boy is at school he is kept neat and clean. Directly, however, he returns to his tribe he is in danger of relapsing into the habits of his forefathers. Too often he is sneered at for his neatness. His short hair is looked upon as an offense, and he is generally willing to fall in with tribal fashions, abandon his neat clothing, and let his hair grow and his face accumulate the regulation amount of dust and dirt.

The Indian trader and the pioneer generally will tell you that the only good Indian is a dead Indian. He will repeat this adage until it becomes wearisome in its monotony. Then, perhaps, he will vary it by telling you that of all the mean Indians the educated one is the meanest. This is only true in some instances, but it is a fact that education does not invariably benefit the Indian at all.

Almost all Indians are passionately fond of dancing. Several books have been written descriptive of the various dances of different tribes. Some of them have a hidden meaning and dangerous significance, while others are merely for the purpose of amusement and recreation. For these dances the Indians generally put on the most fancy costumes they have, and their movements are sometimes graceful and sometimes grotesque. The sign dance, as seen in some of the Southwestern tribes, is a curious one. One of the belles of the tribe leads a man into the dancing apartment, which consists of one of two tepees thrown together. In one are the tomtom beaters, in the other the dancers. In this room the couple begin to dance, making signs to each other, the meaning of which may be: "Well, what do you think of me? Do you like me? Do you think me pretty? How do I affect you?" and so on, the signs all being closely watched by the

Civilized Indians—The Means and the End.

spectators, who applaud, giggle, chuckle or laugh uproariously by turns, as the case may be. Such a dance is a questioning bee, a collision of wits on the part of two really facetious Indians.

Wit is a universal trait of the savage. Some white men draw. All Indians draw. Some white men are cunning. All Indians are cunning. Some white men are humorous. All Indians are witty. Dry wit, with a proverbial philosophy in it which would have delighted the soul of Tupper, is indigenous to the Indian. The Indian is the finest epigrammist on earth. His sentences are pithy and sententious, because short—never long and involved. A book of Indian wit and wisdom would have an enormous sale, and reveal the very core of his thought on a typical scale.

The Indian flirt is sweet, saucy, subtle, seductive. She has the art of keeping in stock constantly about her a score of bucks, each one of whom flatters himself that he, and he alone, is the special object of her admiration. Every tribe has had its belle. Poquite for the Modocs, Ur-ska-te-na for the Navajos, Mini-haha for the Dakotas, Romona for the neighboring bands. These belles have their foes among Indian women, but, however cordially hated, they never brawl or come to blows.

Love-making is one of the interesting night scenes in an Indian camp. When a young man wants to court a pretty red coquette, he stands at the door of his lodge on a bright day and flashes a ray of light from his sun-glass on the face of his sweetheart far away. She sees the ray as it falls on her, and follows in the direction whence it is thrown, right or left. She understands the secret of these flash lights. Soon the lovers meet, each under a blanket;

not a word, not a salutation is exchanged; they stand near each other for a time and then retire, only to repeat the affair day after day.

At last, upon some favorable night, the Indian youth visits the door of her lodge; she comes out and sits down on the ground beside him; still no word is spoken. At last she arises from the ground; he also rises, and standing before her, throws his blanket over both of them. No sooner has he done so than she doffs her blanket, letting it fall upon the ground, which is the admission on her part that she loves him, and does him obeisance as her future lord and master.

Every Indian camp at night is full of such lovers, with wooings as sweet, lips as willing, embraces as fond, lives as romantic, hearts as true, and elopements as daring and desperate as ever graced a Spanish court. The old people come together with their friends and hold a council. "How many ponies can he pay for her?" has a good deal to do with the eligibility of the suitor. That night he brings his articles of dowry to the door of his fiancee. If they are still there next morning, he is rejected; if not, accepted.

No formal marriage ceremony is gone through as a rule. The heart is the certificate and the Great Spirit the priest. Under the tribal government of the Indians, the rights of women were respected and clearly defined. She was the head of the house, and all property, save an insignificant amount, descended at death to her. She was in many tribes personified as the principal object of worship, prayer and adoration, in the tutelary goddess of the tribe. Now all is changed. The Indian of to-day is not the Indian of fifty years ago, and cannot be studied in the same light. His manners, customs and habits are all changed, and polygamy, more and more, creeps in with all its appalling degradations.

On special occasions an entire tribe is gathered under an open space in the cottonwoods to celebrate their principal dances. Hands are wildly waved above the heads of the dancers around a central fire of logs, piled in a conical heap. Around this blazing pile runs the dark circle which was built at sunset, inclosing sacred ground, which must not be trespassed on. The old chanter stands at the gate of the corral and sings. The men built the dark circle in less than an hour. When done, the corral measures forty paces in diameter. Around it stands a fence eight feet high, with a gate in the east ten feet wide.

At night-fall many of the Navajo people move, temporarily, all their goods and property into the corral, and abandon their huts or hogans. Those who do not move in are watchers to protect their property, for there are thieves among the Navajos. At 8 o'clock a band of musicians enters, and, sitting down, begins a series of cacophonous sounds on a drum. As soon as the music begins, the great wood pile is lighted. The conflagration spreads rapidly and lights the whole landscape and the sky. A storm of red, whirling sparks fly upward, like bright golden bees from out a hive, to a height of a hundred feet. The descending ashes fall in the corral like a light shower of snow. The heat soon grows so intense that in the remotest parts of the enclosure it is necessary for a person to screen his face when he looks towards the fire.

Suddenly a warning whistle is heard in the outer darkness, and a dozen forms, lithe and lean, dressed only with the narrow white breech-clout and mocassins, and daubed with white earth until they seem a group of living marbles, come bounding through the entrance, yelping like wolves, and slowly moving round the fire. As they advance, in single file, they throw their bodies into diverse attitudes, some graceful, some strained, some difficult, some menacing, and all grotesque. Now they face the east, now the west, now the south, now the north, bearing aloft their slender wands, tipped with eagle down, holding and waving them with surprising effects. Their course around the fire is to the left, east, west, south, north, a course invariably taken by all the dancers of the night.

When they have circled the fire twice, they begin to thrust their wands toward it. Their object is to try to burn off the tip of eagle down. They dash up to the fire, crawl up to it on their faces, run up holding their heads sidewise, dart up backward and approach it in all sorts of attitudes. Suddenly, one approaching the flaming pile throws himself on his back, with his head to the fire, and swiftly thrusts his wand into the flames. Many are the unsuccessful attempts, but at length, one by one, they all succeed in burning the downy balls from the end of their wands. As each accomplishes his feat, it becomes necessary, as the next duty, to restore the ball of down, which is done by refitting the ring held in the hand with down upon it, and putting it on the head of the aromatic sumac wand.

The dance customs and ideas differ with the tribes and localities. Sometimes the dance is little more than an exhibition of powers of endurance. Men or women, or both, go through fatiguing motions for hours and even days in succession, astounding spectators by their disregard of the traditions of their race, so far as idleness is concerned. Other dances are grotesque and brutal. On special occasions weird ceremonies are indulged in, and the proceedings are sensational in the extreme.

Of the ghost dance and its serious import, readers of the daily papers are familiar. Of the war dances of the different tribes a great deal has also been written, and altogether the dance lore of the American Indian is replete with singular incongruities and picturesque anomalies. Dancing with the Indian is often a religious exercise. It involves hardship at times, and occasionally the participants even mutilate themselves in their enthusiasm. Some of the tribes of the Southwest dance, as we shall see later, with venomous snakes in their hands, allowing themselves to be bitten, and relying on the power of the priests to save them from evil consequences.

The Indians gamble as if by instinct. On one occasion the writer was visiting a frontier town just after its settlement. Indians were present in very large numbers, and in a variety of ways they got hold of a good deal of money. The newcomers from the Eastern States were absolutely unprepared for the necessary privations of frontier life. Hence they were willing to purchase necessary articles at almost any price, while they were easily deluded into buying all sorts of articles for which they had no possible need. The Indians, who are supposed to be civilized, took full advantage of the situation, and brought into town everything that was of a salable character, frequently obtaining three or four times the local cash value.

With the money thus obtained they gambled desperately. One Indian, who boasted of the terrible name of "Cross-Eye," brought in two ponies to sell. One of them was an exceptionally ancient-looking animal, which had long since outlived its usefulness, and which, under ordinary local conditions, could certainly have been purchased for $4.00 or $5.00. A friendly Indian met Mr. "Cross-Eye," and a conversation ensued as to the value of the pony and the probable price that it would realize. The two men soon got angry on the subject, and finally the owner of the pony bet his animal's critic the pony against $20.00 that it would realize at least the last-named sum.

With this extra stimulus for driving a good bargain, the man offered his pony to a number of white men, and finally found one who needed an animal at once, and who was willing to pay $20.00 for the antiquated quadruped. "Cross-Eye" made a number of guttural noises indicative of his delight, and promptly collected the second $20.00.

He had thus practically sold a worthless pony for $40.00, and had it not been for his innate passion for gambling, would have done a very good day's business. A few hours later, however, he was found looking very disconsolate, and trying very hard to sell some supposed curiosities for a few dollars with which to buy a blanket he sorely needed. His impecuniosity was easily explained. Instead of proceeding at once to sell his second pony, he turned his attention first to gambling, and in less than an hour his last dollar had gone. Then, with the gamester's desperation, he had put up his second pony as a final stake, with the result that he lost his money and his stock in trade as well. He took the situation philosophically and stoically, but when he found it impossible in the busy pioneer town to get even the price of a drink of whisky for his curiosities, he began to get reckless, and was finally escorted out of the town by two or three of his friends to prevent him getting mixed up in a fight.

When the Indians have enough energy they gamble almost day and night. The women themselves are generally kept under sufficient subjection by their husbands to make gambling on their part impossible, so far as the actual playing of games of chance is concerned. But they stand by and watch the men. They stake their necklaces, leggings, ornaments, and in fact, their all, on the play, which is done sometimes with blue wild plum-stones, hieroglyphically charactered, and sometimes with playing bones, but oftener with common cards. Above the ground the tom-tok would be sounded, but below ground the tom-tom was buried.

An Indian smokes incessantly while he gambles. Putting the cigarette or cigar to his mouth he draws in the smoke in long, deep breaths, until he has filled his lungs completely, when he begins slowly to emit the smoke from his nose, little by little, until it is all gone. The object of this with the Indian is to steep his senses more deeply with the narcotizing soporific. The tobacco they smoke is generally their own raising.

"The thing that moved me most," writes a traveler, describing a visit to an Indian gambling den, "was the spectacle in the furthest corner of the 'shack' of an Indian mother, with a pappoose in its baby-case peeping over her back. There she stood behind an Indian gambler, to whom she had joined her life, painted and beaded and half intoxicated. The Indian husband had already put his saddle in pawn to the white professional gambler for his $5.00, and it was not five minutes before the white gambler had the saddle and $5.00 both. Then, when they had nothing else left to bet, so intense was their love for gambling, they began to put themselves in pawn, piecemeal, saying: 'I'll bet you my whole body.' That means 'I'll put myself in pawn to you as your slave to serve you as you will for a specified time.'

"So it was that this Indian mother stood leaning back wearily against the wall, half drunk and dazed with smoke and heat, when all at once the Indian who lived with her said to her in Indian: 'Put in the baby for a week. Then pay-day will come.' It was done. The baby was handed over. That is what civilization has done for the Indian. Its virtues escapes him; its vices inoculate him."

One of these vices is gambling. The Indian is kept poor all the year round and plucked of every pinfeather. That is the principal reason why he steals, not only to reimburse himself for loss, but also to avenge himself upon the white man, who he knows well enough has constantly robbed him.

Gambling, as witnessed in the Indian camp at night, is a very different affair from the cache. The tom-tom notifies all that the bouts with fortune are about to begin. During the game the music is steadily kept up. In the intervals between the games the players all sing. Crowds surround the camp. When a man loses heavily the whole camp knows it in a few minutes, and not infrequently the wife rushes in and puts a stop to the stake by driving her chief away. Gambling is the great winter game. It is often played from morning till night, and right along all night long. Cheating and trickery of every sort are practiced.

"Lizwin" or "mescal" are the two drinks made by the Indians themselves, one from corn and the other from the "maguay" plant. The plains Indians drink whisky. To gamble is to drink, and to drink is to lose. Gambling is the hardest work that you can persuade an Indian to do, unless threatened by starvation. Different tribes gamble differently.

The Comanches, undoubtedly, have by far the most exciting and fascinating gambling games. The Comanche puzzles, tricks and problems are also decidedly superior to those of any other nation. The gambling bone is used by the Comanches. The leader of the game holds it up before the eyes of all, so that all can see it; he then closes his two hands over it, and manipulates it so dexterously in his fingers that it is simply impossible to tell which hand the bone is in. In a moment he suddenly flings each closed hand on either side of him down into the outreaching hand of the player next to him.

The game commences at this point. The whole line of players passes, or pretends to pass, this bone on from one to another, until at last every hand is waving. All this time the eyes along the opposite line of gamblers are eagerly watching each shift and movement of the hands, in hopes of discovering the white flash of the bone. At last some one descries the hand that holds the bone, or thinks so. He points out and calls out for his side. The hand must instantly be thrown up. If it is right, the watching side scores a point and takes the bone. The sides change off in this way until the game is won. The full score is twenty-one points. The excitement produced by this game is at times simply indescribable.

The Utes play with two bones in each hand, one of which is wrapped about with a string. The game is to guess the hand that holds the wrapped bone. The plum-stone game is played by the plains Indians. It is only another name for dice throwing. The plum-stones are graved with hieroglyphics, and counts are curiously made in a way that often defies computation by white men. The women gamble quite as much as the men, when they dare, and grow even more excited over the game than their lords. Their game, as witnessed among the Cheyennes, is played with beads, little loops and long horn sticks made of deer foot.

The children look on and learn to gamble from their earliest childhood, and soon learn to cheat and impose on their juniors. Their little juvenile gambling operations are done principally with arrows. Winter breeds sloth, and sloth begets gambling, and gambling, drink. There is no conviviality in Indian drinking bouts. The Indian gets drunk, and dead drunk, as soon as he possibly can, and finds his highest enjoyment in sleeping it off. His nature reacts viciously under drink, however, in many cases, and he is then a dangerous customer.

The women of many tribes are a most pitiable lot of hard working, ragged and dirty humanity. Upon them falls all the drudgery of the camp; they are "hewers of wood and drawers of water," and bend under immense burdens piled upon their backs, while thousands of ponies browse, undisturbed, in every direction. As the troops are withdrawn, the squaws swoop down upon the deserted camps, and rapidly glean them of all that is portable, for use in their domestic economy. An Indian fire would be considered a very cheerless affair by the inmates of houses heated by modern appliances; but such as it is—a few sticks burning with feeble blaze and scarcely penetrating the dense smoke filling the tepee from the ground to the small opening at the top—it consumes fuel, and the demand is always greater than the supply, for the reason that an Indian has no idea of preparation for future necessities. If the fire burns, all right; when the last stick is laid on, a squaw will start for a fresh supply, no matter how cold and stormy the weather may be.

The poetical Indian maiden may still exist in the vivid imagination of extreme youth, but she is not common to-day. The young girls affect gay attire, and are exempt from the hardships of toil which are imposed on their elder sisters, mothers and grandams, but their fate is infinitely worse. Little beauty is to be discerned among them, and in this regard time seems to have effaced the types which were prevalent a few years ago.

Annuity day is a great event in the life of every Agency Indian, and if the reader would see Indian life represented in some of its most interesting features, there is no more suitable time to select for a visit to any Agency. It is a "grand opening," attended by the whole tribe; but the squaws do not enjoy quite the freedom of choice in the matter of dress goods, or receive such prompt attention from the clerks as our city ladies are accustomed to. Even at 9 o'clock in the morning, notwithstanding the fact that the actual distribution would not take place until noon, the nation's wards are there, patiently waiting for the business of the day to begin. Stakes have been driven into the ground to mark the space to be occupied by each band, and behind them, arranged in a semicircle, are the different families, under the charge of a head man. The bands vary in numbers, both of families and individuals, but they all look equally solemn as they sit on the ground, with their knees drawn up under their chins, or cross-legged like Turks and tailors.

The scene now becomes one of bustle and activity on

the part of the Agency people, who begin rapidly filling wagon after wagon with goods from the store-houses. Blankets of dark blue material, cotton cloth, calico of all colors and patterns, red flannel, gay woolen shawls, boots and shoes that make one's feet ache to look at them, coffee pots, water buckets, axes, and numerous other articles, are piled into each wagon in the proportion previously determined by conference with the head men. A ticket is then given to the driver, bearing the number of the stake and the name of the head man. Away goes the wagon; the goods are thrown out on the ground in a pile at the proper stake, and that completes the formal transfer to the head man, who then takes charge of them, and, with the assistance of a few of the bucks designated by himself, divides the various articles, according to the wants of the families and the amount of goods supplied.

During the rush and fury of the issue and division of the goods, the sombre figures in the background have scarcely moved. Not one has ventured to approach the center where the bucks are at work, measuring off the cloth, etc.; they are waiting for the tap of the bell, when they will receive just what the head man chooses to give them. There is no system of exchange there; it is take what you get or get nothing. In a great many cases they do not use the goods at all, but openly offer them for sale to the whites, who, no doubt, find it profitable to purchase at Indian prices.

As soon as the issue is completed, a crowd of Indians gather in front of the trader's store to indulge their passion for gambling, and in a short space of time a number of blankets and other articles change hands on the result of pony races, foot races or any other species of excitement that can be invented. There is a white man on the ground who is, no doubt, a professional runner, and the Indians back their favorite against him in a purse of over $30.00, which the white man covers, and wins the race by a few inches. The Indians will not give up, and make similar purses on the two succeeding days, only to lose by an inch or two. There is a master of ceremonies, who displays a wonderful control over the Indians. He makes all the bets for the red men, collecting different amounts for a score or more, but never forgetting a single item or person.

Ration day brings out the squaws and dogs in full force; the one to pack the rations to camp, and the latter to pick up stray bits. A few at a time the squaws enter the store-house and receive their week's supply of flour, coffee, sugar, salt, etc., for themselves and families. The beef is issued directly from the slaughter-house, and the proceeding is anything but appetizing to watch. The beeves to be killed are first driven into a corral, where they are shot by the Indian butchers; when the poor beasts have been shot to death, they are dragged to the door of the slaughter-house and passed through the hands of half-naked bucks, who seem to glory in the profusion of blood, and eagerly seek the position on account of the perquisites attached to it in the way of tempting (?) morsels which usually go to the dogs or on the refuse heap. The beef is issued as fast as it can be cut up, at the rate of half a pound a day for each person, regardless of age; bacon is also issued as a part of the meat ration.

CHAPTER IX.

CIVILIZATION—ACTUAL AND ALLEGED.

Tried in the Balances and Found Wanting—Indian Archers—Bow and Arrow Lore—Barbarous Customs that Die Slowly—"Great Wolf," the Indian Vanderbilt—How the Seri were Taught a Valuable Lesson—Playing with Rattlesnakes with Impunity.

DOES Prohibition prohibit? is a question politicians and social reformers ask again and again. Does civilization civilize? is a question which is asked almost exclusively by persons who are interested in the welfare of the American Indian, and who come in daily contact with him.

In the preceding chapter we have seen some little of the peculiar habits of the American Indian, civilized and otherwise, and it will be interesting now to see to what extent the white man's teaching has driven away primeval habits of living, hunting and fighting. Within the last few weeks, evidence of a most valuable character on this question has been furnished by the report submitted to the Secretary of the Interior by the Commission sent to investigate matters concerning the five civilized tribes of Indians in the Indian Territory. This says that they have demonstrated their incapacity to govern themselves, and recommends that the trust that has been reposed in them by the Government should be revoked.

The courts of justice have become helpless and paralyzed. Murder, violence and robbery are an every-day occurrence. It was learned by the Commission that fifty-three murders occurred in the months of September and October in one tribe only, and not one of the culprits was brought to justice. The Dawes Commission recommends that a large portion of the Indian reservation be annexed to Oklahoma; this action to be followed by forming that country into a Territory. But to accomplish this, it would be necessary that the consent of the Indians be obtained, and this is doubtful.

The statement that the Indians have cast aside their ancient weapons and adopted more modern ones, and that, through the use of them, they are gradually extending their hunting grounds beyond the lines of their reservations, is false. The report of the Commission makes this clearly known. Throughout the West the Indians still trust to their bows and arrows. On the northwest coast most of the Indians live by hunting and fishing. They use principally the bow and arrow, knife, war club and lance. In the North Pacific Ocean are several islands inhabited only by Indians. In the Queen Charlotte and the Prince of Wales Archipelago is found one of the most remarkable races of aborigines on the American continent. These are the Haida tribes, and consist of strikingly intelligent Indians. They acquire knowledge readily; learn trades and exhibit much ingenuity in following the teachings of missionaries and traders. But for all that, they still cling with something bordering upon affection to the primitive weapons of their race.

During the long winter nights the old Indians seat themselves before the fire and carve bows, ornament club handles, and feather and point arrows. Perhaps in some of the tepees hang polished guns furnished by the Government, but they are more for ornament than use. This evening work is accompanied by the low croaking of some old Indian, who tells over again the legends, folk-lore and nursery tales of their grandfathers and grandmothers.

The Haida tribe is more rapidly advancing in civilization than any of its neighbors, yet they still carve and paint bows, arrows, club handles and paddles. The Indians still cling to other rude implements and take not kindly to metal ones. Rude knives are still used for skinning deer, especially by the old Indians. The axe, of course, is employed for cutting trees and excavating canoes and mortars. It has really taken the place of the stone chisel, yet many old men prefer burning the roots of the tree until it can be made to fall by giving it a few hacks with the rude stone hatchet.

In archery, the Indian has scarcely been excelled. With a quick eye and a powerful muscle, he sends the arrow as unerringly as the archers of olden time.

The Indian bow is usually from three and one-half to four feet in length, with such a difficult spring that one with no experience can scarcely bend it sufficiently to set the string. Different tribes, of course, carry bows of different lengths, the Senecas having the longest. The best of woods for making bows are Osage orange, hickory, ash, elm, cedar, plum and cherry; some of these are strengthened with sinews and glue. Almost every tribe has three sizes, the largest being used for war purposes, and until an Indian can handle this war bow, he is not considered entitled to be called a warrior.

Some claim the Sioux and the Crows make the best bows, although the Apaches come close in the rank. When the Sioux bow is unstrung, it is a straight piece of wood, while the Apaches and the Southern Indians make a

An Uncivilized Savage.

perfect Cupid's bow. The Crows often use elk horns as material, and carve them beautifully. The Sioux, to make the straight piece of wood more elastic, string the backs with sinews. Often these are beautifully beaded and leathered, quite equaling, as a piece of art, the elaborate elk horn bows made by the Crows. The Comanches' bows are covered with sinew, much like those of the Apaches. The object of practice is to enable the bowman to draw the bow with sudden and instant effect. It is seldom that the Indian has need of throwing the arrow to a great distance.

The bow of the Western Indian is small and apparently insignificant, though its owner makes it very powerful, indeed. From his babyhood days he has habituated it to his use, until it has become, as it were, a very part of his nature. The Indian studies to get the greatest power out of the smallest possible compass, and he finds a short bow on horseback far more easily used and much more reliable in its execution. In the Far West, bows are made largely of ash, and are lined with layers of buffalo or deer sinews on the back. The Blackfeet have in use very valuable bows of bone. Other tribes make use of the horns of mountain sheep. Sometimes the bone bows will fetch very large sums of money, and deals have been noticed in which the consideration for one of them was a pair of ponies, with five pounds of butter thrown in as make-weight.

An athletic Indian on a fleet horse can do terrible execution with one of these bows, which, even in these days of repeating rifles, is by no means to be despised as a weapon. No one can estimate the force of a throw from one of them when an artistic archer is in charge. The effects from a wound from an arrow are so distressing that it is quite common to accuse an Indian of using poisoned arrows, when possibly such a fiendish idea never entered his head. Only those who have ridden side by side with an Indian hunter really know how much more powerful an arrow shot is than the average man supposes.

In war the Indians would even now arm themselves in part with bow, quiver, lance, war club and shield. The Northwestern tribes are partial to fighting with the bow and lance, protected with a shield. This shield is worn outside of the left arm, after the manner of the Roman and Grecian shield.

The Western Indians are fonder of horseback riding than the Eastern tribes, and have learned to wield their weapons while mounted. They are taught to kill game while running at full speed, and prefer to fight on horseback. Some of them are great cowards when dismounted, but seated on an Indian pony they are undaunted.

It is a mistake to suppose that arrow-heads are no longer manufactured; the art of fashioning them is not lost. Almost every tribe manufactures its own. Bowlders of flint are broken with a sledge-hammer made of a rounded pebble of hornstone set in a twisted withe. This bone is thought to be the tooth of the sperm whale. In Oregon the Indian arrow is still pointed with flint. The Iroquois also used flint until they laid aside the arrow for the lack of anything to hunt. The Iroquois youth, though the rifle has been introduced largely into his tribe, will have none of it, but takes naturally to the bow and arrow. Steel for arrow-heads is furnished by the fur-traders in the Rocky Mountains, and iron heads are often made from old barrel hoops, fashioned with a piece of sandstone. In shooting with the bow and arrow on horseback, the

Indian horse is taught to approach the animal attacked on the right side, enabling its rider to throw the arrow to the left. Buffalo Bill was an adept at slaughtering game on horseback, and he won his great bet at killing the greatest number of buffaloes, by following the custom of the Indians and shooting to the left. The horse approaches the animal, his halter hanging loose upon his neck, bringing the rider within three or four paces of the game, when the arrow or rifle ball is sent with ease and certainty through the heart.

Indians who have the opportunity to ride nowadays, still exercise with a lance twelve or fifteen feet in length. In their war games and dances they always appear with this lance and shield. The spears are modern and have a blade of polished steel, and the shields are made of skin. Those of old make are of buffalo neck. The skin is soaked and hardened with a glue extracted from the hoofs. The shields are arrow-proof, and will throw off a rifle shot if held obliquely, and this the Indian can do with great skill. Since there is no war or the occasion for the use of these arms, except in games of practice, many of the Indians, for a few bottles of "fire water," have sold their best shields, and now they are seen scattered over the country, preserved as curios.

It is folly to assume that the Indians have wholly or partly done away with their barbaric customs. In their celebrations it is their great joy to cast off their clothing and to paint their bodies all colors of the rainbow, wear horns on their heads and make themselves look as hideous as possible. The arrow game is introduced—never are there demonstrations with the modern weapons—and the man is esteemed above all others who can throw the greatest number of arrows in the sky before the first one falls. In hunting, the Sioux kill muskrats with spears, as they did in early days spear the buffaloes, managing to get close to them by being dressed in wolf skin, and going on all fours. There are Indians who would, on horseback, attack and kill a bear with a lance, but are afraid to molest the animal unless they have the Indian pony as a means of escape.

The arrow-heads of chert used for hunting are peculiarly fastened, in order to make the arrow revolve. The Indian feathers the arrow for the same purpose, and also carves the arrow shaft with a spiral groove. This is not, as has been supposed, to let the blood out of the wound, but to make the arrow carry.

Every tribe has its own arrow. It is claimed that the Pawnees are the best manufacturers. The Comanches feather their arrows with two feathers; the Navajos, Utes and all Apaches, except the Tontos, have three feathers—the Tontos using four feathers for each shaft. The bird arrow is the very smallest made.

"I have practiced" says one traveler, "for hours with the Utes, uselessly trying to blame the twist of the feathered arrow for my bad shots. The Indians say the carving and feathers are so arranged as to give the arrow the correct motion, and one old chief on seeing the twist in the rifle barrel by which the ball is made to revolve in the same manner, claimed that the white man stole his idea from the Indian."

Stones, with grooves around their greatest circumference, are secured to a handle by a withe or thong and become war clubs. They are dangerous weapons in the hand of an Indian. Tomahawks, manufactured by white men, have succeeded the war club in a way, as it is claimed the rifle has the bow and arrow. Recent tomahawks taken from the Indians bear an English trade-mark. They originally cost about 15 cents, and were sold to the Indians for nothing less than a horse, and perhaps two.

Chief "Wolf," an Indian Crœsus, and the Vanderbilt of the red men, though he is worth over $500,000 and drives at times in an elegant coach, clings closely to his tepee, ever demonstrating the savage part of his life.

He lives at Fishhook Bay, on the Snake River, in the State of Washington. He is of the Palouse Snake Indians, and though he has a comfortable house, he never sleeps there, but goes to the tepee, no matter how inclement the weather. In the days when the buffalo were plenty, "Wolf" was a great hunter. He tells a tale of driving 3,000 bison over a bluff near the Snake, where they were all killed by the fall. This is supposed to be true, because until late years the place was a mass of bones. Though he has his guns and all the modern fire-arms, both he and his children cling to the primitive weapons of war.

The correspondence between the Governments of the United States and Mexico over the brutal murder of two men by the Seri Indians, seems to show that some at least of the North American Indians have gained nothing at all from the civilizing influences which are supposed to have extended for so many years. The deed had no other motive than pure fiendishness. Small as is the tribe of Seris—they number only about 200 souls—these savages are the most blood-thirsty in North America. For a long time they have terrorized Sonora, but the Mexican Government seems powerless to control them.

The tribe was visited recently by an expedition from

the Bureau of Ethnology, which has just returned to Washington with some very interesting information. Prof. W. J. McGee, who led the party, says: "It is understood that the Seris are cannibals—at all events they eat every white man they can slay. They are cruel and treacherous beyond description. Toward the white man, their attitude is exactly the same as that of a white man toward a rattlesnake—they kill him as a matter of course, unless restrained by fear. Never do they fight in open warfare, but always lie in ambush. They are copper-colored Ishmaelites. It is their custom to murder everybody, white, red or Mexican, who ventures to enter the territory they call their own."

In many respects the Seris are the most interesting tribe of savages in North America. They are decidedly more primitive in their way than any other Indians, having scarcely any arts worth mentioning. In fact, they have not yet advanced as far as the stone age. The only stone implement in common use among them is a rude hammer of that material, which they employ for beating clay to make a fragile and peculiar kind of pottery. When one of the squaws wishes to make meal of mesquite beans, and she has no utensil for the purpose, she looks about until she finds a rock with an upper surface, conveniently hollow, and on this she places the beans, pounding them with an ordinary stone.

The Seris live on the Island of Tiburon, in the Gulf of California. They also claim 5,000 square miles of the mainland in Sonora. Their dwellings are the rudest imaginable. A chance rock commonly serves for one wall of the habitation; stones are piled up so as to make a small enclosure, and the shell of a single great turtle does for a roof. The house is always open on one side, and is not intended as a shelter from storms, but chiefly to keep off the sun. The men and women wear a single garment like a petticoat, made of pelican skin; the children are naked. Not far from Tiburon, which is about thirty miles long by fifteen miles wide, there is a smaller island where pelicans roost in vast numbers. The Seris go at night and with sticks knock over as many birds as they require.

These Indians are fond of carrion. It makes no difference to them whether a horse has died a natural death a week or a month ago, they devour the flesh greedily. The feet of the animal they boil until those parts are tender enough to bite. The Seris are among the very dirtiest of savages. Their habits in all respects are filthy. They seem to have almost no amusements, though the children play with the very rudest dolls. Before the whites came they used pieces of shells for cutting instruments. They are accustomed to killing deer by running and surrounding the animals. No traditions of sufficient interest to justify recording in print appear to exist among these people. The most interesting ornament seen on any member of the tribe was a necklace of human hair, adorned with the rattles of rattlesnakes, which abound in the territory infested with these remnants of all that is most objectionable among the aboriginal red men of this continent.

Physically speaking, the Seris are most remarkable. They are of great stature, the men averaging nearly six feet in height, with splendid chests. But the most noticeable point about them is their legs, which are very slender and sinewy, resembling the legs of the deer. Since the first coming of the Spaniards they have been known to other tribes as the runners. It is said that they can run from 150 to 200 miles per day, not pausing for rest. The jack rabbit is considered a very fleet animal, yet these Indians are accustomed to catch jack rabbits by outrunning them.

For this purpose, three men or boys go together. If the rabbit ran straight away from the pursuer it could not be taken, but its instinct is to make its flight by zigzags. The hunters arrange themselves a short distance apart. As quickly as one of them starts a rabbit, a second Indian runs as fast as he can along a line parallel with the course taken by the animal. Presently the rabbit sees the second Indian, and dashes off at a tangent. By this time the third hunter has come up and gives the quarry another turn. After the third or fourth zigzag, the rabbit is surrounded, and the hunters quickly close in upon him and grab him.

It is an odd fact that this method of catching jack rabbits is precisely the same as that adopted by coyotes, which work similarily by threes. By this strategy, these wild dogs capture the rabbits, though the latter are more fleet by far. It is believed that no other human being approaches the Seris in celerity of movement. A favorite sport of the boys is lassoing dogs. Mongrel curs are the only animals domesticated by these wild people. For amusement sake, the boys take their dogs to a clear place and drive them in all directions, then they capture the frightened animals by running and throwing the lassos, which are made of human hair. They have no difficulty in overtaking the dogs.

One day, a party of boys returning with their dogs after a bout of this sport, passed near a bush in which there were three or four blackbirds; on spying the birds, they dashed toward the bush and tried to catch them with their hands; they did not succeed, though one of the birds only escaped with the loss of several feathers. Some women of the tribe were watching, and they actually jeered at the boys for their failure. The boys were so mortified that they did not go into camp, but went off and sat by themselves in the shade of a greasewood bush. What white man or boy would think of catching blackbirds in such a way? Yet non-success in an attempt of that kind was the exception and not the rule. The Seris often take birds in this fashion.

Señor Encinas was the pioneer in that region. He found good grazing country in the territory claimed by the Seris, and so established his stock farm there. He brought priests with him to convert the savages, and caught a couple of the latter to educate as interpreters. The plan for civilizing the Indians proved a failure. They did not care to become Christians, and they killed the Señor's stock. So, finally, the Señor decided to adopt a new course of procedure. He summoned the Indians to a council, as many of them as would come, and informed them that from that time on he and his vaqueros would slay an Indian for every head of cattle that was killed. At the same time he sent away the priests and engaged an additional number of vaqueros.

The Indians paid no attention to the warning, and a few days later they killed several head of cattle. Without delay the Señor and his men coralled and killed a corresponding number of the Seris. Then there was war. The savages made ambushes, but they had only bows and arrows, and the vaqueros fought bravely with their guns. Every ambush turned out disastrously for the Indians.

Finally, the Seris made a great ambush, and there was a battle which resulted in the killing of sixty-five savages. The lesson proved sufficient, and the Indians were glad to conclude a permanent peace, agreeing that no further depredations against the Señor or his property should be attempted. From beginning to end the fighting lasted ten years.

After the killing of the two Americans, the Seris were very much afraid of reprisals. For a good while they did not dare to come to the ranch of Señor Encinas, but at length one old woman came for the philosophical purpose of seeing if she would be killed. She was well treated and went away. Eventually confidence was restored, and about sixty of the savages were visiting on the premises.

No other people in North America have so few conceptions of civilization as the Seris. They have absolutely no agriculture. As well as can be ascertained they never put a seed into the ground or cultivate a plant. They live almost wholly on fish, water fowl, and such game as they kill on the main land. The game includes large deer, like black tails, and exquisite species of dwarf deer, about the size of a three months' fawn, peccaries, wild turkeys, prairie dogs, rabbits and quail. They take very large green turtles in the Gulf of California. Mesquite beans they eat both cooked and raw. The mesquite is a small tree that bears seeds in pods.

The snake dance is another evidence of the comparative failure of civilization to civilize. This is seen chiefly in the vicinity of the Grand Cañon of the Colorado. Venomous rattlesnakes are used in the dance, which is an annual affair. Hundreds of snakes are caught for the occasion, and when the great day arrives the devotees rush into the corral and each seizes a rattler for his purpose. Reliable authorities, who have witnessed this dance, vouch for the fact that the snakes are not in any way robbed of their power to implant their poisonous fangs into the flesh of the dancers. It even appears as though the greater the number of bites, the more delighted are the participants, who hold the reptiles in the most careless manner and allow them to strike where they will, and to plant their horrible fangs into the most vulnerable parts with impunity. When the dance is over, the snakes are taken back to the woods and given their liberty, the superstition prevailing that for the space of one year the reptiles will protect the tribe from all ill or suffering.

The main interest attached to this dance is the secret of why it is the dancers do not die promptly. No one doubts the power of the rattlesnake to kill. Liberal potations of whisky are supposed by some people to serve as an antidote, while Mexicans and some tribes of Indians claim to have knowledge of a herb which will also prolong the life of a man stung by a snake and apparently doomed to an early death. Tradition tells us that for the purposes of this dance, a special antidote has been handed down from year to year, and from generation to generation, by the priests of the Moquis. It is stated that one of the patriarchs of old had the secret imparted to him under pledges and threats of inviolable secrecy. By him it has been perpetuated with great care, being always known to three persons, the high priest of the tribe, his vice-regent and proclaimed successor, and the oldest woman among them. On the death of any one of the three trustees of the secret, the number is made up in the manner ordered by the rites of the tribal religion, and to reveal the secret in any other way is to invite a sudden and an awful death.

During the three days spent by the dancers in hunting snakes, it is stated that the secret decoction is freely administered to them, and that in consequence they handle the reptiles with perfect confidence. When they are bitten there is a slight irritation but nothing worse. On the other hand, there is often a heavy loss of life during the year from snake bites, for the sacred antidote is only used on the stated occasion for which it was, so the legend runs, specially prepared or its nature revealed.

The people living within almost sight of the Grand Cañon vary as much in habits and physique as does the scenery and general contour of the cañon vary in appearance. The Cliff Dwellers and the Pueblos do not as a rule impress the stranger with their physical development, nor are they on the average exceptionally tall or heavy. There are, however, small tribes in which physical development has been, and still is, a great feature. Unlike the Pueblos, these larger men wear little clothing, so that their muscular development and the size of their limbs are more conspicuous. Naturally skilled hunters, these powerful members of the human race climb up and down the most dangerous precipices, and lead an almost ideal life in the most inaccessible of spots.

The Maricopa Indians must be included among those whose general appearance seems to invite admiration, however much one may regret the absence of general civilization and education. These men are for the most part honest, if not hard working, and they are by no means unpleasant neighbors. Right near them are the homes of smaller Indians, who have reduced peculation to a fine art, and who steal on general principles. We have all heard of the little boy who prefers to steal poor apples from his neighbor's tree to picking up good ones in his father's orchard. Much the same idea seems to prevail among these Indians. They will frequently spend several hours, and even the greater portion of a day, maneuvering to secure some small article worth but a few cents to any one.

They have a way of ingratiating themselves with white tourists, and offering to act as guides not only to spots of special beauty, but also to mines of great value. When they succeed in convincing strangers of their reliability, they are happy, and at once proceed to exhibit the peculiar characteristics of their race. Pocket handkerchiefs, stockings and hats are believed to be the articles after which they seek with the most vigor. They are, however, not particular as to what they secure, and anything that is left unguarded for but a few hours, or even minutes, is certain to be missed. The perquisites thus obtained or retained are regarded as treasure trove. When first charged with having stolen anything, they deny all knowledge of the offense, and protest their innocence in an amusing manner. When, however, convincing proof is obtained, and the missing article discovered, the convicted thief thinks the matter a good joke, and laughs most heartily at the credulity and carelessness of the white man.

CHAPTER X.

OLD TIME COMMUNISTS.

Houses on Rocks and Sand Hills—How Many Families Dwelt Together in Unity—Peculiarities of Costumes—Pueblo Architecture and Folk Lore—A Historic Struggle and How it Ended—Legends Concerning Montezuma—Curious Religious Ceremonies.

PERHAPS the most peculiar people to be found in our native land are the Pueblos, who live in New Mexico between the Grande and Colorado Rivers. When Coronado, the great explorer, marched through the territory 450 years ago, he found these people in a condition of at least comparative civilization. They were living in large houses, each capable of accommodating several families, and solidly built. Although they had wandering bands of robbers for their nearest neighbors, they were able to defend themselves against all comers, and were content and prosperous. Their weapons, although primitive, were quite scientific, and were handled with much skill as well as bravery.

For two years they were able to withstand the Spanish invaders in their "casas-grandes." It had been reported to the Spanish commanders that several hundred miles in the north lay a great empire named Cibola, which had seven large cities. In these were long streets, on which only gold and silversmiths resided; imposing palaces towered in the suburbs, with doors and columns of pure turquoise; the windows were made of precious stones brilliantly polished. At the sumptuous feasts of the prince of the land, enchanting slaves served the most delicate dainties on golden dishes. There were mountains of opal rising above valleys reveling in jewels, with crystal streams, whose bottom consisted of pure silver sand.

The disappointment of the Spaniards was great. A number of large Indian villages were found, whose inhabitants subsisted upon the fruits of a primitive agriculture. The frugality and thrift of the Pueblos excited the interest of the voluptuous Spaniards. The peculiar architecture of the villages and houses also drew their admiration. Taken as a whole, the circles of houses resembled the cells of a wasp's nest, of which the upper stories were reached on a crude ladder. Entrance could be gained only through a small opening in the roof, not even the sides facing the streets containing doors. A few heavily grated windows served as port-holes for their arrows. These peculiar constructions of baked clay are still fashionable in such old towns as Suni, Taos and others.

Situated as the Moqui villages and Acoma were, on the top of an inaccessible rock, the Spaniards despaired of conquering them. The supposed Cibola not panning out according to expectation, they did not seek reinforcement, and left the Pueblos in peace. Only near the end of the Sixteenth Century the Pueblos had to submit to Spanish rule, under which they remained until 1848, when the territory embracing New Mexico and Arizona was ceded to the United States.

In some respects the Spanish supremacy proved beneficial to the Indians. They virtually maintained their independence. Many innovations in their life and customs can be traced from this period. The only domestic creatures in their villages were large turkeys, whose feathers served as head ornaments for the warriors; but horses, cows, sheep, goats, dogs and last, but not least, the indispensable burros were added to their domestic stock.

The most important change in their communistic mode of living dates from the annexation of New Mexico to the United States, and the introduction of railroads. Their unfriendly neighbors, the Apaches, Comanches, Kiowas and Navajos, were restricted to their own reservations.

Feeling safe under the powerful protection of the Government, these peaceable people have begun to relinquish their old mode of communistic existence in their strange dwellings. Until recently, there was a promiscuous living together of large families in the numerous apartments of a single house, to which access could be only obtained through a small aperture in the roof. More modern cottages are being built for single families now; farming is also carried on on a large scale, and in some parts grape and fruit culture is attempted with good results.

All the villages are characterized by a certain industrial monopoly. In one of them, for instance, the pottery for all the Pueblos is manufactured; in others, like the Moqui villages, all the people are employed in the making of finely woven goats' hair blankets, in which occupation many are great experts. Although a large number are engaged in the sale of blankets and Indian goods in the southwestern part of the Union, in the gold diggings of California, in Mormon settlements, in the small railroad stations of Arizona, the average Pueblo Indian prefers a settled life. He is domestic in his habits, and loves his family, his cattle, his farm and his neighbors as dearly as does his pale-faced brothers. And has he not good cause to

rejoice and be contented with his lot? Has he not a faithful and charming wife? There are some pretty girls of perfect contour among the Pueblo Indians, especially in the Tigua villages. Are not his gleeful children, who are enjoying a romp on the huge sand hills, obedient and reverential in his presence? The impudent spirit of young America has not yet exerted its baneful influence here.

How scrupulously clean are the households! The good housewives of the Netherlands do not excel the Pueblo squaws in cleanliness. Floors are always carefully swept; all along the walls of the spacious rooms seats and couches are covered with finely variegated rugs; the walls are tastefully decorated with pictures and mirrors, and the large cupboards are filled with luxurious fruits, meats, pastry and jellies. Thousands of white bread-winners in the large cities would envy these Indians if they could behold their comparative affluence and their obviously contented state. Nor do they obtain all this without fatiguing toil. The land is barren and dry, which compels them to induce irrigation through long canals from far away streams, and the men are never afraid of work.

The Pueblo pottery of to-day differs but little from that of the Sixteenth Century. In the pottery villages the work is done mostly by men, who sit on the broad, shaded platform and shape their immense vessels in imitation of human beings and every imaginable animal shape. The grotesquely shaped mouth is generally intended for the opening, through which the water, soup or milk is poured.

The squaws are assuming more and more the occupations of the modern housewife, though they still grind their corn in the stone troughs used hundreds of years ago, and they still bake their bread in thin layers on hot, glowing stones. Dressmakers and tailors still go a-begging among the Pueblo people, and no attention whatever is paid to Parisian dictators of fashion. The good Pueblo squaw cuts, fits, and sews all the clothing for the family, which used to be composed mostly of leather. Her husband's wardrobe consists now of a few multi-colored shirts, a pair or two of leather pantaloons, with silver buttons, moccasins and a shoulder blanket.

The head gear, if any be worn, as is often the case, is simply a large colored handkerchief. Girls are usually dressed like the daughters of Southern farmers, but they refuse to discard the bloomers, over which the petticoats are worn a little below the knees. These leather pantalettes are a necessity in a country where poisonous snakes and insects abound in gardens and fields. To see a Pueblo girl at her best, she must be surprised in animated gossip in a bevy of girl friends, or when engaged in mirthful laughter while at work. Then the expressive, deep black eyes sparkle and the white teeth offer a glittering contrast to her fine black tresses, eyes and eyebrows. The Pueblo Indians are to be congratulated on one fact especially, that they permitted their moral improvement through the agency of the black-frocked missionaries and school teachers who came from the East, but also that they are one of the few tribes who resisted the conscienceless rascals who would wreck their homes through "fire water" and gambling devices.

A large number of ancient many-storied, many chambered communal houses are scattered over New Mexico, three of the most important of which are Isletta, Laguna and Acoma. Isletta and Laguna are within a stone's throw of the railroad, ten miles and sixty-six miles, respectively, beyond Albuquerque, and Acoma is reached from either Laguna or Bubero by a drive of a dozen miles. The aboriginal inhabitants of the pueblos, an intelligent, complex, industrious and independent race, are anomalous among North American natives. They are housed to-day in the self-same structures in which their forefathers were discovered, and in three and a half centuries of contact with Europeans their manner of life has not materially changed.

The Indian tribes that roamed over mountain and plain have become wards of the Government, debased and denuded of whatever dignity they once possessed, ascribe what cause you will for their present condition. But the Pueblo Indian has absolutely maintained the integrity of his individuality, and is self-respecting and self-sufficient. He accepted the form of religion professed by his Spanish conquerors, but without abandoning his own, and that is practically the only concession his persistent conservatism has ever made to external influence.

Laborious efforts have been made to penetrate the reserve with which the involved inner life of this strange child of the desert is guarded, but it lies like a dark, vast continent behind a dimly visible shore, and he dwells within the shadowy rim of a night that yields no ray to tell of his origin. He is a true pagan, swathed in seemingly dense clouds of superstition, rich in fanciful legend, and profoundly ceremonious in religion. His gods are innumerable. Not even the ancient Greeks possessed a more populous Olympus. On that austere yet familiar height, gods of peace and of war, of the chase, of bountiful harvest and of famine, of sun and rain and snow, elbow a thousand others for standing room. The trail of the serpent has crossed his history, too, and he frets his pottery with an imitation of its scales, and gives the rattlesnake a prominent place among his deities. Unmistakably a pagan, yet the purity and well being of his communities will bear favorable comparison with those of the enlightened world.

He is brave, honest and enterprising within the fixed limits of his little sphere; his wife is virtuous, his children are docile. And were the whole earth swept bare of every living thing, save for a few leagues surrounding his tribal home, his life would show no manner of disturbance. Probably he might never hear of so unimportant an event. He would still alternately labor and relax in festive games, still reverence his gods and rear his children to a life of industry and content, so anomalous is he, so firmly established in an absolute independence.

Pueblo architecture possesses none of the elaborate ornamentation found in the Aztec ruins in Mexico. The exterior of the house is absolutely plain. It is sometimes seven stories in height and contains over a thousand rooms. In some instances it is built of adobe—blocks of mud mixed with straw and dried in the sun, and in others, of stone covered with mud cement. The entrance is by means of a ladder, and when that is pulled up the latch-string is considered withdrawn.

The pueblo of pueblos is Acoma, a city without a peer. It is built upon the summit of a table-rock, with overhanging, eroded sides, 350 feet above the plain, which is 7,000 feet above the sea. Anciently, according to the traditions of the Queres, it stood upon the crest of the superb Haunted Mesa, three miles away, and some 300 feet higher, but its only approach was one day destroyed by the falling of a cliff, and three unhappy women, who chanced to be the only occupants—the remainder of the population being at work in the fields below—died of starvation, in view of the homeless hundreds of their people who for many days surrounded the unscalable mesa with upturned, agonized faces.

The present Acoma is the one discovered by the Spaniards; the original pueblo on the Mesa Encantada being even then an ancient tradition. It is 1,000 feet in length and 40 feet high, and there is, besides, a church of enormous proportions. Until lately, it was reached only by a precipitous stairway in the rock, up which the inhabitants carried upon their backs every particle of the materials of which the village is constructed. The graveyard consumed forty years in building, by reason of the necessity of bringing earth from the plain below; and the church must have cost the labor of many generations, for its walls are 60 feet high and 10 feet thick, and it has timbers 40 feet long and 14 inches square.

The Acomas welcomed the soldiers of Coronado with deference, ascribing to them celestial origin. Subsequently, upon learning the distinctly human character of the Spaniards, they professed allegiance, but afterwards wantonly slew a dozen of Zaldibar's men. By way of reprisal, Zaldibar headed three-score soldiers and undertook to carry the sky-citadel by assault. The incident has no parallel in American history, short of the memorable and similar exploit of Cortez on the great Aztec pyramid.

After a three days' hand to hand struggle, the Spaniards stood victors upon that seemingly impregnable fortress, and received the submission of the Queres, who for three-quarters of a century thereafter remained tractable. In that interval, the priests came to Acoma and held footing for fifty years, until the bloody uprisal of 1680 occurred, in which priest, soldier and settler were massacred or driven from the land, and every vestige of their occupation was extirpated. After the resubjection of the natives by De Vargas, the present church was constructed, and the Pueblos have not since rebelled against the contiguity of the white man.

All the numerous Mexican communities in the Territory contain representatives of the Penitentes order, which is peculiar by reason of the self-flagellations inflicted by its members in excess of pietistic zeal. Unlike their ilk of India, they do not practice self-torture for long periods, but only upon a certain day in each year. Then, stripped to the waist, these poor zealots go chanting a dolorous strain, and beating themselves unsparingly upon the back with the sharp-spined cactus, or soap-weed, until they are a revolting sight to look upon. Often they sink from the exhaustion of long-sustained suffering and loss of blood. One of the ceremonies among these peculiar people is the bearing of a huge cross of heavy timber for long distances. Martyrs to conscience and religious devotees frequently carry crosses of immense weight for miles, and are watched eagerly by crowds of excited spectators. The man who carries this fanatacism to the greatest length is the hero of the day, and receives the appointment of Chief of the Ceremonies for the following year.

Ceremonies such as these point to the extreme antiquity of the people, and seem to indicate that they must have been descended from tribes which were prominent in biblical narrative. According to many able historians, people have resided in this part of the world for at least twelve hundred years. In other words, when Columbus and Americus Vespucius discovered and explored the new world or portions of it, these peculiar people had been living on the then mysterious continent for the greater part of a thousand years.

According to some authorities these people are aboriginal. According to others, they migrated from some distant clime. The antiquity of China is well known, and there is good reason to believe that the Moquis and Zunis have sprung from Chinese voyagers, or perhaps pirates, who, hundreds of years ago, were wrecked on the western shores of America. Another theory is, that on the occasion of one of the numerous expulsions or emigrations from China, a band of Mongolians turned northward and came into America by crossing the Behring Strait.

Other antiquarians think that Morocco, rather than China, was the original home of these races. The traveler is much struck with the resemblance between the habits and customs of the Moors and of some of the old established tribes of New Mexico. In dress and architecture the Moorish idea certainly prevails very prominently. The white toga and the picturesque red turban are prominent in these resemblances. The jugs used for carrying water are distinctly Moorish in type, and the women carry them on their heads in that peculiar manner which is so characteristic of Moorish habits and customs.

One of the very earliest records of these people has been left us by Spanish explorers. A writer who accompanied one of the earliest expeditions from Spain, says: "We found a great town called Acoma, containing about 5,000 people, and situated upon a rock about fifty paces high, with no other entrance but by a pair of stairs hewn in the rock, whereat our people marveled not a little. The chief men of this town came peaceably to visit us, bringing many mantles and chamois skins, excellently dressed, and great plenty of victuals. Their corn-fields were two leagues distant, and they fetched water out of a small river to water the same, on the brinks whereof there were great banks of roses like those of Castile. There were many mountains full of metals. Our men remained in the place three days, upon one of which the inhabitants made before them a very solemn dance, coming forth in the same gallant apparel, using very witty sports, wherewith our men were exceedingly delighted."

Among the ruins found here, the early use of stone for architectural purposes is clearly manifested, and there are innumerable relics of ingenuity in periods upon which we are apt to look with great contempt. Arrow-heads made of flint, quartz, agate and jaspar, can easily be found by the relic hunter. Hatchets made of stone, and sharpened in a most unique manner, are also common, and the ancestors of the Pueblos undoubtedly used knives made of stone hundreds of years ago.

One of the most interesting of the ancient houses is in the Chaco Cañon. This edifice was probably at one time 300 feet long, about half as wide and three stories high. From the nature of the rooms, it is evident that the walls were built in terrace-form out of sandstone. There were about 150 rooms, and judging from the present habits of the people, at least 500 human beings lived in this mammoth boarding-house. Another very interesting structure of a similar character is found on the Upper Grande River, about two hours' drive from Santa Fe. It was about 300 feet square originally, and most of the foundations are still in fairly good condition, though much of the exposed portion of the stone has yielded by degrees to the friction caused by continual sandstorms. It is believed that more than 1,000 people lived in this one house.

Of recent years a good deal has been written concerning the possibilities of the future in regard to saving expense by large numbers of families occupying one house. Most of these ideas have been ridiculed, because experience has proved that families seldom reside comfortably in crowded quarters. The tribes of which we are writing, while they destroy the originality of the communistic ideas of the Nineteenth Century, also disprove the arguments which are principally brought against them. In these singular houses or colonies, several families live together in perfect harmony. There are no instances on record of disputes such as are met with in boarding-houses patronized by white people, and in this one respect, at any rate, quite a lesson is taught us by the Pueblo tribes. The people are quiet and peaceable in disposition, and one secret of their peaceful dwelling together is found in the absence of jealousy, a characteristic or vice which does not seem to have penetrated into the houses on the cliffs, or to have sullied the dispositions of these people with such a remarkable and creditable history. It requires a good deal of dexterity and agility to enter or leave a communal house of this character, and a door, from what we are apt to term a civilized point of view, is unknown.

The visitor is told a number of legends and stories about these houses and the people who live in them. The coming of Montezuma is the great idea which permeates all the legends and stories. According to many of the people, Montezuma left Mexico, during the remote ages, in a canoe built of serpent-skins. His object was to civilize the East and to do away with human sacrifice. He communicated with the people by means of cords in which knots were tied in the most ingenious manner. The knots conveyed the meaning of the Prophet, and his peculiar messages were carried from pueblo to pueblo by swift messengers, who took great delight in executing their tasks.

A number of exceedingly romantic legends are centered around the Pueblo de Taos, which is about twenty miles from Embudo. Taos is considered the most interesting and the most perfect specimen of a Pueblo Indian fortress. It consists of two communistic houses, each five stories high, and a Roman Catholic church (now in a ruined condition) which stands near, although apart from the dwellings. Around the fortress are seven circular mounds, which at first suggest the idea of being the work of mound-builders. On further examination they prove to be the sweating chambers or Turkish baths of this curious people. Of these chambers, the largest appears also to serve the purpose of a council chamber and mystic hall, where rites peculiar to the tribe (about which they are very reticent) are performed.

The Pueblo Indians delight to adorn themselves in gay colors, and form very interesting and picturesque subjects for the artist, especially when associated with their quaint surroundings. They are skilled in the manufacture of pottery, basket-making and bead work. The grand annual festival of these Indians occurs on the 30th of September, and the ceremonies are of a peculiarly interesting character.

Jesuitism has grafted its faith upon the superstitions of the Montezumas, and a curious fruitage is the result. The mystic rites of the Pueblo Indians, performed at Pueblo de Taos in honor of San Geronimo (St. Jerome), upon each succeeding 30th day of September, attract large concourses of people, and are of great interest to either the ethnologist, ecclesiastic or tourist. A brief description can give but a faint idea of these ceremonies, but may serve to arouse an interest in the matter. In the early morning of St. Jerome's day, a black-robed Indian makes a recitation from the top of the pueblo to the assembled multitude below. In the plaza stands a pine tree pole, fifty feet in height, and from a cross-piece at top dangles a live sheep, with legs tied together and back down. Besides the sheep, a garland of such fruits and vegetables as the valley produces, together with a basket of bread and grain, hang from the pole. The bell in the little adobe chapel sounds and a few of the Indians go in to mass.

A curious service follows. A rubicund Mexican priest is the celebrant, while two old Mexicans in modern dress, and a Pueblo Indian in a red blanket, are acolytes. When the host is elevated, an Indian at the door beats a villainous drum and four musket shots are discharged. After the services are concluded, a procession is formed and marches to the race track, which is three hundred yards in length. The runners have prepared themselves in the estufas, or underground council chambers, and soon appear. There are fifty of them, and all are naked except a breech-clout, and are painted no two alike. Fifty other runners to contest with these, arrive from the other pueblo. They form in line on either side of the course, and a slow, graceful dance ensues. All at once three hundred mad young Mexicans rush through the throng on their wild ponies, the leader swinging by the neck the gallo or cock. Then the races begin, two runners from each side darting down the track cheered by their companions. No sooner do they reach the goal than two others start off, and thus for two hours, until the sum of victories gained by individuals entitles one party or the other to claim success. The race decided, the runners range themselves in two facing lines, and, preceded by the drum, begin a slow zig-zag march.

Excitement now runs riot. The dancers chant weird songs, break the ranks and vie with each other in their antics and peculiarities. A rush is made upon the crowd of spectators through whom the participants in the orgies force their way, regardless of consequences. The women, who hitherto have taken but little part in the excitement, now come forward and throw cakes and rolls of bread from the pueblo terraces. Everybody rushes after these prizes in a headlong manner, and the confusion becomes still greater.

An adjournment is then taken for dinner, and in the afternoon, six gorgeously painted and hideously decorated clowns come forward and go through a series of antics calculated to disgust rather than amuse the spectator. The unfortunate sheep, which is still hanging to the pole, is finally thrown to the ground after several attempts have been made to climb the pole. The fruits and products are seized by the clowns, who rush off with them, and every one connected with the tribe seem to be highly satisfied with the outcome of the day's proceedings, and the culmination of the spectacle.

CHAPTER XI.

HOW CUSTER LIVED AND DIED.

"Remember Custer"—An Eye Witness of the Massacre—Custer, Cody and Alexis—A Ride over the Scenes of the Unequal Conflict—Major Reno's Marked Failure—How "Sitting Bull" Ran Away and Lived to Fight Another Day—Why a Medicine Man did not Summon Rain.

"REMEMBER Custer" was the watchword and battle-cry of the small army of American soldiers who early in the present decade advanced against hostile Indians in the Northwest, who after indulging for weeks in a series of fantastic dances and superstitious rites, were finally called to time by the Government and punished for their disregard of treaty rights and reasonable orders. Every American child should know who Custer was and why the troopers called upon each other to remember him on the occasion referred to. It is less than twenty years since he died. His name should be remembered by civilians as well as soldiers for almost as many centuries to come.

There are some men who seem to defy and even court death. Custer was one of these. He was so recklessly brave that he often caused anxiety to his superior officers. Time and again he led a handful of men apparently into the jaws of death and brought them out safely, after having practically annihilated the foe. As the pitcher which is carried safely to the well ninety-nine times sometimes gets broken at the hundredth attempt, so was it with General Custer. In June, 1876, his detachment was outnumbered twenty to one at a little ford near Crazy Horse Creek, in Dakota, and his entire command was wiped out. An adopted son of "Sitting Bull," the famous Indian, states that he saw Custer die, adding that he twice witnessed the hero lying on his back fighting his foes. The third time he saw him a blanket was drawn over the hero, who was apparently dead.

On another page is given an admirable illustration of the camp and ford, as well as of the monument erected in Custer's memory, with typical Indian camp scene. This picture is from photographs taken specially for Mr. Charles S. Fee, General Passenger Agent of the Northern Pacific Railroad, whose tracks run close by this scene of such sad history.

A volume could be devoted to the life of Custer, the adventures he encountered, and the risks he ran in the course of his eventful and useful career. His works and his memoirs bristle with information concerning the actual truths of border life and Indian warfare, bereft of romance and exaggeration. Like almost all Indian fighters, Custer entertained a supreme contempt for the red man generally, although his naturally kind disposition led him to give credit to individual red men for bravery, gratitude, and other characteristics generally believed to be inconsistent with their character and nationality.

Besides being a gallant fighter, Custer was also a great lover of recreation and fun, while a genuine hunting expedition drew him out from his almost habitual quiet and made him the natural leader of the party. Among his friends was William Cody, better known to the amusement loving world as Buffalo Bill, on account of his alleged excessive prowess in the shooting and destruction of buffalo. If Mr. Cody were consulted, he would probably prefer to be called Indian Bill, as his hatred of the average red man was very largely in excess of his anxiety to kill the hump-backed oxen, which were, at one time, almost in sole possession of the Western prairies. On one occasion, he and Custer had a very delightful time together, and Cody has given a pleasing description of what took place.

This was on the occasion of the visit to this country of the Grand Duke Alexis. Some twenty-three years ago this European celebrity enjoyed a tour through the United States, and visited most of the grandest features of our native land. Before coming to the country, he had heard of its great hunting facilities, and also of the sport to be obtained from shooting buffalo on the prairie. He mentioned this fact to the officers of the Government, who were detailed to complete arrangements for his benefit, and, acccordingly, it was arranged that the Grand Duke should be conducted into buffalo land, and initiated into the mysteries of buffalo hunting, by the officer who has since been annihilated by the Sioux, and the irrepressible hunter who has since developed into a prince among showmen.

These two somewhat rough, but very kind, chaperones, took with them on this trip a party of Indians, including "Spotted Tail," with whose daughter Custer carried on, we are told, a mild flirtation on the march. A great deal of amusement was derived from the trip, as well as very much important information.

It was but four years later that Custer was engaged on a more serious and less entertaining mission. The scene of the tragedy was visited some three years ago by Mr.

L. D. Wheeler, to whom we are indebted for the following very graphic and interesting description of the visit and of the thoughts it called forth:

"A rather lengthy ride found us at Reno's crossing of the river, the ford where he crossed to make his attack. Fording the stream, we dismounted among the young timber and bushes lining the stream, and ate lunch. Before lunch was finished, two Indian girls came down the river. The younger, tall, slender and graceful, dressed in bright, clean scarlet, was a picture. With her jet black hair hanging in shining plaits, her piercing eyes and handsome face, she was the most comely, sylph-like Indian maiden I have ever seen.

"Mounting our horses, lunch over, we cantered back on the trail that Custer and Reno followed, for a ride of several miles to Lookout Hill, or Point, which we ascended. This was the point where Custer and his officers obtained their first view of the valley of the Greasy Grass, as the Sioux call the Little Horn.

"After a survey of the region, spurring our horses forward, we in time found ourselves climbing the gentle acclivities which led up to Reno's old rifle-pits, now almost obliterated. The most noticeable feature of the spot is the number of blanched bones of horses which lie scattered about. A short distance from the pits—which are rather rounded, and follow the outline of the hills in shape—and in a slight hollow below them, are more bones of horses. This is where the wounded were taken, and the hospital established, and the horses kept. From the wavy summit line of the bluffs, the ground slopes in an irregular broken way back to the northeast and east, into a coulee that forms the passage to the ford which Custer aimed for and

Custer Battle Field and Monument.

never reached. The ground about the battle-field is now a national cemetery. It is enclosed by a wire fence, and there are several hundred acres of it. It might be cared for in a manner somewhat better than it is. During one of my visits there, a Crow Indian rode up to the gate and deliberately turned his herd of horses into the inclosure to graze.

"As I rode into the grounds, after fording and recrossing the river where Custer failed, the first object to greet my sight was a small inclosure, with large mound and headstone, which marked the spot where Lieutenant Crittenden fell. At one corner, and outside of it, stood the regulation marble slab which marks the place where each body on the field was found. This one stated that there Lieutenant Calhoun was killed. At numbers of places down the western slope, but near the ravines, the surface is dotted with the little gravestones. In some places, far down the descent, and far from where Custer, Van Reilly, Tom Custer and others fell, they are seen singly; in other spots three or four, or half a dozen. At one point there are over thirty, well massed together. Down in this part of the field, in the ravine running towards the monument, is the stone marking where Dr. Lord's body was found, and with it are four others.

"In the shallow coulee east of the ridge, and almost at the bottom of the slope, some distance northwest of where Calhoun and Crittenden were killed, and on the main ridge slope of it, is a large group of stones. Here is where Captain Miles Keogh and thirty-eight men gave up their lives. On this side of the ridge—the eastern side—between where Keogh and his men died and where Custer fell, there are numerous stones. On the opposite side of the Custer ridge—that which faces the river—and close to its crest, there are very few stones, and those are much scattered, and not in groups. At the northern extremity of the ridge is a slight elevation which overtops everything else, and slopes away in all directions, save where the ridge lies. Just below this knoll, or hillock—Custer Hill—facing southwest, is where Custer and the larger part of his men fell."

On the right bank of the Missouri River—the Big Muddy—in North Dakota, almost within rifle shot of the town of Mandan, on the Northern Pacific Railroad, there existed in the '70s a military post named after the nation's great martyr President, Fort Abraham Lincoln. On the morning of the 17th of June, 1876, there went forth from here among others, with the pomp and ceremony for which they were distinguished, a cavalry regiment famed in the army for dash, bravery and endurance—the noted Seventh Cavalry.

At the head of the Seventh Cavalry was a man who was unquestionably the most picturesque character for long years, and perhaps for all previous and present time, in the army. Entering the army in active service during the Civil War, his career was a continual round of successes and advances, and at its close, aside from the peerless Sheridan, no cavalryman had a greater reputation for magnificent dash than he. Transferred to the plains—the war over—his success as an Indian campaigner naturally followed, and at the time he moved out upon his latest and fated expedition, George Custer had a reputation as an Indian fighter second to none.

On June 22d, Custer and the Seventh Cavalry left camp on the Rosebud in compliance with their instructions. On the 23d and 24th, many of the camping places of the Indians, in their migration westward, were passed. By evening of June 24th, the trail and signs had become so hot and fresh that a halt was ordered to await tidings from the scouts. Their information proved that the Indians were across the divide, over in the valley of the Little Horn. Custer, confident of his ability to whip the Indians single-handed, prepared for fight at once. He pushed ahead on the trail, and created the impression that it was his determination to get to the spot, and have one battle royal with the Indians, in which he and the Seventh should be the sole participants on our side, and in consequence the sole heroes. The idea of defeat seems never to have occurred to him.

Early on the morning of June 25th, Custer resumed his march. Up to that time the command was maneuvered as a whole. Now, however, it was divided into four detachments. One under Major Reno, consisting of three troops of cavalry and the Indian scouts, forty in number, held the advance; the second battalion, composed also of three troops, moved off some miles to the left of Reno, scouting the country to the southward; a third detachment, comprising the pack train which carried the reserve ammunition—some 24,000 rounds—was under the command of Captain McDougall, and had one troop as an escort; the fourth battalion was that under Custer himself, and was the largest, having five troops, and it marched parallel to Reno and within easy supporting distance to the north, the pack train following the trail in rear of Reno and Custer.

Reno advanced from the ford across the valley in column of fours for some distance, then formed in line of battle, and afterwards deployed the command as skirmishers. The bulk of the Indians and their camp were hidden by a bend of the river, and Reno, instead of charging round the bend and into the Indian camp, halted and dismounted his command to fight on foot. At this point two or three of the horses could not be controlled, and carried their riders into the Indian camp; one account stating that they plunged over the river bank, injuring the men, who were afterwards killed by the Indians. Here at Ash Point, or Hollow, the command soon got sheltered in the timber, and were on the defensive; the Indians now pouring in from all sides. The Indian scouts with Reno had before now been dispersed, and were making back tracks fast as their ponies could carry them. Accounts differ as to how long they remained in this timber, but it was probably not to exceed half an hour. The "charge" out—as Reno termed it—was virtually a stampede, and many did not know of the departure until too late to start, no well-defined and well-understood order having been given to that effect. There was no systematic attempt to check the pursuit of the Indians, who now, directed by "Gall," swarmed down upon them and prevented them from reaching the ford at which they had crossed. Many were killed on this retreat, and many others wounded, among the former being Lieutenant Donald McIntosh. Reno headed the retreat, and they tore pell mell across the valley, and at the new ford they were lucky to strike, there was great confusion, it being every man for himself, and the devil take the hindmost; and, as is usually the case, the (red) devil got his clutches on more than one. Crossing the stream as best they could, Lieutenant Hodgson being killed after having crossed, men and horses climbed the steep, almost inaccessible bluffs and ravines, upon the top of which they had a chance to "take account of stock." Many had attempted to scale the bluffs at other points hard by. The Indians were up there in some force, and by them, when almost up the cliffs, Dr. DeWolf was killed.

After remaining on the bluffs at least an hour, probably longer, a forward movement down stream was made for a mile or mile and a half. Previous to this, heavy firing had been heard down the river in the direction Custer had gone. Two distinct volleys were heard by the entire command, followed by scattering shots, and it was supposed Custer was carrying all before him. When Reno had reached the limit of this advance north toward Custer, they saw large numbers of Indian horsemen scurrying over what afterward proved to be Custer's battle-field. Soon these came tearing up toward Reno, who hastily retreated from what would seem to have been a strong position, back to near the point where he had originally reached the bluffs. Here they sheltered themselves on the small hills by the shallow breastworks, and placed the wounded and horses in a depression. That night, until between 9 and 10 o'clock, they were subjected to a heavy fire from the Indians, who entirely surrounded them. The firing again began at daylight of the 26th, and lasted all day, and as the Indians had command of some high points near by, there were many casualties. Reno's total loss, as given by Godfrey, was fifty killed, including three officers, and fifty-nine wounded. Many of those left in the river bottom when the retreat began, eventually reached the command again, escaping under cover of night.

Of Custer's movements, opinions of what he did or should have done, are many and various. The theory first entertained and held for years, but not now tenable nor, indeed, probably held by many, was that Custer reached the ford and attempted to cross; was met by a fire so scorching that he drew back and retreated to the hill in the best form possible, and there fought like an animal at bay, hoping that Reno's attack in the bottom and Benton's timely arrival would yet relieve him. The Indians, however, strenuously assert that Custer never attempted the ford, and never got anywhere near it. No dead bodies were found any nearer than within half a mile of the ford, and it seems undoubted that the Indians tell the truth.

When Custer rode out on the bluff and looked over into the valley of the Greasy Grass, he must have seen at once that he had before utterly misapprehended the situation. The natural thing to do would have been to retrace his trail, join Reno by the shortest route, and then, united, have pushed the attack in person or, if then too late for successful attack, he could, in all likelihood, have extricated the command and made junction with Terry. Indian signals travel rapidly, and as soon as Reno was checked and beaten, not only was this fact signaled through the camp, but every warrior tore away down stream to oppose Custer, joining those already there, and now, at least, alert.

It is probable, then, that before Custer could reach the creek valley the Indians had made sufficient demonstrations to cause him to swerve from where he would otherwise, and naturally, strike it, and work farther back toward the second line of bluffs, even perhaps as far back as Captain Godfrey gives the trail. The only thing to militate against this would be the element of time, which seems hardly to oppose it. However he got there, Custer is at last upon the eminence which is so soon to be consecrated with his life's blood. What saw he? What did he? The sources of information are necessarily largely Indian. At the southeastern end of the Custer ridge, facing, apparently, the draw, or coulee, of the branch of Custer Creek, Calhoun and Crittenden were placed. Some little distance back of them, in a depression, and down the northern slope of the Custer Ridge, Keogh stood. Stretched along the north slope of the ridge, from Keogh to Custer Hill, was Smith's command, and at the culminating point of the ridge, or Custer Hill, but on the opposite ridge from where the others were placed, were Tom Custer and Yates, and with them Custer himself. Yates' and Custer's men evidently faced northwest. It would appear from the Indians' statements that most of the command were dismounted.

The line was about three-quarters of a mile in length, and the attack was made by two strong bodies of Indians. One of these came up from the ford named after the hero and victim of the day. It was led by a daring Indian, with some knowledge of generalship, and his followers were of a very superior class to the average red man. This body of attackers did great execution and succeeded in almost annihilating the white men against whom they were placed, and whom they outnumbered so conspicuously. From the meagre information concerning what took place that is accessible, it appears as though the execution of these men was almost equal to that of skilled sharpshooters. A reckless Indian named "Crazy Horse" was at the head of a number of Cheyennes who formed the principal part of the second attacking body. These encountered Custer himself, and the men immediately under his orders. Outnumbering the white men to an overwhelming extent, they circled around, and being reinforced by the first column, which by this time was elated by victory and reckless as to its brutality, it commenced the work of blotting out of existence the gallant cavalrymen before them.

Most of Custer's men knew the nature of their destroyers too well to think of crying for quarter or making any effort to escape. There was a blank space between the ridge on which the battle was fought and the river below. Some few men ran down this spot in hopes of fording the river and finding temporary hiding places; they prolonged their lives but for a few minutes only, for some of the fleetest Indians rushed after them and killed them as they ran. The horse upon which Captain Keogh rode into the battle escaped the general slaughter, and found its way back once more to civilization. Of the way it spent its declining years we have already spoken.

With this exception, it is more than probable that no living creature which entered the fight with Custer came out of it alive. A Crow scout named "Curley," claims that he was in the fight, and that after it was over he disguised himself as a Sioux, held his blanket around his head and escaped. "Curley's" statement was never received with much credence. The evidence generally points to the fact that, prior to the battle, nearly all the Indian scouts who were with Custer on the march ran away when they saw the overpowering nature of the foe. "Sitting Bull," who has since met the fate many believe he deserved, also claimed to be in the fight on the other side. His story of the prowess of Custer, and of his death, was probably concocted with a view to currying favor with white men, as it appears evident that "Sitting Bull" showed his usual cowardice, and ran away before there was a battle within twenty-four hours' distance.

Major James McLaughlin, during his experience as Indian Agent at Standing Rock Agency, North Dakota, had an opportunity of gathering a great deal of important information with reference to the battle-field and incidents connected with it. At the request of Mr. Wheeler, whose researches into the legends and history of interesting spots within easy access by means of the Northern Pacific Railroad were most successful, obtained from the Major the following valuable information concerning many points of detail which have been the subject of debate and dispute:

"It is difficult," says this undoubted authority, "to arrive at even approximately the number of Indians who were encamped in the valley of the Little Big Horn when Custer's command reached there on June 25th, 1876; the indifference of the Indians as to ascertaining their strength by actual count, and their ideas at that time being too crude to know themselves. I have been stationed at this Agency since the surrendered hostiles were brought here in the summer of 1881, and have conversed frequently with many of the Indians who were engaged in that fight, and more particularly with 'Gall,' 'Crow King,' 'Big Road,' 'Hump,' 'Sitting Bull,' 'Gray Eagle,' 'Spotted Horn Bull,' and other prominent men of the Sioux, regarding the Custer affair. When questioned as to the number of Indians engaged, the answer has invariably been, 'None of us knew; nina wicoti,' which means 'very many lodges.' From this source of information, which is the best obtainable, I place the number of male adults then in the camp at 3,000; and that on June 25th, 1876, the fighting strength of the Indians was between 2,500 and 3,000, and more probably approximating the latter number.

" 'Sitting Bull' was a recognized medicine man, and of

great repute among the Sioux, not so much for his powers of healing and curing the sick—which, after he had regained such renown, was beneath his dignity—as for his prophecies; and no matter how absurd his prophecies might be, he found ready believers and willing followers, and when his prophecies failed to come to pass, he always succeeded in satisfying his over-credulous followers by giving some absurd reason. For instance, I was in his camp on Grande River in the spring of 1888, sometime about the end of June. There had been no rain for some weeks, and crops were suffering from drouth, and I remarked to him, who was in an assemblage of a large number of Indians of that district, that the crops needed rain badly, and that if much longer without rain the crops would amount to nothing. He, 'Sitting Bull,' replied: 'Yes, the crops need rain, and my people have been importuning me to have it rain. I am considering the matter as to whether I will or not. I can make it rain any time I wish, but I fear hail. I cannot control hail, and should I make it rain, heavy hail might follow, which would ruin the prairie grass as well as the crops, and our horses and our cattle would thus be deprived of subsistence.' He made this statement with as much apparent candor as it was possible for a man to give expression to, and there was not an Indian among his hearers but appeared to accept it as within his power.

"'Sitting Bull' was dull in intellect, and not near as able a man as 'Gall,' 'Hump,' 'Crow,' and many others who were regarded as subordinate to him; but he was an adept schemer and very cunning, and could work upon the credulity of the Indians to a wonderful degree, and this, together with great obstinacy and tenacity, gained for him his world-wide reputation. 'Sitting Bull' claimed in his statement to me that he directed and led in the Custer fight; but all the other Indians with whom I have talked contradict it, and said that 'Sitting Bull' fled with his family as soon as the village was attacked by Major Reno's command, and that he was making his way to a place of safety, several miles out in the hills, when overtaken by some of his friends with news of victory over the soldiers, whereupon he returned, and in his usual style, took all the credit of victory to himself as having planned for the outcome, and as having been on a bluff overlooking the battlefield, appeasing the evil spirits and invoking the Great Spirit for the result of the fight.

"And, when considering the ignorance and inherent superstition of the average Sioux Indian at that time, it is not to be wondered at that the majority, if not all, were willing to accept it, especially when united in common cause and what they considered as their only safety from annihilation. As a matter of fact, there was no one man who led or directed that fight; it was a pell mell rush under a number of recognized warriors as leaders, with 'Gall' of the Hunkpapas and 'Crazy Horse' of the Cheyennes the more prominent.

"The Indians with whom I have talked deny having mutilated any of the killed, but admit that many dead bodies were mutilated by women of the camp. They also claim that the fight with Custer was of short duration. They have no knowledge as to hours and minutes, but have explained by the distance that could be walked while the fight lasted. They vary from twenty minutes to three-quarters of an hour, none placing it longer than forty-five minutes. This does not include the fight with Reno before his retreat, but from the time that Custer's command advanced and the fight with his command commenced. The opinion of the Indians regarding Reno's first attack and short stand is, that it was his retreat that gave them the victory over Custer's command. The helter skelter retreat of Reno's men enthused the Indians to such an extent that, flushed with excitement and this early success, they were reckless in their charge upon Custer's command, and with the slight number of Indians thus fully enthused, that small command was but a slight check to their sweeping impetuosity. The Indians also state that the separated detachments made their victory over the troops more certain."

Thus Custer fell. The mystery surrounding his death will probably never be solved in a satisfactory manner, owing to the impossibility of placing any reliance on statements made by the Indians. The way in which the command was annihilated and the soldiers' bodies mutilated, should go a long way towards disproving many of the theories now in existence concerning the alleged ill treatment of Indians, and their natural peacefulness and good disposition. Custer had so frequently befriended the very men who surrounded his command and annihilated it, that the baseness of their ingratitude should be apparent even to those who are inclined to sympathize with the red men, and to denounce the alleged severity with which they have been treated. Travelers through the Dakota region find few spots of more melancholy, though marked, interest than the one illustrated in connection with this chapter.

CHAPTER XII.

AMONG THE CREOLES.

Meaning of the Word "Creole"—An Old Aristocratic Relic—The Venice of America—Origin of the Creole Carnivals—Rex and His Annual Disguises—Creole Balls—The St. Louis Veiled Prophets—The French Market and Other Landmarks in New Orleans—A Beautiful Ceremony and an Unfinished Monument.

NEW ORLEANS is known throughout the world for the splendor of its carnivals. As one of the great Creole cities of the world, it has for more than half a century made merry once a year, and given quite a business aspect to carnival festivities. The Creole is one of the interesting characters to be met with in a tour through the United States. As a rule, he or she is joyous in the extreme, and believes most heartily in the wisdom of the command to "laugh and grow fat." The genuine Creole scarcely knows what it is to be sad for more than a few hours at a time, a very little pleasure more than offsetting a very great deal of trouble and suffering. A desire to move around and to enjoy changes of scene is a special feature of the Creole, and hence the spectacular effects of the carnival procession appeal most eloquently to him.

Many Eastern and Northern people confound the term "Creole" and "Mulatto," believing that the former name is given to the offspring of mixed marriages, which take place in spite of the vigilance of the laws of most of the Southern States. This is entirely a mistake, for the genuine Creole, instead of being an object of contempt and pity, is rather an aristocrat and of a higher caste than the average white man. Strictly speaking, the term implies birth in this country, but foreign parentage or ancestry. It was originally applied to the children of French and Spanish settlers in Louisiana, and in that application applied only to quite a handful of people. As time has worn on, and French emigration has ceased, and the Spaniard has been gradually pushed south, the number of actual Creoles has of course diminished rapidly. The name, however, by common consent, has been perpetuated and is retained by descendants in the third and fourth generations of original Creoles. Some of the Creoles of to-day are very wealthy, and many of the others are comparatively poor, changes in modes and conditions of life having affected them very much. Although the very name Creole suggests Spanish origin, there is more French blood among the Creoles of to-day than that of any other nation. The vivacious habits and general love of change so common among French people, continue in their descendants. The old plan of sending the children over to France to be educated has been largely abandoned in these later days, but the influences of Parisian life still have their effect on the race.

This is largely the reason why it is that New Orleans has been often spoken of as the American Venice. To that beautiful European city, with its gondolas and picturesque costumes, belongs the honor of having originated high-class comedy. To New Orleans must be given the credit of planting, or at any rate perpetuating, the idea in a tangible shape in this country, and of having, for fully two generations, kept up the annual celebration almost without a break. Masquerading came across the Atlantic from Venice by way of France, where the idea took strong hold. When emigration from France to the old Territory of Louisiana became general, the idea came with it, and the practice of sending children to Paris to be educated resulted in the latest ideas of aristocratic festivities being brought over to the home which has since sheltered them.

History tells us that on New Year's Eve of 1831, a number of pleasure-seeking men spent the entire night in a Creole restaurant at Mobile arranging for the first mystic order in that city, and from this beginning the long line of Creole comedies sprang up. In 1857, the Mystic Krewe of Comus made its first appearance upon the streets of New Orleans. "Paradise Lost" was the subject selected for illustration. Year after year the revelry was repeated on Shrove Tuesday, but the outbreak of the war naturally put a stop to the annual rejoicing. Southern enthusiasm is, however, hard to down, and directly the war was over, Comus reappeared in all his glory. A few years later the Knights of Momus were created, and in 1876 the Krewe of Proteus had its first carnival. Many other orders have followed, but these are the more magnificent and important.

It is difficult to convey an adequate idea of the feeling which prevails in regard to these comedies. The mystery which surrounds the orders is extraordinary, and the secret has been well kept, a fact which cynics attribute to the exclusion of ladies from the secret circle. It is well known that on many occasions men have pretended to leave the city on the eve of the comedy, and to have returned to their homes a day or two later, not even their own families knowing that they took a leading part in the procession.

The Carnival Kings issue royal edicts prior to their arrival, commanding all business to cease on the occasion of the rejoicings. The command is obeyed literally. Banks, courts of justice and business houses generally suspend operations, and old and young alike turn out to do homage to the monarch of the day.

Let us imagine for a moment we are privileged to see a Creole carnival. Every inch of available space has been taken up. Every balcony overlooking the royal route is crowded with pleasure parties, including richly dressed ladies, all the flower and beauty of the Sunny South being represented. The course is illuminated in the most attractive manner, and every one is waiting anxiously for the procession. Bands of music, playing sprightly tunes, finally reward the patience of the watchers. Then come heralds, bodyguards and marshals, all gorgeously arrayed for the occasion. Their horses, like themselves, are richly adorned for the occasion, and the banners and flags are conspicuous for the artistic blending of colors.

Then riding in state comes the Lord High Chamberlain, bearing the golden key of the city, delivered over to him in state twenty-four hours previously by the Mayor. Next comes the hero of the parade, the King himself. All eyes are riveted upon him. Thoroughly disguised himself, he is able to recognize on the balconies and among the crowds his personal friends and most devoted admirers. To these he bows with great solemnity. Mystified to a degree, and often disputing among themselves as to the probable identity of the monarch, the richly dressed young ladies and their cavaliers bow in return, and look as though they would fain hold the monarch among them much longer than the necessity of keeping order makes it possi-

The Old French Market at New Orleans.

ble. Following the King are the bodyguards and crowds of holiday makers.

Rex generally makes a display now of some special theme, appearing this year as a crusader, another year as the discoverer of America, and a third year as some other mystic individual. But no matter what the subject of the carnival may be, the underlying principle is the same. Sometimes a great deal of instruction is imparted with the mirth-making, but in every case the procession is but a signal for general rejoicing. Directly the procession is disbanded, which always takes place in military order, the entire city gives way to fun and mirth of every character. Liberty abounds throughout the city without license. By common consent every one is careful to prevent disturbance or trouble. All are happy, and every one seems to appreciate the fact that the very life of the comedy depends upon its respectability. There is nothing vulgar or common about any of the proceedings, or about the countless tableaux which pass along the private streets. Everything is what has been described as orderly disorder. Everything is attractive and easy.

The ball, which is a prominent feature of a Creole carnival, is a wonderful combination of Nineteenth Century aristocratic ideas and of Oriental humor. The guests are in full dress, and represent the highest elements of Southern society. Around the carpeted floor, those who have taken part in the pageant march in their grotesque costumes. An apparently blood-thirsty Indian, brandishing a club over his head, darts for a second from the line to go through the motions of dashing out the brains of perhaps a most intimate friend, who has no idea who has thus honored him by a recognition.

Another man, who in everyday life is, perhaps, a sedate banker or a prominent physician, is masquerading in some extraordinary attire with a mask of extraordinary dimensions and significance. He sees in the throng a young lady of his acquaintance, and proceeds to shake hands with her with great effusion. So well is the secret kept, that she has no idea that the apparently frolicsome youth is a middle-aged man of business, and she spends perhaps half the night wondering which of her beaus this fearfully and wonderfully disguised man was.

Of the balls which succeed carnivals in the cities which delight in these temporary divorces from the cares of business and finance, pages might be written. One ball only need be mentioned in any detail. This is the ball given by the "Knights of Revelry," in connection with and at the expense of the Mobile clubs. The entire theatre was rearranged in illustration of the theme of the club's pageant for the year. All around the halls were hung tapestries and banners, artistically decorated, and arranged so as to convey the idea of forests and gardens. The very doors were converted into mimic entrances to caves and parterres, and the general effect was entrancing as well as sentimental. The band was hidden from the guests in a most delightfully arranged little Swiss chalet, and refreshments were served from miniature garden pavilions. The very floors upon which the dancing was to take place were decorated so as to present the appearance of a newly mown lawn.

The height of realism was attained by means of an imitation moat over the orchestra well. Across this was a drawbridge, which was raised and dropped at fitting intervals, and the drop curtain was made to represent a massive castle door. There was a banquet chamber, with faultless reproductions of mediæval grandeur and wonder. Stained glass windows represented well-known and attractive ladies, and there were other marvelous and costly innovations which seemed practically impossible within a theatre.

At this ball, as at all others, the revelry proceeded until midnight. Just as Cinderella left the ball when the clock struck 12, so do the holders of the Creole revels stop dancing immediately that Lent has commenced. The next day all is over. Men who the night before were the leaders in the masquerade, resume their commonplace existence, and are seen at the ordinary seats of custom, buying and selling and conducting themselves like Eastern rather than Southern men.

The carnival idea has not been confined to strictly Southern cities. St. Louis has, for many years in succession, enjoyed the pageants and balls of its Veiled Prophets, an organization as secret and mysterious as any to be found in a Creole section. Instead of being a Mardi Gras celebration, the St. Louis pageant is given during the Indian summer days of the first week of October. The parade takes place after night-fall, and consists of very costly pageants and displays. It is no exaggeration to say that hundreds of thousands of dollars have been spent in illuminating the streets through which the processions have passed, the money for this purpose being freely subscribed by business men and private citizens. But in St. Louis, as in New Orleans, no one knows who finds the money to pay for the preparation of the pageant, the rich and varied costumes, the exquisite invitations and souvenirs, and the gorgeous balls. Readers of the "Pickwick Papers" will remember that when certain members of the club proposed to make a tour of the country, with a view to noting matters of special interest, it was unanimously resolved not to limit the scope of the investigations, and to extend to the investigators the privilege of paying their own expenses. Very much the same rule prevails in regard to the Creole carnivals and balls, and the adaptation of the idea in other cities. The utmost secrecy is preserved, and it is considered bad form in the extreme to even hint at belonging to any of the secret orders. The members subscribe all expenses themselves without a moment's hesitation, and there has never been such a thing seen as a list of the amounts donated.

There are not lacking people who say that these celebrations are childish, and beneath the dignity of a business community. The answer to criticisms of this kind is, that no one being asked to contribute to the expense of the revelries, or being even asked or allowed to purchase a ticket of admission to the balls, any criticisms are very much like looking a gift horse in the mouth. If it be agreed that life is made up of something more than one stern, continuous race for wealth, then it must be conceded that these carnivals occupy a most important part in the routine of life. The absolute unselfishness of the entire work commends it to the approval of the most indifferent. Those who raise the expense have to work so hard during the parades and balls that they get comparatively little pleasure from them, while they are also prevented by the absolute secrecy which prevails from securing so much as a word of thanks or congratulation from the outside public. In this material age, there is a danger of celebrations of this kind wearing themselves out. When they do so, the world will be the poorer in consequence.

New Orleans, to which we have referred as the great home of the Creole carnival, is a city known the world over by reputation. It is situated at the very mouth of the great Mississippi River, and its history dates back to the year 1542, when a gallant band of adventurers floated down the river into the Gulf of Mexico. In 1682, La Salle sailed down the river and took possession of the country on both sides of it in the name of France. In the closing days of the Seventeenth Century a French expedition landed not far from New Orleans, which was founded in 1718, with a population of sixty-eight souls. Three years later, the city, which now contains a population of more than a quarter of a million, was made the capital of the Territory of Louisiana, and it at once became a place of considerable importance.

In 1764, it was ceded to Spain, and this resulted in the people taking possession of New Orleans and resisting the change in government. Five years later, the new Spanish Governor arrived with ample troops, suppressed the rebellion, and executed its leaders from the Place d'Armes. In 1804, the territory of Orleans was established, and in 1814, a British army, 15,000 strong, advanced on the city after which the Territory was named. A great deal of confusion followed, but the city held its own, and the invading army was repulsed.

During the Civil War New Orleans again saw active campaigning. The occupancy of the city by General Butler, and the stern measures he adopted to suppress the loyalty even of the women of the town, has formed the subject of much comment. There are many interesting stories concerning this epoch in the city's history, which are told with many variations to every one who sojourns for a while in the great port at the gate of the greatest river in the world.

To-day, New Orleans is perhaps best known as the second largest cotton mart in the world, some 2,000,000 bales of the product of the Southern plantations being received and shipped out every year. More than 30,000,000 pounds of wool and 12,000,000 pounds of hides also pass through the city every year, to say nothing of immense quantities of bananas and costly transactions in sugar and lumber.

Although New Orleans is really some little distance from the ocean, the river at this point is more than half a mile wide, and the great ships of all nations are seen loading and unloading at its levee.

New Orleans naturally abounds in ancient landmarks and memorials. The old Spanish Fort is one of the most interesting among these. Warfare of the most bitter character was seen again and again at this place. The fortifications were kept up largely to afford protection against raids from Mexican pirates and hostile Indians, though they were often useful against more civilized foes. It was at this port that Andrew Jackson prepared to receive the British invaders. The magnificent use he made of the fortifications should have given to the old place a lasting standing and a permanent preservation. Some forty years ago, however, the fort was purchased and turned into a kind of country resort, and more lately it has become the home of a recreation club.

Better preserved, and a most interesting connecting link between the past and the present, is the world-renowned French Market in New Orleans. A story is told of a great novelist, who traveled several thousand miles in order to find representatives of all nationalities grouped together in one narrow space. For a work he had in contemplation he was anxious to select for his characters men of all nationalities, whom chance or destiny had thrown together. He spent several days in Paris, journeyed throughout sunny Italy, got lost in some of the labyrinths of the unexplored sections of London, and finally crossed the Atlantic without having found the group of which he was in search. Not even in the large cities of America could he find his heart's desire, and it was not until he strayed into the old French Market of New Orleans that he found that for which he searched. He spent several days, and even weeks, wandering through the peculiar market, and making friends with the men of all nationalities who were working in different parts of it. He found the Creole, full of anecdote, superstition and pride, even when he was earning an occasional meal by helping to unload bananas, or to carry away the refuse from the fish stores. The negro, in every phase of development, civilization and ignorance, could, and always can, be found within the confines of the market. The amount of folk-lore stored up in the brains covered by masses of unkempt wool astounded the novelist, who distributed dollars, in return for information received, so lavishly, that he began to be looked upon after a while as a capitalist whose wealth had driven him insane. Then, again, he met disappointed emigrants from nearly all the European countries, men, and even women, who had crossed the Atlantic full of great expectations, but who had found a good many thorns among the looked-for roses.

The Indian is not often seen now around the French Market, although he used to be quite a feature of it.

Some of the most exceptionally idle loungers, however, show evidence of Indian blood in their veins, in the shape of exceptionally high cheek-bones, and abnormally straight and ungovernable hair.

Almost every known language is spoken here. There is the purest French and the most atrocious patois. There is polished English, which seems to indicate high education, and there is the most picturesque dialect variation that could be desired by the most ardent devotee of the everlasting dialect story. Spanish is of course spoken by several of the market traders and workers, while Italian is quite common. At times in the day, when trade is very busy, the visitor may hear choice expletives in three or four languages at one time. He may not be able to interpret the peculiar noises and stern rebukes administered to idle help and truant boys, but he can generally guess pretty accurately the scope and object of the little speeches which are scattered around so freely.

If it be asked what special function the market fulfills, the answer is that it is a kind of inquire-within for everything. Many of the poorer people do all their trading here. Fruit is a great staple, and on another page a picture is given of one of the fruit stands of the old market. The picture is reproduced from a photograph taken on the spot by an artist of the National Company of St. Louis, publishers of "Our Own Country," and it shows well the peculiar construction of the market. The fruit sections are probably the most attractive and the least objectionable of the entire market, because here cleanliness is indispensable. In the vegetable section, which is also very large, there is not always quite so much care displayed or so much cleanliness enforced, refuse being sometimes allowed to accumulate liberally. Fish can be obtained in this market for an almost nominal consideration, being sometimes almost given away. Macaroni and other similar articles of diet form the staple feature of the Italian store of trade, which is carried on on the second floor of the market. The legitimate work called for alone provides excuse for the presence of many thousand people, who run hither and thither at certain hours of the day as though time were the essence of the contract, and no delay of any kind could be tolerated. As soon, however, as the pressing needs of the moment are satisfied, a period of luxurious idleness follows, and rest seems to be the chief desideratum of the average habitue or employe. The children, who are sitting around in large numbers, vie with their elders in matters of idleness, though they are occasionally aroused to a condition of pernicious activity by the hope of securing donations or compensation of some kind from newcomers and guests.

Structurally, the French Market is very well preserved. There are evidences of antiquity and of the ravages of time and weather on every side, but for all that the market seems to have as its special mission the reminding of the people that when our ancestors built, they built for ages, and not entirely for the immediate present, as is too often the case nowadays. The market also serves as a link between the present and the past. It is only of late years that the bazaar, which used to be so prominent a feature, has fallen into insignificance. Formerly it retained the importance of the extreme Orient, and afforded infinite fund for reflection for the antiquarian and the lover of history.

The cemeteries of New Orleans are of exceptional interest, and are visited every year by thousands of people. Owing to the proximimity of the water mark to the surface of the ground, the dead are not buried as in other cities, and the vaults are above instead of under ground. They are well arranged, and the antiquity of the burial grounds, and the historic memories connected with the tablets, combine to make them of more than ordinary interest. The local custom of suspending business on the first day of November of each year for the purpose of decorating graves in all the cemeteries, is also worthy of more than a passing notice. Not only do people decorate the last resting places of their friends and relatives on this specially selected day, but even the graves of strangers are cared for in a spirit of thankfulness that the angel of death has not entered the family circle, and made inroads into bonds of friendship.

A few years ago a young woman died on the cars just as they were entering the world-renowned Creole city. There was nothing on the body to aid identification, and a stranger's grave had to be provided. In the meantime the friends and relatives of the missing girl had been making every effort to locate her, no idea having occurred to them that she was going South. A loving brother finally got hold of a clew, which he followed up so successfully that he at last solved the mystery. He arrived in New Orleans on November 1st, and when taken out to the grave that had been provided for the stranger who had died just outside the gates, he was astounded to find several handsome bouquets of flowers, with wreaths and crosses, lying upon it. Such a sight could hardly have been met with in any other city in the world, and too much can hardly be said in praise of the sentiment which suggests and encourages such disinterested kindness and thought.

The cemetery which occupies a site close to the great battle-field, is always specially decorated, and crowds go out in thousands to pay tribute to honored memories. Close to this spot there is a monument to celebrate the great battle during which General Pakingham was shot, and at which General Jackson galloped excitedly up and down the lines, and almost forced the men on to victory. The monument has not received the care which it deserves. More than half a century ago work was commenced on it, and a great deal was accomplished. But after a year or two of effort the project was abandoned for the time, and it has never been renewed. In the long interval that has ensued the roof has, in a large measure, disappeared, as well as several of the steps leading up to the front. Hundreds of people have cut their names in the stone work, and the monument, which ought to be preserved in perpetuity, looks so disreputable that little regret would be caused were the entire fragment to be swept away by some unusually heavy gust of wind.

More than 1,500 soldiers were buried in the Chalmette Cemetery after the battle referred to. Since the war it has been well nigh forgotten, but several duels and affaires d'honneur have been settled on the historic spot.

CHAPTER XIII.

THE HEATHEN CHINEE IN HIS ELEMENT.

A Trip to Chinatown, San Francisco—A House with a History—Narrow Alleys and Secret Doors—Opium Smoking and its Effects—The Highbinders—Celestial Theatricals—Chinese Festivals—The Brighter Side of a Great City—A Mammoth Hotel and Beautiful Park.

CHINATOWN, San Francisco, is such a remarkable place, and contrasts so strangely with the wealth and civilization of the great city on the Pacific Coast, of which it is a part, that its peculiarities cannot be ignored in a sketch of the most remarkable features of our native land. Writers and artists have for years made this blot on San Francisco's splendor the subject for sarcasm and cartoon, and, indeed, it is difficult to handle the subject without a considerable amount of severity. Californians are often blamed for their harshness towards the Chinese, and the way in which they have clamored from time to time for more stringent exclusion laws. It takes a trip to Chinatown to make it clear to the average mortal why this feeling is so general in San Francisco, and why it extends throughout the entire Pacific Slope.

There are about 25,000 Chinese in and around San Francisco. A small proportion of these have abandoned the worst features of their race, and make themselves comparatively useful as domestic servants. In order to retain their positions they have to assimilate themselves more or less to the manners and customs of the country, and they are only objectionable in certain respects. But the one-time dwellers in the Celestial Empire, who make their homes in Chinatown, have very few redeeming qualities, and most of them seem to have no tangible excuse whatever for living.

They adhere to all the vices and uncivilized habits of their forefathers, and very frequently add to them equally objectionable vices of so-called civilization. At one time all the streets in Chinatown were little more than elongated ash pits and garbage receptacles. The public outcry at length became so vigorous that the strong hand of the law was brought to bear, and now the principal through streets are kept fairly clean. The side streets and alleys are, however, still in a deplorable condition, and no American or European could possibly live many days in such filth without being stricken with a terrible disease. The Mongolians, however, seem to thrive under conditions which are fatal to civilized humanity. They live to quite the average age, and the children seem to be very healthy, if not conspicuously happy.

Chinatown covers an area of about eight large squares, in the very heart of San Francisco. Again and again attempts have been made to get rid of the drawback and nuisance. But the "Melica Man" has allowed himself to be outwitted by the "Heathen Chinee," who has secured property rights which cannot be overcome without a measure of confiscation, which would appear to be scarcely constitutional. The area is probably one of the most densely populated in the world. The Chinese seem to sleep everywhere and anywhere, and the houses are overcrowded to an extent which passes all belief. It is known as an actual fact, that in rooms twelve feet square as many as twelve human beings sleep and eat, and even cook what passes with them for food. The houses themselves are so horrible in their condition, and have been so remodeled from time to time, to meet Celestial ideas and fall in with notions which are but a relic of barbarism, that not even a colored man of the most degraded type can be persuaded to live permanently in a house which has ever been occupied by an unregenerated denizen of Chinatown.

At the entrance to this peculiar, and, indeed, disreputable quarter, there is a house with a peculiar history. It was built more than a quarter of a century ago, by a wealthy banker, who selected the site because of the admirable view that could be obtained from it of the leading features of the city. He spared no expense in its erection, and when it was completed he was able to gaze from the upper windows upon some of the most beautiful scenery in the world. For a while the banker lived in the most magnificent style, and earned for himself a reputation as a prince of entertainers. He spent thousands of dollars on entertainments, and appeared to have everything that a human being could desire. His end was a tragic one, and it has never been ascertained for certain whether he died by his own hand, or by the hand of one of his alleged friends or avowed foes. The house which was once his great pride is now occupied by the Chinese Consul.

It is still, by far, the finest house in the Chinese quarter. The moment it is passed the sight-seeker or slummer finds himself in the midst of a horrible collection of Oriental filth and squalor. There are a number of stores which excite his contempt the moment his eyes light upon them. They are chiefly devoted to the retailing of such food as the occupants of Chinatown delight in, and over many of them the Chinese national emblem can be seen flying. Fish are on sale in large numbers, and as they are kept until sold, regardless of their condition, the effluvia of some of the fish markets can be very easily imagined. Vegetables also form a very large proportion of the daily bills of fare, and these add materially to the malodorous condition of the neighborhood. The streets are all of them very narrow, and there are also a number of exceptionally narrow and complicated passages and alleys, which have been the scenes of crimes innumerable in days gone by.

Some of these alleys are but three or four feet wide, and, owing to their almost countless turns and angles, they afford an easy means for the escape of a fugitive who is being hunted by the police, or by one of those blood-thirsty Chinese societies of which the Highbinders is a type. One writer who has investigated the matter very thoroughly, tells us that most of the houses have secret doors leading from one to the other in such a manner that if a fugitive should determine to make his escape, he can always do so by means of these secret doors, and the underground passages to which they lead.

The stores, workshops and other apartments are generally exceedingly small, and the proverbial economy of the Chinaman is proved by the fact that every square foot of floor space and ground is put to some practical use, and one finds cobblers, barbers, fortune-tellers and a multitude of small tradesmen carrying on a business in a jog, or niche in the wall, not as large as an ordinary bootblack's stand. Along the narrow sidewalks are seen many of these curbstone merchants. Some have their goods displayed in glass show-cases, ranged along the wall, where are exhibited queer-looking fancy articles of Chinese workmanship, of a cheap grade, all sorts of inexpensive ornaments for women and children's wear, curiously fashioned from ivory, bone, beads, glass and brass, water and opium pipes galore.

The opium pipe is something so unlike any European conception of a pipe that it is difficult to describe it. It consists of a large bamboo tube or cylinder, with a bowl about midway between the extremities. The bowl is sometimes a very small brass plate, and sometimes an earthen cup-shaped contrivance, with the top closed or decked over, having only a tiny hole in the center. Into this little aperture the opium, in a semi-liquid state, after being well melted in a lamp flame, is thrust by means of a fine wire or needle. The drug is inserted in infinitesimal quantities. It is said that all the Chinese smoke opium, although all do not indulge to excess. Some seem to be able to use the drug without its gaining the mastery over them.

There are more than a hundred opium dens in the Chinese quarters. These places are used for no other purpose whatever at any time. If it were the Chinese alone who frequented them, but little would be thought of it. Hundreds of white people, men, women and the youth of both sexes, have, however, become victims to this loathsome habit. So completely enslaved are they, that there is no escape from the tyrant. For all the poverty and untold misery this has brought upon these unfortunates, the Chinese are responsible. Vices cluster around Chinese social life, and nearly every house has its opium-smoking apartment, or rooms where the lottery or some kind of gambling is carried on.

The Prettiest Chinese Woman in America.

The residents of Chinatown have a government of their own, with its social and economic regulations, and its police and penal department, and they even inflict the death penalty, but in such a secret way that the outside world seldom hears of these acts of high authority. This social and commercial policy is controlled by six companies, to one of which every Chinaman in the country owes allegiance and is tributary. These companies severally represent different provinces in the Chinese Empire, and upon every arrival of a steamer from that country, and before the passengers are landed, the Chinese portion of them are visited by an official of the six companies, who ascertains what province each arriving coolie is from. That decides as to which company he will belong.

Every Chinaman who comes is assured of his return to China, or, if he is so unfortunate as to die while in exile, that his bones will be sent home. This very important matter is one of the duties of the six companies. This comforting assurance, however, is not shared in by the women, whom, excepting those who are the wives of men of the better class, are brought over by a vile class of traders, and sold as chattels, or slaves, having no relation to the six companies.

There is in the Chinese quarters a ghastly underground place, where the bones of the departed are conveyed, after they have remained a certain time in the ground. Here they are scraped, cleaned and packed, preparatory to their last journey back to the fatherland, and their final resting place. Among the Chinese residents of San Francisco there are comparatively few of those of the higher class. The difference between them and the masses is very pronounced, and they appreciate the difference to the fullest extent. They are educated, well-bred gentlemen. The coolie and lower class are an ignorant, repulsive and ill-mannered people. They seem to be mere brutes, and not a gleam of intelligence is apparent in their dull, expressionless faces.

The "Highbinders" are bound together by solemn obligations, and are the instruments used by other Chinamen to avenge their real or fancied wrongs. The Highbinders are organized into lodges or tongs, which are engaged in constant feuds with each other. They wage open warfare, and so deadly is their mutual hatred, that the war ceases only when the last individual who has come under the ban of a rival tong has been sacrificed. These feuds resemble the vendettas in some of the Southern States of Europe, and they defy all efforts of the police to suppress them. Murders are, consequently, frequent, but it is next to impossible to identify the murderers, and if a Chinaman is arrested on suspicion, or even almost positive evidence of guilt, the trial uniformly ends in a failure to convict.

The theatres are, to the visitor, probably the most interesting feature of the Chinese quarters. A few years ago there were several of these playhouses, but the number is now reduced to two. The charge of admission is 25 cents or 50 cents.

The white people who, out of curiosity, attend a performance, generally pay more, and are given more comfortable seats upon the stage. The stage is a primitive affair. It boasts of no curtain, footlights or scenery of any kind.

When, during the progress of a play, a man is killed, he lies upon the stage until the scene is ended, and then gets up and walks off. Sometimes an attendant will bring in and place under his head a small wooden pillow, so that the dead man may rest more comfortably. After an actor has been beheaded, he has been known to pick up the false head and apostrophize it while making his exit from the stage. The orchestra is at the back of the stage. It usually consists of one or two ear-splitting flageolets and a system of gongs and tom-toms, which keep up an infernal din during the entire performance.

Chinese plays are usually historical, and vary in length from a few hours to several months. The costumes are gorgeous after the Chinese ideas of splendor. No females are allowed on the stage at all, young men with falsetto voices invariably impersonating the women.

The restaurants of Chinatown are a very unsatisfactory feature of the unsavory quarter. Many of the laborers board at them, and the smaller ones are nothing in the world but miserable little chop-houses, badly ventilated and exceedingly objectionable, and, indeed, injurious to health and good morals. There are larger restaurants, which are more expensively equipped. Shakespeare's advice as to neatness without gaudiness is not followed. There is always a profusion of color in decoration, but there is never anything like symmetry or beauty.

There are an immense number of joss-houses in Chinatown. Each company has one of its own. Others belong to the societies, tongs and to private parties. The appointments of these temples are gorgeous in their way. One has recently been opened on Waverly Place, which far surpasses all the others in the grandeur of its sacred equipments and decoration. The idols, bronzes, carvings, bells, banners and the paraphernalia of the temple are said to have cost about $20,000, and represents the highest degree of Chinese art. In front of the throne in each of these temples, where the principal god is seated, burns a sacred flame that is never extinguished. In a cabinet at the right of the entrance is a small image called "the doorkeeper," who sees that no harm befalls the temple of those who enter.

The temple doors are always open, and those who are religiously inclined can come in at any hour of the day. Prayers are written or printed on red or blue paper. These are lighted and deposited in a sort of furnace with an opening near the top, and as the smoke ascends the bell near by is sounded to attract the attention of the gods. The women have a favorite method of telling their fortunes. They kneel before the altar, holding in either hand a small wooden block, about five inches long, which resembles a split banana. These they raise to their closed eyes, bow the head and drop. If they fall in a certain position, it is an indication that the wish or prayer will be granted. If they fall in an unfavorable position, they continue the effort until the blocks fall as desired. When business is dull and times hard with the Chinaman, they attribute it to the displeasure of their gods. They try to propitiate the offended deity by burning incense sticks, and offering fruits and other things which have no Christian equivalent, and which are supposed to be grateful to the divine palate.

The Chinese observe a great many holidays. The most important are those of the New Year. This is a movable feast, and occurs between the 21st of January and the 19th of February. The New Year must fall on the first new moon after the sun has entered Aquarius. It is customary at this time to have all business straightened out, and all debts contracted during the year paid. Unless this is done, they will have no credit during the year, and consequently a great effort is made to pay their creditors. There are some, however, who have been unfortunate and have laid by nothing for this day of settlement, and knowing well that there are a number of those troublesome little bills that are liable to be presented at any time, they keep themselves out of sight until the sun has risen upon the New Year.

They then reappear in their accustomed haunts, feeling safe for a few days at least, for while the merry-making is going on there is no danger of being confronted with a dun. All gloomy subjects are tabooed, and everybody devotes himself to getting all the enjoyment he possibly can out of this festal day. To some this is the only holiday in the whole year, and they are obliged to return to their labors the following day. Others will celebrate three or four days, and so on up the scale. The rich and the independent keep it up for fully two weeks, and begin to settle down to everyday life about the sixteenth day.

The night preceding New Year's day is spent in religious ceremonies at the temples or at home. Out of doors the air is filled with the smoke and roar of exploding fire-crackers. But when the clock has tolled the death of the old and announced the birth of the New Year, one would think that Pandemonium was let loose. Unless one has heard it, no idea can be formed as to what this unearthly noise really is. We are told it is to frighten away evil spirits, to invoke the favor of the gods, to bid, as they fondly hope, a final farewell to ill-luck; and, again, simply because they are happy, and when in this frame of mind, they love to manifest their joy in noisy demonstrations. A certain time in the early morning is spent in worship at the shrines at home and in the temples. They place before their sacred images, offerings of tea, wine, rice, fruits and flowers. The Chinese lily is in full bloom at this season, and it occupies a conspicuous place in the joss-houses. It is for sale on every street corner.

The day is spent in feasting, pleasure seeking, and in making New Year's calls. The Chinamen are always greatly pleased to receive calls from white men with whom they have business dealings, and they exhibit their cards with much pride. They are very punctilious and even rival the Frenchmen in politeness, and it is considered an offense if any of their proffered hospitalities are declined.

But while Chinatown is the most extraordinary feature of San Francisco, and is visited by tourists who naturally look upon it somewhat in the light of forbidden and hence exceptionally attractive fruit, it is not by any means the most interesting or most important feature of one of the finest cities in the world. San Francisco is the metropolis of the Pacific Slope. It occupies the point of a long peninsula between the bay and the ocean, and so unique is its site that it includes some magnificent hills and peaks. The history of San Francisco bristles with border and gold mine stories and tales of the early troubles of pioneers. Whole pages could be written concerning the adventures of the early days of this remarkable city. The time was when a few frame buildings constituted the entire town. The rush of speculators following discovery after discovery of gold, converted the quiet little port into a scene of turmoil and disturbance.

Every ship brought with it a cargo of more or less

desperate men, who had come from various points of the compass determined to obtain a lion's share of the gold which they had been told could be had for the taking. The value of commodities went up like sky-rockets. The man who had a few spare mules and wagons on hand was able to realize ten times the price that was tendered for them before the boom. Many men who were thus situated did not consider it advisable to throw away their chances by accepting grave risks in search of gold, and many who stayed at home and supplied the wants of those who went up country realized handsome competences, and in some cases small fortunes.

That there was a good deal of lawlessness and violence is not to be wondered at. It has been said that for every bona fide miner there was at least one hanger-on or camp follower, who had no intention of doing any digging or washing, but who was smart enough to realize that a veritable thief's paradise would be built up by the hard workers. Sometimes these men went to the trouble of digging tunnels under the ground and into the tents of successful miners, frequently passing through rich deposits of gold on the way. At other times they waylaid wagons and coaches coming into San Francisco from the mining camps. History tells us of the fights which ensued, and we have all heard of the successful miners who were murdered while asleep at half-way houses, and the result of their hard toil turned to base uses and vicious purposes.

In San Francisco itself robbery and violence could not be suppressed. We have all heard of the way in which the decent element finally got together, formed special laws and executed offenders in short order. No one of course approves lynch law in the abstract, but when the circumstances of the case are taken into consideration, it is difficult to condemn very severely the men who made it possible for San Francisco to become a great and honored city.

The population of San Francisco to-day is about a third of a million. A greater portion of its growth has been during the last quarter of a century, and it was the first city in this country to lay cable conduits and adopt a system of cable cars. For several years it had practically a monopoly in this mode of street transportation, and, although electricity has since provided an even more convenient motive power, San Francisco will always be entitled to credit for the admirable missionary work it did in this direction. At the present time, almost every portion of the city and its beautiful parks can be reached easily by a system of transportation as comfortable and rapid as it is inexpensive.

Among the wonders of San Francisco must be mentioned the Palace Hotel, a structure of immense magnitude and probably two or three times as large as the average Eastern man imagines. The site of the hotel covers a space of more than an acre and a half, and several million dollars were spent on this structure. Everything is magnificent, expansive, huge and massive. The building itself is seven stories high, and in its center, forming what may be described as the grandest enclosed court in the world, is a circular space 144 feet across and roofed in with glass at a great height. Carriages are driven into this enclosure, and, in the nearest approach to severe weather known in San Francisco, guests can alight practically indoors.

There are nearly 800 bed-rooms, all of them large and lofty, and the general style of architecture is more than massive. The foundation walls are 12 feet thick, and

31,000,000 brick were used above them. The skeleton of wrought iron bands, upon which the brick and stone work is constructed, weighs more than 3,000 tons. Four artesian wells supply pure water to the house, which is not only one of the largest hotels in the world, but also one of the most complete and independent in its arrangements.

A pleasant ride of nearly four miles in length brings the rider to Golden Gate Park. The Golden Gate, from which the park takes its name, is one of the world's beauty spots, and here some of the most exquisite sunsets ever witnessed can be seen. The Gate is the entrance from the Pacific Ocean to San Francisco Bay, which varies in width from ten to fifteen miles. At the Gate the width is suddenly reduced to less than a mile, and hence at ebb and flow the current is very swift. Near the Gate sea lions can be seen gamboling in the surf, and the waves can be observed striking on the rocks and boulders, and sending up spray of foamy whiteness to a height of a hundred feet.

Golden Gate Park is like everything else on the Pacific Coast, immense and wonderful. It is not the largest park in the world, but it ranks amongst the most extensive. Its acreage exceeds a thousand, and it is difficult to appreciate the fact that the richly cultivated ground through which the tourist is driven has been reclaimed from the ocean, and was but once little more than a succession of sand bars and dunes.

When the reader goes to San Francisco, as we hope he will go some day, if he has not already visited it, he will be told within a few minutes of his entering the city, that he has at least reached what may be fairly termed God's country. Of the glorious climate of California he will hear much at every step, and before he has been in the city many days, he will wonder how he is to get out of it alive if he is to see but a fraction of the wonderful sights to which his attention is called.

California is frequently spoken of as the Golden State. The name California was given to the territory comprising the State and Lower California as long ago as 1510, when a Spanish novelist, either in fancy or prophecy, wrote concerning "the great land of California, where an abundance of gold and precious stones are found." In 1848, California proper was ceded to the United States, and in the same year the discovery of gold at Colomo put a stop to the peace and quiet which had prevailed on the fertile plains, the unexplored mountains and the attractive valleys. Shortly after, a hundred thousand men rushed into the State, and for the first few years as many as a hundred thousand miners were kept steadily at work.

It was in 1856 that the famous Vigilance Committee was formed. In the month of May of that year murderers were taken from jail and executed, the result being that the Governor declared San Francisco to be in a state of insurrection. The Vigilance Committee gained almost sovereign power, and before it disbanded in August, it had a parade in which over 5,000 armed, disciplined men took part.

Two years later, the overland mail commenced its journeys and the celebrated pony express followed in 1860. Railroads followed soon after, and instead of being a practically unknown country, several weeks' journey from the old established cities, the lightning express has brought the Pacific so near to the Atlantic that time and space seem to have been almost annihilated.

CHAPTER XIV.

BEFORE EMANCIPATION AND AFTER.

First Importation of Negro Slaves into America—The Original Abolitionists—A Colored Enthusiast and a Coward—Origin of the word "Secession"—John Brown's Fanaticism—Uncle Tom's Cabin—Faithful unto Death—George Augustus Sala on the Negro who Lingered too long in the Mill Pond.

THE American negro is such a distinct character that he cannot be overlooked in a work of this nature. Some people think he is wholly bad, and that although he occasionally assumes a virtue, he is but playing a part, and playing it but indifferently well at that. Others place him on a lofty pedestal, and magnify him into a hero and a martyr.

But the Afro-American, commonly called a "nigger" in the South, is neither the one nor the other. He is often as worthless as the "white trash" he so scornfully despises, and he is often all that the most exacting could expect, when his surroundings and disadvantages are taken into consideration. Physiologists tell us that man is very largely what others make him, many going so far as to say that character and disposition are three parts hereditary and one part environment. If this is so, a good deal of allowance should be made. It is less than 300 years since the first negroes were brought over to this country, and it is but little more than thirty years since slavery was abolished. Hence, from both the standpoints of descent and environment, the negro is at a great disadvantage, and he should hardly be judged by the common standard.

It was in the year 1619 that a Dutch ship landed a cargo of negroes from Guinea, but that was not really the first case of slavery in this country. Prior to that time paupers and criminals from the old world had voluntarily sold themselves into a species of subjection, in preference to starvation and detention in their own land; but this landing in 1619 seems to have really introduced the colored man into the labor world and market of America.

We need not trace the history of the negro as a slave at any length. That he was occasionally abused goes without saying, but that his condition was approximately as bad as a majority of writers have attempted to prove is not so certain. It was the policy of the slave owner to get as much work out of his staff as he possibly could. He knew from experience that the powers of human endurance were necessarily limited, and that a man could not work satisfactorily when he was sick or hungry. Hence, even on the supposition that all slave owners were without feeling, it is obvious that self-interest must have impelled them to keep the negro in good health, and to prevent him from losing strength from hardship and want.

On some plantations the lot of the slave was a hard one, but on others there was very little complaining or cause for complaint. Thousands of slaves were better off by far than they have been subsequent to liberation, and it is a fact that speaks volumes for the much discussed and criticized slaveholders, that numbers of emancipated slaves refused to accept their freedom, while many more, who went away delighted at the removal of withstraint, came back of their own option very soon after, and begged to be allowed to resume the old relations.

The average negro obeys, literally obeys, the divine instruction to take no thought for the morrow. If he has a good dinner in the oven he is apt to forget for the time being that there is such a meal as supper, and he certainly does not give even a passing thought to the fact that if he has no breakfast in the morning he will be "powerfu' hungry." This indifference as to the future robbed slavery of much of its hardship, and although every one condemns the idea in the abstract, there are many humane men and women who do not think the colored man suffered half as much as has so often and so emphatically been stated.

Abolition was advocated with much earnestness for many years prior to Lincoln's famous emancipation proclamation. The agitation first took tangible shape during the administration of General Jackson, a man who received more hero worship than has fallen to the lot of any of his successors. To a zealous, if perhaps bigoted, Quaker belongs the credit of having started the work, by founding a newspaper, which he called the "Genius of Universal Emancipation." William Lloyd Garrison, subsequently with "The Liberator," was connected with this journal, and in the first issue he announced as his programme, war to the death against slavery in every form. "I will not equivocate; I will not excuse; I will not retreat a single inch, and I will be heard," was the announcement with which he opened the campaign, which he subsequently carried on with more conspicuous vigor than success.

Garrison handled the question of the relation between the white and colored people of the country without gloves, and his very outspoken language occasionally got him into trouble. The people who supported him were known as Abolitionists, a name which even at that early date conjured up hard feeling, and divided household against household, and family against family. Among these Garrison was regarded as a hero, and to some extent as a martyr, while the bitterness of his invective earned for him the title of fanatic and crank from the thousands who disagreed with him, and who thought he was advocating legislation in advance of public sentiment.

The debates of the days of which we are speaking were full of interest. Many of the arguments advanced teemed with force. The Abolitionists denounced the Republic for inconsistency, in declaring that all men were equal, and then keeping 3,000,000 colored people in enforced subjection. In reply the Bible was freely quoted in defense of slavery, and the fight was taken up by ministers of religion with much zeal. It was not, by any means, a sectional question at that time. While the slaves were owned by Southern planters and landed proprietors, they were purchased and kept on borrowed capital, and many of the men in the North, who were supposed to sympathize with the Abolitionists, were as much interested in the perpetuation of slavery as those who actually owned the slaves themselves.

In the year 1831, a negro named Turner, supported by six desperate and misguided fellow countrymen, started out on what they regarded as a practical crusade against slavery. Turner professed to have seen visions such as inspired Joan of Arc, and he proceeded to fulfill what he regarded as his divine mission, in a very fanatical manner. First, the white man who owned Turner was murdered, and then the band proceeded to kill off all white men in sight or within convenient reach. Within two days nearly fifty white men were destroyed by those avenging angels, as they were called, and then the insurrection or crusade was terminated by the organizing of a handful of white men who did not propose to be sacrificed as had been their fellows.

Turner's bravery was great when there was no resistance, but he recognized that discretion was the better part of valor the moment organized resistance was offered. Taking to the woods, he left his followers to shift for themselves. For more than a week he lived on what he could find in the wheat fields, and then, coming in contact with an armed white man, he speedily surrendered. A week later he was hanged, and seventeen other colored men suffered a like penalty for connection with the conspiracy. The murderous outbreak had other dire results for the negro, and caused many innocent men to be suspected and punished.

A year later, Garrison started the New England Anti-Slavery Society, which was followed by many similar organizations. So intense did the feeling become that President Jackson thought it advisable to recommend legislation excluding Abolition literature from the mails. The measure was finally defeated, but in the Southern States, particularly, a great deal of mail was searched and even condemned. Rewards were offered in some of the slave-holding States for the apprehension of some of the leading Abolitionists, and feeling ran very high, every outbreak being laid at the doors of the men who were preaching the new gospel of equal rights, regardless of color.

Mobs frequently took a hand in the proceedings, and several men were attacked and arrested on very flimsy pretexts. In 1836, the Pennsylvania Hall, in Philadelphia, was burned, because it had been dedicated by an anti-slavery meeting. So bitter did the feeling become that every attempt to open schools for colored children was followed by disturbance, the teachers being driven away and the books destroyed. Numerous petitions on the subject were sent to Congress, and there was an uproar in the House when it was proposed to refer a petition for the abolition of slavery in the District of Columbia to a committee. The Southern Congressmen withdrew from the House as a formal protest, and the word "secession," which was subsequently to acquire such a much more significant meaning, was first applied to this action on their part.

A compromise, however, was effected, and the seceding members took their seats on the following day. Feeling, however, ran very high. Some people returned fugitive slaves to their owners, while others established what was then known as the underground railway. This was a combination between Abolitionists in various parts, and involved the feeding and housing of slaves, who were passed on from house to house and helped on their road to Canada. Much excitement was caused in 1841 by the ship "Creole," which sailed from Richmond with a cargo of 135 slaves from the Virginia plantation. Near the Bahama Islands one of the slaves named Washington, as by the way a good many thousand slaves were named from time to time, headed a rebellion. The slaves succeeded in overpowering the crew and in confining the captain and the white passengers. They forced the captain to take the boat to New Providence, where all except the actual members of the rebelling crowd were declared free.

Joshua Giddings, of Ohio, offered a resolution in the

Yellowstone Falls.

House of Representatives claiming that every man who had been a slave in the United States was free the moment he crossed the boundary of some other country. The way in which this resolution was received led to the resignation of Mr. Giddings. He offered himself for re-election, and was sent back to Congress by an enormous majority. As Ohio had been very bitter in its anti-negro demonstrations, the vote was regarded as very significant. The Supreme Court decided differently from the people, and a ruling was handed down to the effect that fugitive slaves were liable to re-capture. The court held that the law as to slavery was paramount in free as well as slave States, and that every law-abiding citizen must recognize these rights and not interfere with them. Feeling became very intense after this, and for a time it threatened to extend far beyond rational limits. In the church the controversy waxed warm, and in more than one instance division as well as dissension arose.

In 1858, a new phase was given to the controversy by John Brown. Every one has heard of this remarkable man, who was regarded by some as a martyr, and by others as a dangerous crank. As one writer very aptly puts it, John Brown was both the one and the other. That his intentions were in the main good, few doubt, but his methods were open to the gravest censure, and according to some deep thinkers he was, in a large degree, responsible for the bitter feeling which made war between the North and the South inevitable. Probably this is giving undue importance to this much-discussed enthusiast, who regarded himself as a divine messenger sent to liberate the slaves and punish the slave-holders.

He conceived the idea of rallying all the colored people

around him in the impregnable mountains of Virginia, and having drafted a constitution, he proceeded to unfurl his flag and call out his supporters. In October, 1859, he took possession of the United States Armory at Harper's Ferry, interfered with the running of trains, and practically held the town with a force of some eighteen men, of whom four were colored. Colonel Robert E. Lee quickly came on the scene with a detachment of troops and drove the Brown following into an engine-house. They declined to surrender, and thirteen were either killed or mortally wounded. Two of Brown's sons were among those who fell, and the leader himself was captured. He treated his trial with the utmost indifference, and went to the scaffold erect and apparently unconcerned. His body was taken to his old home in New York State, where it was buried.

Abraham Lincoln must not be included in the list of enthusiastic Abolitionists, although he eventually freed the slaves. In speeches made prior to the war he expressed the opinion that in slave States general emancipation would be ill-advised, and although his election was looked upon as dangerous to slave-holders' interests, the fear seems to have been prophetic in a large measure. It was not until the war had lasted far longer than originally anticipated that Lincoln definitely threatened to liberate the colored slaves. That threat he carried into execution on January 1st, 1863, when 3,000,000 slaves became free. The cause of the Confederacy had not yet become the "lost cause," and the leaders on the Southern side were inclined to ridicule the decree, and to regard it rather as a "bluff" than anything of a serious order. But it was emancipation in fact as well as in deed, as the colored orator never tired of explaining.

Such in outline is the history of the colored man during the days of enforced servitude. Of his condition during that period volumes have been written. Few works printed in the English language have been more widely circulated than "Uncle Tom's Cabin," which has been read in every English-speaking country in the world, and in many other countries besides. It has been dramatized and performed upon thousands of stages before audiences of every rank and class. As a descriptive work it rivals in many passages the very best ever written. Much controversy has taken place as to how much of the book is history—how much of it is founded upon fact and how much is pure fiction. The ground is a rather dangerous one to touch. It is safest to say that while the brutality held up to scorn and contempt in this book was not general in the slave States or on plantations in the South, what is depicted might have taken place under existing laws, and the book exposed iniquities which were certainly perpetrated in isolated cases.

That all negroes were not treated badly, or that slavery invariably meant misery, can be easily proved by any one who takes the trouble to investigate, even in the most superficial manner. When the news of emancipation gradually spread through the remote regions of the South, there were hundreds and probably thousands of negroes who declined absolutely to take advantage of the freedom given them. Many most pathetic cases of devotion and love were made manifest. Even to-day there are numbers of aged colored men and women who are remaining with their old-time owners and declining to regard emancipation as logical or reasonable.

Not long ago, a Northern writer while traveling through

the South found an aged negro, whom he approached with a view to getting some interesting passages of local history. To his surprise he found that the old man had but one idea. That idea was that it was his duty to take care of and preserve his old master's grave. When the war broke out, the old hero was the body-servant or valet of a man, who, from the very first, was in the thick of the fight against the North. The colored man followed his soldier-master from place to place, and when a Northern bullet put an end to the career of the master, the servant reverently conveyed the body back to the old home, superintended the interment, and commenced a daily routine of watching, which for more than thirty years he had never varied.

All the relatives of the deceased had left the neighborhood years before, and the faithful old negro was the only one left to watch over the grave and keep the flowers that were growing on it in good condition. As far as could be learned from local gossip, the old fellow had no visible means of subsistence, securing what little he needed to eat in exchange for odd jobs around neighboring houses. No one seemed to know where he slept, or seemed to regard the matter as of any consequence. There was about the jet black hero, however, an air of absolute happiness, added to an obvious sense of pride at the performance of his self-imposed and very loving task.

Instances of this kind could be mutiplied almost without end. The negro as a free man and citizen retains many of the most prominent characteristics which marked his career in the days before the war. Now and again one hears of a negro committing suicide. Such an event, however, is almost as rare as resignation of an office-holder or the death of an annuitant. Indifference to suffering and a keen appreciation of pleasure, make prolonged grief very unusual among Afro-Americans, and in consequence their lives are comparatively joyous.

One has to go down South to appreciate the colored man as he really is. In the North he is apt to imitate the white man so much that he loses his unique personality. In the Southern States, however, he can be found in all his original glory. Here he can be regarded as a survival of preceding generations. In the South, before the war, the truism that there is dignity in toil was scarcely appreciated at its full worth. The negro understood, as if by instinct, that he ought to work for his white master, and that duties of every kind in the field, on the road and in the house, should be performed by him. For a white man who worked he entertained feelings in which there was a little pity and a great deal of contempt. He has never got over this feeling, or the feeling which his father before him had. Down South to-day the expression "po' white trash" is still full of meaning, and the words are uttered by the thick-lipped, woolly-headed critics with an emphasis and expression the very best white mimic has never yet succeeded in reproducing.

George Augustus Sala, one of England's oldest and most successful descriptive writers, talks very entertainingly regarding the emancipated slave. The first trip made to this country by the versatile writer referred to was during the war.

He returned home full of prejudices, and wrote up the country in that supercilious manner European writers are too apt to adopt in regard to America. Several years later he made his second trip, and his experiences, as recorded in "America Revisited," are much better reading, and much freer from prejudice.

"For full five and thirty years," he writes, "had I been waiting to see the negro 'standing in the mill pond.' I saw him in all his glory and all his driving wretchedness at Guinneys, in the State of Virginia. I own that for some days past the potential African, 'standin' in de mill pond longer than he oughter' had been lying somewhat heavily on my conscience. My acquaintance with our dark brethren since arriving in this country had not only been necessarily limited, but scarcely of a nature to give me any practical insight into his real condition since he has been a free man—free to work or starve; free to become a good citizen or go to the devil, as he has gone, mundanely speaking, in Hayti and elsewhere. Colored folks are few and far between in New York, and they have never, as a rule, been slaves, and are not even generally of servile extraction. In Philadelphia they are much more numerous. Many of the mulatto waiters employed in the hotels are strikingly handsome men, and on the whole the sable sons of Pennsylvania struck me as being industrious, well dressed, prosperous, and a trifle haughty in their intercourse with white folks.

"In Baltimore, where slavery existed until the promulgation of Lincoln's proclamation, the colored people are plentiful. I met a good many ragged, shiftless, and generally dejected negroes of both sexes, who appeared to be just the kind of waifs and strays who would stand in a mill pond longer than they ought to in the event of there being any convenient mill pond at hand. But the better class darkeys, who have been domestic slaves in Baltimore families, seemed to retain all their own affectionate obsequiousness of manner and respectful familiarity. Again, in Washington, the black man and his congeners seemed to be doing remarkably well. At one of the quietest, most elegant and most comfortable hotels in the Federal Capital, I found the establishment conducted by a colored man, all of whose employes, from the clerks in the office to the waiters and chambermaids, were colored. Our chambermaid was a delightful old lady, and insisted ere we left that we should give her a receipt for a real old English Christmas plum pudding.

"But these were not the mill pond folk of whom I was in quest. They were of the South, as an Irishman in London is of Ireland, but not in it. I had a craving to see whether any of the social ashes of slavery lived their wonted fires. Away down South was the real object of my mission, and in pursuit of that mission I went on to Richmond."

Mr. Sala proceeds to give a most amusing account of his ride from New York to Richmond, with various criticisms of sleeping-car accommodation, heartily endorsed by all American travelers who have read them. Arriving at Richmond he asked the usual question: "Is not the negro idle, thriftless and thievish?" From time immemorial it has been asserted that the laws of meum and tuum have no meaning for the colored man. It is a joke current in more than one American city, that the police have standing orders to arrest every negro seen carrying a turkey or a chicken along the street. In other words, the funny man would have us believe that the innate love of poultry in the Ethiopian's breast is so great that the chances are against his having been possessed of sufficient force of character to pass a store or market where any birds were exposed for sale and not watched.

It is doubtless a libel on the colored race to state that even the majority of its members are chicken thieves by descent rather than inclination, just as it is a libel on their religion to insinuate that a colored camp meeting is almost certain to involve severe inroads into the chicken coops and roosts of the neighboring farmers. Certain it is, however, that chicken stealing is one of the most dangerous causes of backsliding on the part of colored converts and enthusiastic singers of hymns in negro churches. The case of the convert who was asked by his pastor, a week after his admission to the church, if he had stolen a chicken since his conversion, and who carefully concealed a stolen duck under his coat while he assured the good man that he had not, is an exaggerated one of course, but it is quoted as a good story in almost every State and city in the Union.

Mr. Sala objects very much to judging a whole class of people by a few street-corner or cross-road loungers. The negro he found to be superstitious, just as we find them to-day. Even educated negroes are apt to give credence to many stories which, on the face of them, appear ridiculous. The words "Hoodoo" and "Mascot" have a meaning among these people of which we have only a dim conception, and when sickness enters a family the aid of an alleged doctor, who is often a charlatan of the worst character, is apt to be sought. It will take several generations to work out this characteristic, and perhaps the greatest complaint the colored race has against those who formerly held them in subjection, is the way in which voodoo and supernatural stories were told ignorant slaves with a view to frightening them into obedience, and inciting them to extra exertions.

For absolute ignorance and apparent lack of human understanding, the negro loafer to be found around some of our Southern towns and depots may be quoted as a signal and quite amusing example. The hat, as Mr. Sala humorously puts it, resembles an inverted coal scuttle or bucket without handles, and pierced by many holes. It is something like the bonnet of a Brobdingnagian Quakeress, huge and flapped and battered, and fearful to look upon.

"Hang all this equipment," this interesting writer goes on to say, "on the limbs of a tall negro of any age between sixteen and sixty, and then let him stand close to the scaffold-like platform of the depot shanty and let him loaf. His attitude is one of complete and apathetic immobility. He does not grin. He may be chewing, but he does not smoke. He does not beg; at least in so far as I observed him he stood in no posture and assumed no gestures belonging to the mendicant. He looms at you with a dull, stony, preoccupied gaze, as though his thoughts were a thousand miles away in the unknown land; while once in every quarter of an hour or so he woke up to a momentary consciousness that he was a thing neither rich nor rare, and so wondered how in thunder he got there. He is a derelict, a fragment of flotsam and jetsam cast upon the not too hospitable shore of civilization after the great storm had lashed the Southern sea to frenzy and the ship of slavery had gone to pieces forever. Possibly he is a good deal more human than he looks, and if he chose to bestir himself and to address himself to articulate discourse, could tell you a great many things about his wants and wishes, his views and feelings on things in general which, to you, might prove little more than amazing.

As things go, he prefers to do nothing and to proffer no kind of explanation as to why he is standing there in a metaphorical mill pond very much 'longer than he oughter.'"

One turns with pleasure from the severe, but perhaps not overdrawn, character sketch of the colored loafer, to the better side of the modern negro. The intense desire for education, and the keen recognition of the fact that knowledge is power, point to a time when utter ignorance even among the negroes will be a thing of the past. Prejudice is hard to fight against, and the colored man has often a considerable amount of handicap to overcome. But just as Mr. Sala found the typical negro, "standing in the mill pond longer than he oughter," a sad memento of the past, so the traveler can find many an intelligent and entertaining individual whose accent betrays his color even in the darkest night, but whose cute expressions and pleasant reminiscences go a long way towards convincing even the sternest critic that the future is full of hope for a race whose past has in it so little that is either pleasing or satisfactory.

CHAPTER XV.

OUR NATIONAL PARK.

A Delightful Rhapsody—Early History of Yellowstone Park—A Fish Story which Convulsed Congress—The First White Man to Visit the Park—A Race for Life—Philosophy of the Hot Springs—Mount Everts—From the Geysers to Elk Park—Some Old Friends and New Ones—Yellowstone Lake—The Angler's Paradise.

YELLOWSTONE PARK is generally included in the list of the wonders of the world. It is certainly unique in every respect, and no other nation, modern or ancient, has ever been able to boast of a recreation ground and park provided by nature and supplied with such magnificent and extraordinary attractions and peculiarities. It is a park upon a mountain, being more than 10,000 feet above the level of the sea. Irregular in shape, it may be said to be about sixty miles across on the average, and it contains an area of 3,500 square miles.

Mr. Olin D. Wheeler, in an admirable treatise on this park, in which he describes some of the many wonders in the marvelous region traversed by the Northern Pacific Railroad, thus rhapsodizes:

"The Yellowstone Park! The gem of wonderland. The land of mystic splendor. Region of bubbling caldron and boiling pool with fretted rims, rivaling the coral in delicacy of texture and the rainbow in variety of color; of steaming funnels exhaling into the etherine atmosphere in calm, unruffled monotone and paroxysmal ejection, vast clouds of fleecy vapor from the underground furnaces of the God of Nature; sylvan parkland, where amidst the unsullied freshness of flower-strewn valley and bountiful woodland, the native fauna of the land browse in fearless joy and wander wild and free, unfretted by sound of huntsman's horn, the long-drawn bay of the hound, and the sharp crack of the rifle.

"Land of beauteous vale and laughing water, thundering cataract and winding ravine; realm of the Ice King and the Fire King; enchanted spot, where mountain and sea meet and kiss each other; where the murmurs of the river, as it meanders through heaven-blest valleys, becomes harsh and sullen amid the pine-covered hills which darken and throttle its joyous song, until, uncontrollable, it throws itself, a magnificent sheet of diamond spray and plunging torrent, over precipices, and rolls along an emerald flood betwixt cañon walls, such as the eye of mortal has seldom seen."

The history of this park is involved in a good deal of mystery. About ninety years ago it was first discovered, but the information brought back to civilization by the explorers was apparently so exaggerated that it excited general ridicule. No one believed that the wonders described really existed. Even later, when corroborative evidence was forthcoming, skepticism continued. It was almost as difficult then to make people believe the truth about the hot springs and geysers, as it is now to make people believe that it is possible for a man to stand on the edge of a hot spring, catch the choicest kind of fish in the cool waters of the lake surrounding him, and then cook his fish in the boiling water of the spring without taking it off the hook, or walking a single step.

This latter fish story has the peculiar feature of being true. Several reliable men, including some who have not allowed the ardent pursuit of Isaac Walton's pet pastime to blunt their susceptibility of veracity, have performed this apparently impossible feat, or have seen it done right before their very eyes. A year or so ago, when an appropriation was asked for in Congress for the further preservation of Yellowstone Park, a member made this extraordinary possibility an argument in support of his plea. A roar of laughter succeeded his recital, and when the orator stopped to explain that he was merely recording an actual fact and not telling a fish story, there seemed to be danger of wholesale convulsion within the legislative walls. Several of the amused Congressmen subsequently made inquiries and ascertained to their astonishment that, instead of exaggeration, the half had not been told, and that if a full summary of the attractions of Yellowstone Park were to be written, the immense shelves of the Congressional Library itself would scarcely hold the books that would have to be written to contain it.

This little divergence is to afford an excuse for the incredulity of our forefathers, who made sarcastic remarks as to the powers of wild Western whisky, when pioneers returned from the Rocky Mountains and told them that there existed away up in the clouds an immense natural park, where beauty and weirdness could be found side by side.

John Colter, or Coulter, is said to have been the first white man who ever entered the natural portals of this glorious park. It was in the early days of the century that this remarkable man had his adventure. He was a member of the Lewis and Clark expedition, which was sent out to explore the sources of the Missouri and Columbia Rivers. He was naturally an adventurer, and a man who had no idea of the meaning of the word "danger." The party had a glimpse of Yellowstone Park, and Coulter was so enamored with the hunting prospects that he either deserted from the expedition party or obtained permission to remain behind.

However this may have been, it is certain that Coulter remained, with but one companion, in the vicinity of the Jefferson Fork of the Missouri River. According to fairly authentic records, he and his companion were captured by hostile Blackfeet, who showed their resentment at the intrusion upon the privacy of their domains by depriving Coulter of his clothing, and Coulter's companion of his life. The chronic adventurer, however, spent four years among the more friendly Bannock Indians, who probably for centuries had lived in or near the park. He had a very enjoyable time in the newly discovered region, and his adventures crowded upon each other, one after the other, with great rapidity. When at last he decided to return to the abode of the white man, he took with him a fund of recollection and incident of the most sensational character, and before he had been at home with his own kindred a week, he had earned the reputation of being a modern Ananias, ten times more mendacious than the original article.

Twenty or thirty years elapsed before any reliable information was obtained about the park. James Bridger, the daring scout and mountaineer, went through the park more than once, and in his most exaggerated rhapsodies told of its beauties and of its marvels. But Bridger's stories had been tried in the balances and found wanting before this, and nobody worried very much over them. In 1870, Dr. F. V. Hayden and Mr. M. P. Langford explored the park on a more rational basis, and gave to the world, in reliable shape, a resume of their discoveries. Mr. Langford was himself an experienced Western explorer. For many years he had desired to either verify or disprove the so-called fairy tales which were going the rounds concerning Yellowstone Park. He found a number of equally adventurous gentlemen, including the Surveyor-General of Montana, Mr. Washburn, after whom the expedition was generally known. In 1871, Dr. Hayden, who was then connected with the United States Geological Survey Department, undertook a scientific exploration of the park. He was accompanied by Mr. Langford, and the two men together tore away the veil of mystery which had overhung the wonderful resort among the hills, and gave to the country, for the first time, a reliable description of one of the most magnificent of its possessions.

The report was not confined to eulogy. It included drawings, photographs and geological summaries, and wound up with an earnest appeal to the National Government to reserve the beauty spot as a National Park forever. Several men arose to endorse the request, and in March, 1872, Congress passed an act dedicating Yellowstone Park to the public for all time, declaring it to be a grand national playground and a museum of unparalleled and incomparable marvels.

Since that time the park has gradually become better known and more highly appreciated. The Northern Pacific Railroad runs a branch line to which the name of the park has been given, and which connects Livingston, Montana, with Cinnabar, at the northern edge of the park. The road is about fifty miles long, and the scenery through which it passes is astounding in its nature.

From Cinnabar the tourist is driven in large stages throughout the park. If at all reminiscent by nature, he thinks about the experiences of Coulter, to whom we have already referred as the pioneer white man of Yellowstone. Early in the century the park was occupied by Indians, who had scarcely come in contact with white men, and who had not learned that in the unavoidable conflict between races, the weaker must inevitably succumb to the stronger. Around the limpid streams and at the borders of the virgin forests, containing untold wealth, tents made of skin drawn over boughs cut roughly from trees, could be seen in every direction. All around there were rough-looking, utterly uncivilized Indians, who were carrying out their usual occupation of doing nothing, and doing it with exceptional ability.

The women or squaws were more active, but frequently paused in their work to look at the unfortunate Coulter, who, deprived of his clothing and absolutely naked, was waiting, bound hand and foot, for the fate that he had every reason to believe awaited him. His only companion had been killed the day before, and he expected every minute to meet the same fate. According to his own description of what followed, strategy saved his life. An Indian, sent for the purpose, asked him if he could run fast. Knowing himself to be an athlete of no mean ability, but guessing the object of the question, he assured the Indian that he was not a speedy runner. The answer had the effect he anticipated.

His thongs were almost immediately cut, and he was taken out on the open prairie, given a trifling start, and then told that he might save himself if he could. Coulter had run many a fast mile before, but he never ran as on

Scenes In and Around Yellowstone Park.

this occasion. He knew that behind him there were, among the indolent young Indians, many who could run with great speed, and his only hope lay in getting to cover ahead of these. Every long stride meant that much space between him and death, and every stride he took was the longest in his power. Again and again he looked around, only to discover to his astonishment that he had but just held his own. At last, however, all his pursuers except one were tired of the pursuit, and when he found this to be the case, he turned like a stag at bay and overpowered him.

Then seeing that others of the Indians were taking up the chase, after a brief rest, Coulter made another great run, plunged into the river in front of him, and finally entered the labyrinth of forests and craters now known to the world as Yellowstone Park. Here, if his story is to be believed, he succeeded in making for himself clothing of some character out of the skins of beasts that he shot, and finally he fell into the hands of less hostile red men.

So much of the early days of Yellowstone, and of the reminiscences which a first visit naturally conjure up. The park as it exists to-day is overcrowded with modern interests, and one only refers to these reminiscences by way of contrast. There are in the park at least 100 geysers, nearly 4,000 springs, and an immense number of miniature parks, large and small rivers, and other marvels.

The park is about equi-distant from the cities of Portland and St. Paul, and so many people have been attracted to it in recent years that a large number of very fine hotels have been built at a great expense. The hotels are open about four months a year, and the help to run them is brought from different States. The expenses are naturally heavy, and hence the hotel charges are not nominal, although the tourist can generally limit the expenses incurred to the bulk of his pocket-book, should he so desire. If he includes in his calculations the absolutely free sights that he witnesses, the expense of a trip is certainly moderate, and ought not to be taken into much consideration.

The Mammoth Hot Springs is one of the leading sources of attraction of the park, a tour of which is something no American of means can afford to miss. The springs are very hard to describe. They consist of a number of irregular terraces, some as large as five acres in extent, and others very small. Some are a few feet high, and others stand forty or sixty feet above the one next below. Few people really understand what these springs are, or how the terraces are formed. One authority of eminence says that the rocks underlying the particular point are calcareous in character, consisting mainly of carbonated lime, which is somewhat soluble in percolating earth water. The hot subterranean water dissolves a large amount of mineral matter in passing through the earth, which it deposits on the surface in passing through the air. By this process walls, embankments and terraces are built up, and as the minerals through which the water passes are varying greatly in color, so the deposits left on the surface are some of them red, other pink and others black, with yellows, greens, blues, chocolates and mixed colors abounding in immense numbers, sometimes harmonizing beautifully and sometimes presenting the most astounding contrasts.

The water in the springs is not warm, but hot, and hence the name. Frequently the temperature exceeds 160 degrees, in which case the coloring matter seems to be washed out, and the terraces present a white appearance. On other occasions, where the temperature is less severe, the varying hues already referred to abound on every side. Sometimes this whiteness, or bleached-out appearance, is astounding in its effects. The true artist will stand for hours gazing upon it, and wishing that he could reproduce, ever so inaccurately, the intense beauties which surround him.

Behind the springs, and blocking up the view on the south, is the mountain known as Bunsen Peak, the highest within the range of the eye. Just across the open space, in front of the hotel at the springs, are the quarters of the National soldiers who patrol the park, and, to a certain extent at any rate, protect it from the vandal and the purloiner.

In an admirable description of this scene contained in "Indian Land and Wonderland," a very delightful story is told of the long, low, flat and lava-capped mountain known as Mount Everts, in honor of Mr. T. C. Everts of Helena. Few know the story upon which the mountain owes its name, which is given as follows:

Among the members of the first party that ever explored Yellowstone Park were Messrs. M. P. Langford, S. T. Hauser and T. C. Everts. There was also a military escort under Lieutenant Doane. The party proceeded up the Yellowstone River to the Grand Cañon, thence across to Yellowstone Lake, around its eastern edge to the southern end, whence turning west they followed down the Firehole River through the Upper Geyser Basin to the Madison River. Following this river out from the park, they returned to Western civilization—all but one of them.

On the nineteenth day out, September 9th, when moving across the country bordering the southern shore of the lake, Mr. Everts became lost. The traveling here was difficult, owing to fallen timber, rugged heights and no trails, and he was not missed until camp was made at night. Mr. Everts was not seen again for thirty-seven days, when he was found by two mountaineers on the verge of what is now known as Mount Everts, perfectly exhausted, and partly deranged through exposure and suffering. On the very first day of his absence his horse, left standing and unfastened, with all the man's arms and camp equipments attached, became frightened and ran away. Everts was near-sighted, had not even a knife for use or defense, and only a field glass to assist him in escaping. He first managed to reach Heart Lake, the source of Snake River. Here he remained for twelve days, sleeping close by the Hot Springs to keep from freezing. His food was thistle roots, boiled in the springs. One night he was forced into a tree by a mountain lion, and kept there all night.

Finally, he bethought himself of the lenses of his field glasses, and thus was enabled to kindle fires. He wandered all along the western side of the lake and down the Yellowstone to where he was providentially found. He gave the story of his terrible experience in the old "Scribner's Magazine," since become "The Century," and a thrilling tale it makes. In a country filled with a network of streams, abundantly supplied with animal life for food, gorged with timber for fuel, the man nearly froze and starved and perished from thirst. Twice he was five days without food; once three days without water. It was late in the season, and the storms swept down on him and chilled him to the bone; the snows kept him prisoner in camp, or, when on his painful marches, blocked his progress.

Naturally, he lost strength, and became hourly in danger of succumbing to the vast difficulties which confronted him. His sufferings were increased by the fear which was created by a large mountain lion, which got on his trail and followed him, evidently with a view to making him a feature of the menu of his next meal. It seems incredible that Mr. Everts should ever have escaped with his life. Fortune, however, came to his rescue at last. He was rescued and nursed back to life by good friends. To the plateau on which he was found, his name was given, although there are few who will remember the significance of the name.

Norris Geyser is another of the almost miraculous features of the park. The basin of the geyser has been described as a weird, uncanny place, and the words seem well chosen. Of vegetation there is practically none, because the underground heat keeps the ground always warm, and steam breaks out into the atmosphere at several points. The general aspect is drear and desolate, gray and dull, and yet there is something about it beautiful as well as uncanny.

A geyser is always a source of wonder. The word is of Icelandic derivation, and signifies gushing. As applied to phenomena such as we are now describing, its applicability is good, for, from the mouth of the geysers, there rushes from time to time an immense mass of boiling water and steam, creating a disturbance of no ordinary character. It is assumed that the water hurled into the air to a great height while at boiling point, has risen to the surface through masses of lava, which are reminiscent of volcanic ages far beyond the memory of mankind. The mystery of geological formation is too great to be gone into in a work of this character, but the bare contemplation of geysers, such as are seen at Yellowstone Park, reminds one of the wonders deeply hidden in the bowels of the earth, unappreciated and unknown by and to 99 per cent. of the human race.

At the Norris Geyser basin the noise is extraordinary, and people who are superstitiously inclined are awed at the rumblings and grumblings which seem to issue from the bowels of the earth. Eruptions of hot water and steam at irregular intervals burst forth, and the very road which crosses the adjoining plain has been bleached to almost perfect whiteness by the vapors. The crust of ground is very thin all around here, and indiscriminate exploring is dangerous. To slip through the crust into the boiling water beneath would inevitably involve being scalded to death, and the man who allows the guide to show him where to tread exhibits the greater wisdom.

In direct contrast to this basin is the Elk Park. Yellowstone is celebrated among other things for being the home of an immense number of the most remarkable specimens of North American animals. The Government herd of buffalo in the park is of countless value, because it is really the only complete representation at the present time of the practically extinct species of flesh and hide producing animals which used to graze by the million on the prairie. The buffalo are comparatively tame. Most of them were born within the confines of the park, and seem to have realized that the existence of their kind in perpetuity is one of the greatest desires of the Government. There are a number of bears around as well, but they have lost their viciousness, and enjoy life very hugely under somewhat changed conditions. They seldom hurt any one, but prowl around the hotels at night, and by eating up the scraps and leavings solve the garbage problem in a satisfactory manner.

Deer, elk, antelope and mountain sheep climb the mountains, and very frequently find their way into Elk Park or Gibbon Meadow. This is an exceptionally desirable wintering ground, because it is surrounded by hills and mountains which keep off the worst of the winds, and there is, moreover, a perpetual spring of pure water. The meadow is probably the prettiest spot in the entire park. There is less of the awful and more of the picturesque than can be found elsewhere, and it is, in many respects, an oasis in a vast and somewhat dreary expanse of land.

Golden Gate is another of the exquisite spots every visitor to Yellowstone Park seeks and finds. To reach the Golden Gate one must be a great climber, for it is high up, and the road to it is built along the edge of a cliff, which, in places, seems to be absolutely perpendicular. The gate is, however, worth reaching, and one is not surprised to hear that as much as $14,000 were spent in cutting out a single mile of the road to it through the rock.

Leaving the Golden Gate, and continuing the tour of inspection, a valley of large dimensions is seen. The contrast between the rich green of almost faultless verdure, and the dreariness of the rocks left behind, is striking. It would seem as though nature had built up an immense barrier between the weird and the natural, so that the one could not affect the other. The Bible speaks of the intense comfort of the shade of a great rock in a dry and thirsty land. A sensation of equal, if not greater, relief is experienced in Yellowstone Park when one leaves the grand, death-like desolation around the Hot Springs, and encounters the exquisite beauty of shrub land and timber but a few paces away. The groves of trees are in themselves sources of great delight, and also of immense wealth. Fortunately, they will be preserved in perpetuity for the American people. The lumber king cannot get here. His ravages must be confined to other regions.

The valley into which the tourist has entered takes its name from the Swan Lake, a very delightful inland mountain scene. The lake is about two miles from Golden Gate. It is not a very large body of water, but its rippling surface extracts expressions of admiration from all who behold it. It has been described as a demure looking sheet of water, and there is something about the appearance of the lake which seems to justify the peculiar definition. The cañon forming the valley is like everything else in Yellowstone Park—a little out of the ordinary. On the one side there are lofty mountains, with eminences and peaks of various formation and height, while in the distance the great Electric Peak can be easily seen. We have already spoken of Yellowstone Park as being about 10,000 feet above the sea level. Electric Peak, well described as the sentinel of the park, is more than 11,000 feet high. Viewed from a distance, or along the line of the valley, it is calculated to excite both admiration and awe.

Willow Creek Park, or Willow Park, as it is sometimes called, lies due south. It takes its name from the immense growth of willow bushes which hide the ground from view, and monopolize the scenery and groundwork entirely. None of these bushes can claim the right to be called trees, as the average height is inconsiderable. But they make up in density what they lack in altitude. The peculiar green of the willow is the predominating color, without any variation of any kind. The idea conveyed to the mind is of a huge green carpet or rug, and when the wind blows freely across the valley, it divides up the bushes into little ridges or furrows, which add to the uniqueness of the scene. Springs of remarkably pure water, many of them possessed of medicinal power, abound in this neighborhood, and tourists slake an imaginary thirst with much interest at different ones of these.

The Obsidian Creek runs slowly through this valley. Obsidian Cliff is the next object of special interest which is witnessed. It is half a mile long and from 150 to 200 feet high. The southern end is formed of volcanic glass, or obsidian, as true a glass as any artificially produced. The roadway at its base is constructed across the talus, and is emphatically a glass road. Huge fragments of obsidian, black and shining, some of it streaked with white seams, line the road. Small pieces are also plentiful. This flow of glass came from a high plateau to the east-northeast. Numerous vent pits, or apparent craters, have been discovered on this plateau. Mr. J. P. Iddings, of the Unites States Geological Survey, who has made a special study of Obsidian Cliff, contributes to the survey report for 1885-86 a paper that has in it much that is of interest to the unscientific mind.

The Lower Geyser Basin is in some respects more pleasing than the Norris, although the desolation is perhaps even more apparent. People who have seen districts in which salt is made out of brine extracted from wells, state that the appearance in the Lower Geyser Basin is very similar to what is seen around manufacturing districts of that character. This basin is in the valley of the Firehole River, a strangely named stream, of a very beautiful character. In the basin itself the branches of the Firehole unite, and with the Gibbon River form one of the three sources of the Missouri, called the Madison, after the President of that name. The Fountain Geyser is the largest in the neighborhood, and is one of the best in the park. It is very regular in its eruptions, and seldom fails to perform on time for the benefit of the onlooker. It sends an immense volume of water into the air, and resembles a fountain very closely. Its basin is very interesting, and gives a good example of the singular deposits left by a geyser.

When the fountain is busy throwing out its volumes of water, the appearance is very peculiar. Little notice is given of an eruption, which takes place suddenly, although at stated intervals. All at once the watcher is rewarded for his patience by having the stillness changed into activity of the most boisterous character. The water is hurled upwards in a mass of frothing, boiling and foaming crystals. The actual height varies, but frequently goes as far as thirty feet. In a moment the wall of water becomes compact, oblong and irregular. Crystal effects are produced, varying according to the time of day and the amount of light, but always delightful and peculiar.

Close at hand are the Mammoth Paint Pots, in the center of the Firehole Geyser. We can explain the appearance of the Paint Pot or Mud Bath much more easily than we can account for the phenomenon. It is well named, because it resembles a succession of paint pots of enormous size more than anything else that the imagination can liken it to. The basin measures forty by sixty feet, with a mud boundary three or four feet high on three sides of it. The contents of the basin have kept scientists wondering for years. The substance is white, looking very much like ordinary paint, but, unlike paint, it is constantly in motion, and the agitation is so persistent that an idea is given that the Paint Pot's basin is the bed of a crater. The continual bubbling and vibration is very interesting in its effects, and the noise it makes is quite peculiar, not unlike a subdued hiss or a badly executed stage-whisper. Mixed among the white substance is a quantity of silicious clay of all sorts and conditions of color. This produces a variation in the appearance, but is merely in addition to what is otherwise marvelous in the extreme. Pearl gray, with terra cotta, red and green tints is the basic color of this boiling, seething mass, which seems to be continually at unrest and in a course of worry.

The Excelsior Geyser is the most conspicuous feature of the Midway Basin, a collection of hot springs and pools. They are situated in the Midway Basin, and were originally called Cliff Caldron. Excelsior Geyser is in a continual state of anarchy, without law, government or regulation. It does just as it likes and when it likes. It seldom performs when wanted to, but when it does break out into a condition of fermentation, the effect is very magnificent. As one writer puts it, the beauties and exhibitions of this geyser are as far superior to those of all the others as the light of the sun seems to that of the moon.

The geyser was for years regarded as the grandest spring in the park, before its exeptionally great features prevailed or became apparent. In the years 1881-82, the eruptions from this geyser became so terrific that it spouted water as high as 250 feet, and converted the generally inoffensive Firehole River into a torrent of storming water. Rocks of large size and heavy enough to be very dangerous were hurled headlong from within the mysterious confines of the earth, and were dashed around in all directions. For miles the terrific noise could be heard, and people who had been waiting for a phenomenon of this character, hurried across country to witness it. It is only now and again that a phenomenon of this kind is repeated, and the most skillful geologists are unable to give us any adequate forecasts as to when the next performance will take place.

Rehearsals seem always in progress. Vast masses of steam rise from the crater or hole. Many people crowd to the edge of the basin and strive to penetrate into the mysteries of subterranean happenings. The day may come when some scientific method of seeing through smoke and steam and enduring scalding heat without difficulty may be devised. Until then the mystery must remain unsolved.

In exact contrast with the irregular and spasmodic action of the Excelsior, is the methodical, persevering action of Old Faithful. This is another of the great and popular geysers of Yellowstone Park. It is so uniform in its appearance that a man can keep his watch regulated by it. Every sixty-five minutes the well-named geyser gives forth a peculiar noise to warn the world that it is about to perform. Then for about five minutes a vast stream of water and steam is hurled into the air to the height of about 150 feet. The mass of boiling water measures six feet in diameter, and the volume discharged exceeds a hundred thousand gallons each hour. Day by day and hour, for nearly twenty years, this industrious geyser has regularly done its duty, and afforded entertainment for visitors. No one knows how long prior to that time it commenced operations, or for how long it will continue.

Leaving for the moment the consideration of geysers and hot springs and other wonders of this character, the sightseer gets a view of a very different nature. At Keppler's Cascades the stage coach generally stops to enable passengers to walk to the edge of the cliff and watch the cascades and foaming river in the black cañon below. Then the journey proceeds through the Firehole Valley, and through leafy forests and open glades, until the narrow and tortuous cañon of Spring Creek is reached. The scenery here is decidedly unconventional and wild.

We soon reach the summit of the Continental Divide. Now the outlook is much expanded, and it becomes more majestic and dignified. The mountains overhang the roadway on one side and drop far below on the other. Heavy, shaggy forests cover the slopes and peaks, while tiny island parks, as it were, and cheerful openings are occasionally seen. The road winds about the mountain-flanks, now climbing up, now descending; the whole aspect of nature grows more grand, more austere; the air grows more rarified, and one becomes more and more exalted in spirit. Occasionally the mountains break away and you obtain a view far out beyond the narrow limits round about. Distant mountains are seen, and the feeling that there are nothing but mountain-walls about you impresses itself strongly upon one, and it is just about true. After several miles of such riding, and when you have begun to imagine that nothing finer can come, the road leads up to a point that, almost before you know it, simply drives from your thoughts all else seen on this ride.

It is a wonderful picture, and produces a state of exultation that to some must seem almost too strong to endure. The mountains, which rise high above, stretch also far below, and in every direction are at their very best. Proud and regal in their strength and bearing, they are still, from summit to the depths, heavily covered with the primeval forest. It would seem as if they really knew what a view was here unfolded, and to rejoice in the grandeur of the scene. Like a thread, you can trace the turns and lines of the road along which the stage has come. But that which adds the softer, more beautiful element to a picture otherwise almost overpowering in its grandeur, and withal stern and unyielding, is seen through a break or portal off to the south.

Far away, far below, lies a portion of Shoshone Lake. Like a sleeping babe in its mother's lap, nestles this tiny lakelet babe in the mountains. It shines like a plate of silver or beautiful mirror. It is a gem worth crossing a continent to see, especially as there runs between the lake and the point of view a little valley dressed in bright, grassy green as a kind of foreground in the rear. There is thus a silvered lake, a lovely valley, with bright and warm green shades, and rich, dark-black forests in the rear. No one can gaze upon such a combination and contrast without being impressed, and without recognizing the sublime beauty and grandeur of the park and its surroundings.

Yellowstone Lake is another of the extraordinary attractions of our great National Park. It is described as the highest inland sea in the world, and more than 7,000 feet above the sea level. It is, really, nearly 8,000 feet above the sea, and its icy cold water covers an area some thirty miles in length and about half as wide or about 300 square miles. This glorious inland ocean is perched up at the summit of the Rocky Mountains, just where no one would expect to find it. Several islands of varying sizes are dotted over the surface of the water, which at times is as smooth as a little mill pond, and at others almost as turbulent as the sea. The shores are entirely irregular in their formation, and Promontory Point extends out into the water a great distance, forming one of the most peculiar inland peninsulas in the entire world. Along the southern shore, inlets and bays are very numerous, some of them natural in character, and others full of evidence of brisk, and even terrific, volcanic action.

From the peculiar rocks and eminences along the shore, reflections are cast into the water of an almost indescribable character. They are varied in nature and color, and, like the lake itself, differ from anything to be seen elsewhere. Another unique feature of this lake, and one that has to be seen to be understood, is the presence on the banks, and even out in the lake itself, of hot springs and geysers full of boiling water and steam. Some of these springs have wide and secure edges, or banks, on which a man can stand and fish. Then, on his right hand, he has the icy-cold water of the lake, from which he can obtain trout and other fish, until he begins to dream of a fisherman's paradise. Dr. Hayden, the explorer, already referred to, was the first man to take advantage of the opportunity and to cook his fish unhooked in the boiling water to his left, merely making a half turn in order to do so. When the Professor first mentioned this fact, he was good humoredly laughed at, but, as stated in an earlier part of this chapter, the possibility has been so clearly demonstrated, that people have long since admitted as a possibility what they had first denounced as an utter absurdity.

A Marvel of Magnificence.

CHAPTER XVI.

THE HEROES OF THE IRON HORSE.

Honor to Whom Honor is Due—A Class of Men Not Always Thoroughly Appreciated at their Worth—An Amateur's Ride on a Flying Locomotive—From Twelve Miles an Hour to Six Times that Speed—The Signal Tower and the Men who Work in it—Stealing a Train—A Race with Steam—Stories about Bewitched Locomotives and Providential Escapes.

NO one who has not given the matter special consideration has the remotest idea of the magnitude and importance of the railroad system of the United States. Nor has any one who has not studied the statistics bearing on the question the faintest conception of the cost of the roads built and in operation. The cost in dollars and cents for a mile of track has been ascertained to a fractional point. Expert accountants have figured out to a hundredth part of a cent the cost of hauling a passenger or a ton of merchandise any given distance. There are even tables in existence showing the actual expense incurred in stopping a train, while such details as the necessary outlay in wages, fuel, repairs, etc., have received the attention which the magnitude of the interests involved deserves.

But the cost in human life and suffering of the great railroad system of the United States is quite another matter, and one that does not come within the scope of the calculations of accountants, expert or otherwise. It has been said repeatedly that a man is safer in a railroad train than on the streets. In other words, the percentage of death and serious injury is said by statisticians to be lower among men habitually traveling than among people who are classed as stay-at-homes, and who seldom take a railroad journey. But while this is doubtless correct, so far as passengers are concerned, the rule does not apply to railroad employes, and those who by their never-wavering care and energy protect the life and limbs of passengers, and make railroad traveling safe as well as comfortable.

A celebrated divine, when preaching on the subject of faith, once took a railroad journey for an illustration. As he pointed out, with much eloquence and force, there could be no more realistic personification of faith than the man who peacefully lay down to sleep at night in his berth of a Pullman car, relying implicitly upon the railroad men to avert the thousands of dangers which had to be encountered during the still hours of the night.

Whenever there is a strike, a great deal is written about the men employed in various capacities by railroads, and every misdeed is exaggerated, and every indiscretion magnified into a crime. But very little is said on the other side of the question. The men to whom railroad travelers, and especially those who ride at night, commend their safety, are worked to the full extent of their powers, and are paid very small wages, when the nature of their duties and the hours they have to make are taken into consideration.

The commendation of these men takes the form of deeds, rather than words, and while so few have ever stopped to consider the loyalty and devotion of the poorly paid and hard-worked railroad man, every traveler who enters a railroad car pays silent tribute to their reliability. The passenger, as he lounges comfortably in a luxurious seat, or sleeps peacefully in his state-room, thinks nothing of the anxiety and annoyances of the men in charge of the train, or of those who are responsible for the track being kept clear, and proper orders being given to the engineer.

This official is a man of many hardships and dangers. To him is entrusted daily the lives of hundreds of human beings. He knows not how many, but he knows that the slightest error on his part will hurl perhaps ten, perhaps twenty, and perhaps fifty human beings into eternity, besides maiming for life two or three times as many more. He knows, too, that not only is he responsible for the safety of the men, women and children who are riding behind him, but also for the occupants of other trains on the same track. He knows exactly where he must run on to a side track to allow the express in the other direction to pass, and he knows just where he must slacken speed in order to get safely around a dangerous curve, or cross a bridge which is undergoing repairs, or which is not quite as substantial as it would be if he, instead of millionaire railroad directors, had the control of the bridge construction and repair fund.

To catch an idea of the responsibility of a locomotive engineer, it is necessary to ride a hundred miles or so in an engine. The author was given this privilege on a bleak, frosty day, early last winter. He was told by the officials that he took the ride at his own risk, and as a matter of personal favor, and that he must not interfere with the engineer or fireman in the execution of their duties. The guest was received kindly by both engineer and fireman, and was given a seat whence he could see a long expanse of track over which the locomotive had to draw the train of cars. To a novice the sensation of a first ride on a locomotive is a very singular one, and to say that there is no tinge of fear intermingled with the excitement and pleasure, would be to make a statement not borne out by fact. On the occasion referred to, the train was a special one, carrying a delegation half way across the continent. It was about fifteen minutes late, and in order to make the run to the next division point it was necessary to maintain an average speed of more than forty-five miles an hour. As is almost always the case, when there is need for exceptional hurry, all sorts of trifling delays occurred, and several precious minutes were wasted before a start could be made.

Finally, the conductor gives the necessary word, the engineer pulls the lever, and the irregular passenger finds for the first time in his life how much more difficult it is to start a locomotive than he ever imagined.

First, there is a distinct tremble on the huge locomotive. Then there comes a loud hiss, with a heavy escape of steam, as the huge pistons tug and pull at the heavy wheels, which slip round and round and fail to grip the rail. Then, as gradually scientific power overcomes brute force, there is a forward motion of a scarcely perceptible character. Then, as the sand-box is brought into requisition, the wheels distinctly bite the rail, and, in the words of the race-track, "They're off." For a few seconds progress is very slow, indeed. Then the good work of the trusted locomotive becomes apparent, and before we are well out of the yards quite a good speed is being obtained. The fireman is busy ringing the bell, and the engineer, from time to time, adds to the warning noise by one of those indescribable toots made only by a steam engine.

Now we are outside the city limits, and the train is making excellent time. We take out our watch and carefully time the speed between two mile-posts, to ascertain that about seventy seconds were occupied in covering the distance. Regardless of our instructions we mention this fact to the fireman, who has just commenced to throw a fresh supply of coal on to the roaring fire, adding a word of congratulation.

"Why, that's nothing," he replies, laughing, "we are going up grade now. Wait until we get along the level or go down grade, and we will show you a mile away inside of sixty."

We are not particularly glad to hear this. Already the locomotive is rocking a good deal more than is quite pleasant to the uninitiated, and the contrast between the hard seat and the pleasant one at our disposal in the Pullman car is becoming more and more obvious. Just as we are wondering how it will be possible to preserve one's equilibrium while going around a curve in the distance, a cow strays sheepishly on to the track, apparently some 200 yards ahead. The engineer plays a tune with his whistle, and the cow proceeds to trot down the track in front of us. That singularly misnamed appendage, the cow-catcher, strikes her amidships. She is thrown twenty feet in the air, and all that is left of her rolls into the ditch by the side of the track.

For the moment we had forgotten George Stephenson's reply to the member of the British Parliament, who asked him what would happen in the event of a cow getting in front of one of the trains George was proposing to run, if necessary powers could be obtained. His reply, which has long since become historical, was that it would be very bad for the cow. We remembered this, and agreed with the pioneer railroad man when we saw the unfortunate bovine turn a quadruple somersault and terminate her existence in less than a second. But a moment previously we had been wondering what would happen when the inevitable collision took place.

The fireman observes that the occurrence has somewhat unnerved us, and in a good-natured way assures us that a little thing of that kind doesn't amount to anything. It is pretty bad, he says, when a bunch of cows get on a track, and he remembers once, several years ago, having a train stopped out in the Far West by a bunch of fat steers, which blocked up the track. "But," he adds, by way of parenthesis, "that was on a very poor road with a broken-down freight locomotive. If we had had "87," with a full head of steam on, we could have got through all right, even if we had to overload the market with beef."

Now the train rushes around a curve in one direction and now in another. The engineer never relaxes his vigilance, and, although he affects to make light of the responsibility, and assures his somewhat nervous passenger that there is no danger of any kind, his actions do not bear out his words. We are running special, a little ahead of the mid-day express schedule, and at every station there are waiting passengers who herald our approach with delight, and, gathering together their packages, advance to the edge of the platform evidently supposing we are going to stop for them. That we are to dash through the station at a speed of fifty or sixty miles an hour, does not occur to them as a remote possibility, and the looks of astonishment which greet us as we rush past the platform are amusing. Finally, we reach a long stretch of level track, where the rails are laid as straight as an arrow for apparently several miles ahead.

"Now's your time, if you want to take a good mile," says the friendly fireman.

We take his advice, and by aid of a stop watch, especially borrowed for the occasion, we ascertain the fact that a mile is covered in fifty-two seconds. The next mile is two seconds slower, but the speed is more than maintained on the third mile. Reduced to ordinary speed figures, this means that we are making something like seventy miles an hour, and doing vastly better than was even anticipated. Our good work is, however, interfered with by the sudden application of the air brakes and the shutting off of steam as we approach a little station, where the signal is against us. A change in train orders proves to be the cause of the hindrance to our progress, and the engineer grumbles somewhat as he finds he will have to wait at a station some twenty miles further on, provided a train coming in the opposite direction is not on the side track before he gets there. The execution of this order involves a delay of five or ten minutes, but when we have the line clear again such good time is made that we accomplish our task and pull into the depot, where locomotives are to be changed, on time to the second.

Such is a ride on a locomotive in broad daylight. At night of course the dangers and risks are increased ten-fold. The head-light pierces into the inky darkness, and frequently exaggerates the size of objects on and near the track. The slightest misunderstanding, the most trivial misinterpretation of an order, the least negligence on the part of any one connected with or employed by the road, may involve a wreck, to the total destruction of the train and its passengers, and the engineer feels every moment the full extent of his responsibilities and the nature of the risks he runs.

These responsibilities are increased ten-fold by the great speed necessary in these days of haste and hurry. Few of our great-grandfathers lived to see steam applied as a motive power for locomotion. Most of our grandparents remember the first train being run in this country. Many of those who read these lines can recollect when a philosopher placed himself on record that a speed of twenty miles was impossible, because, even if machinery could be constructed to stand the wear and tear, the motion would be so rapid that the train men and passengers would succumb to apoplexy or some other terrible and fatal malady.

It is less than seventy years ago since the time that the so-called crank, George Stephenson, ventured modestly to assert that his little four-and-a-half-ton locomotive, "The Rocket," was actually capable of whirling along one to two light carriages at the astounding velocity of twelve miles an hour. He was laughed to scorn by the highly intelligent British Parliamentary Committee engaged in the investigation of his new method of land-traveling. At the present day, with regularly scheduled trains on many lines thundering across wide continents tirelessly hour after hour, at the rate of a mile a minute, it is the deliberate judgment of the most conservative students of railway science that the ultimate limit of speed is still in the far distance, and that 100 miles per hour will not be deemed an extraordinary rate of travel by the time the first decade of the Twentieth Century shall have closed.

It is true that railroad schedules seldom call for mile-a-minute traveling, but the engineer is called upon very frequently to go even faster. The majority of people, even the most intelligent among those who habitually travel, obtain their conceptions of speed from the figures of the time-table, forgetting that in nearly every instance considerable portions of the route must be traversed at much more than the average speed required to cover the total distance in the schedule time. There are very few, if any, of the fast express trains which do not, on some part of each "run," reach or exceed a speed of a mile a minute. Yet, by reason of superior roadway and well constructed cars, the accelerated velocity is unnoticed; while running at from sixty to seventy miles an hour the passenger calmly peruses his paper or book, children play in the aisle, and a glass brim full of water may be carried from one end to the other of the smoothly rolling coach without the spilling of a drop. All the while the nerves of those in charge of the train are kept at high tension, and, oblivious as the passengers may be as to the danger, actual and imaginary, the risks incurred are never for a moment lost sight of by the two men on the locomotive.

The man in the signal tower has an equal responsibility. In some respects the burden upon his shoulders is even greater, because he has the fate of perhaps a score of trains in his hands, with the lives of hundreds of passengers. Now and then, when the wrong lever has been pulled and a train is wrecked, we hear of a signal man sleeping at his post, but few of us stop to think how many thousand times a day the right lever is pulled, and how exceptional is the lapse from duty. There are heroes of the sea, and there are heroes of the battle-field, but there are ten times as many heroes who perform their deeds of heroism on locomotives, in switch and signal towers, and in railroad yards. It may not be fashionable to compare these savers of human life with those who destroy life on the battle-field, but the valor and endurance of the former is at least as conspicuous and meritorious as the daring and suffering of the latter.

In "Scribner's Magazine" there recently appeared a most graphic description of a two-storied, square signal tower at "Sumach Junction."

"This tower," says the contributor to the magazine named, "had two rows of windows on all sides and stood at the intersection of branches. At this point the trunk line resolved itself from four tracks into two, and here the gravel track, which looked as if it had been laid by a palsied contractor, left the main line and respectability behind, and hobbled out of sight behind the signal station with an intoxicated air. Beneath the tower, to the right hand, a double-tracked branch tapped a fertile country beyond the sand hills. And beneath the signal tower, to the left, a single-tracked branch, only a mile long, brought South Sumach, one of those tiresome towns that manufacture on water-power, in touch with the middle man. This petty branch (as if the case had been with petty people), made more trouble than all the rest of the lines put together. The signal man found this out.

"So Sumach Junction had its place in the world, and, perhaps, it was a more important one than that of many a complacent and opulent suburb. The heart of this little community did not center, as a thoughtless person might suppose, in the church, or the commandery, or the grocery store, or the school, but in the signal tower. It was the pulse of the section. It was the life-blood of thousands of unconcerned travelers, whose lives and happiness depended on the intelligent vigilance of three men. These three took turns up there in the tower, locking and unlocking switches and signals until one might expect them to faint for dizziness and confusion. It was no uncommon thing in the signal tower, when one of the three wanted a day off, for the other two to double up on twelve-hour shifts. As long as the service was well performed, the Superintendent asked no questions."

The story came to be written on account of the prolonged sickness of one of the three, which compelled the remaining two to remain on duty until their eyes were often dim, and their brain power exhausted. One of these finally worked until nature overcame force of habit and reliability, and a collision would have resulted but for the returning consciousness of the overworked and thoroughly exhausted man.

While this hero of everyday life slept, or rather lost the power of thought from extreme exhaustion, the heavy snow storm which was making the night doubly dark had so blocked the machinery of the semaphore that it refused to respond to the desperate efforts of the weary signal man, who heard a freight train approaching, and knew that unless it was flagged at once it would dash into the rear end of a passenger train, which was standing in sight of the signal box, with its locomotive disabled. Finally, abandoning the attempt to move the lever, he rushed out into the night and forced his way through the snow in the direction of the approaching train. He was in time to avert the collision that appeared inevitable, but in his excitement overlooked his own danger, and was knocked down and terribly injured by the train he flagged.

Within the last year the largest railroad station in the world, in the yards of which there is an immense amount of traffic, and from whose signal towers are worked switches and signals innumerable, has been opened. This immense station is situated at St. Louis. It covers an area of about twelve acres, and is larger than the two magnificent depots of Philadelphia combined. The second largest railroad station in the world is at Frankfort, Germany. The third in order of size is the Reading Station at Philadelphia. The four next largest being the Pennsylvania Depot at Philadelphia, St. Pancras Station in London, England, the Pennsylvania Depot in Jersey City, and the Grand Central Depot in New York City.

We have all heard of peculiar thefts from time to time, and the records of stolen stoves and other heavy articles seem to show that few things are sufficiently bulky to be absolutely secure from the peculator or kleptomaniac. But to steal a train seems to the average mind an impossibility, though under some conditions it is even easy. During the crusade of the Commonwealers in 1894, more than one train was stolen. All that was required was a sufficient force to overcome the train crew at some small station or water tank, and one or two men who knew how to turn on steam and keep up a fire.

History tells of a much more remarkable case of train stealing, with events of startling bravery and hair-breadth escapes connected with it. We refer to the great railroad raid in Georgia during the year 1862, when a handful of intrepid heroes invaded a hostile country, deliberately stole a locomotive, and came within an ace of getting it safely delivered into the hands of their friends.

A monument, surmounted by the model of a locomotive, was erected four or five years ago to commemorate an event without precedent and without imitation. The story of the raid reads like fiction, but every incident we record is one of fact. Every danger narrated was run. Every difficulty was actually encountered, and the ultimate failure came about exactly as stated.

Generals Grant and Buell were at the time marching towards Corinth, Mississippi, where a junction was to be made. The Confederate troops were concentrating at the same point, and there was immediate trouble brewing. General Mitchell, who was in command of one of Buell's divisions, had advanced as far as Huntsville, Alabama, and another detachment had got within thirty miles of Chattanooga. It was deemed advisable, and even necessary, to cut off the railway communication between Chattanooga and the East and South, and James J. Andrews was selected by General Buell for the task.

Andrews picked out twenty-four spirits like unto himself, who entered the enemy's territory in ordinary Southern dress, and without any other arms than revolvers.

Their purpose was to capture a train, burn the bridges on the northern part of the Georgia State Railroad, and also on the East Tennessee Railroad, where it approaches the Georgia State line, thus completely isolating Chattanooga, which was then virtually ungarrisoned. These men rendezvoused at Marietta, Georgia, more than 200 miles from the point of departure, having (with the exception of five, who were captured en route or belated) made their way thither in small detachments of three and four. The railroad at Marietta was found to be crowded with trains, and many soldiers were among the passengers.

After much reconnoitering, it was determined to capture a train at Big Shanty, a few miles north of Marietta, and, purchasing tickets for different stations along the line in the direction of Chattanooga, the party, which included two engineers, reached Big Shanty.

While the conductor, the engineer, and most of the passengers were at breakfast, the train was seized, and being properly manned, after the uncoupling of the passenger cars, was started on its fierce race northward. Think of the exploit—twenty men, with a hostile army about them, setting out thus bravely on a long and difficult road crowded with enemies.

Of course the theft of the train produced great consternation, but the captors got away in safety, stopping frequently for the purpose of tearing up the track, cutting telegraph wires, etc. Andrews informed the people at the stations that he was an agent of General Beauregard, running an impressed powder train through to Corinth, and generally this silenced their doubts, though some acted suspiciously.

The first serious obstacle was met at Kingston, thirty miles on the journey. Here the captors and their train were obliged to wait until three trains south-bound passed by. For an hour and five minutes they remained in this most critical position, sixteen men being shut up in the box-car, personating Beauregard's ammunition. Just as the train got away from Kingston two pursuers appeared, being Captain W. A. Fuller, the conductor of the stolen train, and an officer who happened to be aboard of it at the time it was run out from Big Shanty. Finding a hand-car, they had manned it and pushed forward until they had found an old locomotive standing with steam up on a side track, which they immediately loaded with soldiers and hurried forward with flying wheels in pursuit, until Kingston was reached, where they took the engine and a car of one of the waiting trains, and with forty armed Confederates continued the journey.

It was now nip and tuck, with one engine rushing wildly after another. To wreck the pursuing train was the only tangible hope of the fugitives, who stopped again and again in order to loosen a rail. Had they been equipped with proper tools they could have done this easily, but as it was, they simply lost precious time. Once they were almost overtaken by the pursuing engine, and compelled to set out again at a terrible speed. At one point at Adairsville, they narrowly escaped running into an express train. Fuller, the conductor of the stolen train, and his companions, being arrested by the obstructions of the track, left their engine behind and started on foot, finally taking possession of the express passed at Adairsville, and turning it back in pursuit.

When Calhoun was passed, the trains were within sight of each other. The track was believed to be clear to Chattanooga, and if only the pursuing train could be wrecked, the end would be gained. Again the lack of tools hampered the daring little band. They made desperate effort to break a rail, but the pursuers were upon them before they had accomplished it, and Andrews hurried on his engine, dropping one car and then another, which were picked up and pushed ahead, by the pursuers, to Resaca Station.

Both engines were, at the time, at the highest rate of speed. Andrews at last broke off the end of his last box car and dropped crossties on the track as he ran. Several times he almost lifted a rail, but each time the coming of the Confederates within rifle range compelled him to desist.

A participant in the feat, in his narrative of the affair, published in "Battles and Leaders of the Civil War," by the Century Company, says:

"Thus we sped on, mile after mile, in this fearful chase, around curves and past stations in seemingly endless perspective. Whenever we lost sight of the enemy beyond a curve, we hoped that some of our obstructions had been effective in throwing him from the track, and that we would see him no more; but at each long reach backward the smoke was again seen, and the shrill whistle was like the scream of a bird of prey. The time could not have been so very long, for the terrible speed was rapidly devouring the distance, but with our nerves strained to the highest tension, each minute seemed an hour. On several occasions the escape of the enemy from wreck seemed little less than miraculous. At one point a rail was placed across the track so skillfully on the curve, that it was not seen till the train ran upon it at full speed. Fuller says that they were terribly jolted, and seemed to bounce altogether from the track, but lighted on the rail in safety. Some of the Confederates wished to leave a train which was driven at such a reckless rate, but their wishes were not gratified."

At last, when hope was well nigh exhausted, a final attempt was made. Additional obstructions were thrown on the track, the side and end boards of the last car were torn into shreds, all available fuel was piled upon it, and blazing brands were brought back from the engine. Reaching a long, covered bridge, the car, which was now fairly ablaze, was uncoupled; but before the bridge was fully on fire the pursuers came upon it, pushed right into the smoke, and ran the burning car before them to the next side track.

Climbing Pike's Peak by Rail.

So this expedient also failed. With no car left, no fuel—every scrap of it having been thrown into the engine or upon the burning car—and with no means of further obstructing the track, the pursued party were reduced to desperation, and as a last resource, when within eighteen miles of Chattanooga, abandoned the train and dispersed to the woods, each to save himself.

The good old locomotive, now feeble and useless, was left. According to some accounts it was reversed, in order to cause a collision with the on-coming train, but according to others, the steam was exhausted, and the engine just stopped for want of power. However this may have been, the hunters of the train become at once hunters of the train stealers, several of whom were captured the same day, and all but two within a week. Two of those who had failed to connect with the party were also captured. Being in citizen's dress within the enemy's lines, the whole party were held as spies. A court-martial was formed and the leader and seven out of the remaining twenty-two were condemned and executed. The others were never brought to trial. Of the remaining fourteen, eight succeeded by a bold effort in making an escape from Atlanta, and ultimately reaching the North. The other six failed in this effort, and remained prisoners until March, 1863, when they were exchanged.

All sorts of stories have been heard from time to time concerning the supernatural side of railroading, and the peculiar and apparently hidden antics which locomotives occasionally are guilty of. The following story is well worth reproducing, and may serve as an illustration of hundreds of others. It was told by an engineer, who worked on the Utah & Northern Railroad years ago, before that road became part of the Union Pacific system. The road was very rough, and save for a long stretch of sage brush along the Snake River north of Pocatello, it ran in cañons, over mountains, and through heavy cuts of clay, which was often washed down on to the tracks by the spring rains. It was, as it is now, a railroad rushed with business.

It was the only line into Butte City, which had been struck a short time before, and was then giving promise of its future distinction as the greatest mining camp in the world. The shipments of gold and bullion were very heavy, and all the money for the banks in Butte and Helena was sent over this road. There were no towns along the line. The only stops were made at water-tanks, and such eating-houses as the railroad company had built at long intervals. It was a rough, hard run, and was made especially lonely by the uninhabited stretches of sand and sage brush, and the echoes from the high granite walls of the narrow cañon. It was a dangerous run besides. The James gang of train robbers and the Younger brothers had been operating so successfully in Missouri, Kansas and Minnesota that other bandits had moved West to attempt similar operations.

Finally, word came from the general offices of Wells, Fargo & Co. that several train robbers had been seen in Denver, and might work their way north in the hope of either securing gold bullion from one of the down trains from Butte, or money in exchange on an up train. After detailing these conditions, the engineer went on.

"We got a new manager for the road, an Eastern man, who had some high notions about conducting railroad travel on what he called a modern basis. One of the first results of his management was a train, which he called the 'Mormon Flyer,' running from Butte to Salt Lake, and scheduled on the time card to run forty miles an hour. We told him he never could make that time on a rough mountain road, where a train had to twist around cañon walls like a cow in the woods, but he wouldn't believe it. He said that if a train could run forty-five miles an hour in the East it could run forty on that road. The train was made up with a heavy 'hog' engine, a baggage car, express car and two sleepers. The first train down jumped the track twice, and the up train from Salt Lake was wrecked and nearly thrown into the Snake River. Then the trains ran from four to six hours behind time, and the people and the papers began to jest about the 'Mormon Flyer,' and ask for a return of the old Salisbury coach line. The manager complained from time to time, and said it was all the fault of the engineers; said that we did not know our business, and that he would get some men from the East who would make the 'Mormon Flyer' fly on time.

"Well, one evening in Butte I had made up my train and was waiting for orders, when the station-master handed two telegrams to me. One was from the manager at Salt Lake, and read: 'You bring the "Flyer" in on time to-morrow, or take two weeks' notice.' The other was from the Wells, Fargo & Co. agent, at Salt Lake, and read: 'No. 3 (the north-bound "Flyer") held up this afternoon near Beaver Cañon. Treasure box taken and passengers robbed.' The best description of the robbers that could be had, was given. I showed both telegrams to the conductor, who held the train until he could get a dozen Winchesters from the town. In the meantime I had put the fireman on, and we put the finishing touches on the engine, No. 38—a big, new machine, with eight drivers, and in the pink of condition. I told my fireman that if we couldn't pull her through on time we would leave the train on the side of the road, and thus teach a trick or two to the man who wanted to run a mountain road on Eastern methods. I pulled that train out of Butte as though it had been shot out of a gun, and when we reached the flat below Silver Bar Cañon I had her well set and flying like a scared wolf. The train was shaking from side to side like a ship at sea, and we were skipping past the foothills so fast that they looked like fence posts. The cab shook so that my fireman couldn't stand to fill the fire-box, so he dumped the coal on the floor and got down on all fours and shoveled it in. No. 38 seemed to know that she was wanted to hold down my job, and quivered like a race horse at the finish. We made up the lost time in the first 100 miles, and got to Beaver Cañon with a few minutes to spare.

"It was when I slowed her up a bit in the cañon that I noticed something the matter with her. She dropped her steady gait and began to jerk and halt. The fire-box clogged and the steam began to drop, and when I reached a fairly long piece of road in the dark and silent cañon, she refused to recover. She spit out the steam and gurgled and coughed, and nothing that I could do would coax her along. I told the fireman that the old girl was quitting us, and that we might as well steer for new jobs. He did his best to get her into action, but she was bound to have her own way. She kept losing speed every second, and wheezed and puffed like a freight engine on a mountain grade, and moved about as fast. Finally, we came to a corner of a sharp turn, almost at the mouth of the cañon, and then No. 38 gave one loud, defiant snort and stopped.

"'She's done for now,' I said to the fireman, and we got out of the cab with our lanterns.

"The cylinder-heads were almost opposite a high rock at the turns. Well, when we got there, what do you think we saw? Not a hundred yards ahead of the mouth of the cañon, and as plain as day in the moonlight, was a pile of rocks on the track. On either side was a bunch of half a dozen masked men, with Winchester rifles half raised. Ten rods further on were a dozen or more horses picketed at a few cottonwood trees.

"Well, you bet your life we couldn't get back to that train too quick. It was not midnight, and in two minutes we had the crew and passengers out with enough guns and revolvers to furnish the Chinese army. Passengers, in those days, and in that country, carried guns. When the robbers saw that the train had stopped they started forward, to be met by a rattling fire. One of them dropped, but the rest ran for their horses and got away.

"Now, then, you can't tell me that there isn't something in an engine besides machinery," concluded the engineer, as he turned to the other members of the Roundhouse Club.

"The man who says there isn't, is a fool," was the answer from one, and the others nodded their heads in approval.

CHAPTER XVII.

A RAILROAD TO THE CLOUDS.

Early History of Manitou—Zebulon Pike's Important Discovery—A Young Medicine Man's Peril and Final Triumph—A Health Resort in Years Gone By—The Garden of the Gods—The Railroad up Pike's Peak—Early Failures and Final Success—The Most Remarkable Road in the World—Riding Above the Clouds.

MANITOU is a name which conjures up reminiscences of legend and history, and it also reminds the traveler of some of the most remarkable scenes of the Rocky Mountains. It has been said that the man who knows how to appreciate natural grandeur and beauty, can spend six months in the vicinity of Manitou, and then come back six month later to find undiscovered joys and treasures of beauty on every side.

The earliest reliable records concerning this spot date back to the year 1806, when Major Zebulon Pike discovered what he called the Great Snow Mountain. This, one of the loftiest of the Rockies, is now known as Pike's Peak after its discoverer, or at any rate after the man who first described it for the benefit of the public.

It is on record that when Major Pike was crossing Colorado, nearly a hundred years ago, he saw on the horizon what he regarded as a misty cloud. When he finally realized that there was a mountain in front of him, he was at least a hundred miles away from it, and there were two or three smaller hills to be crossed before reaching it. After marching for over a week the party reached the Cheyenne Mountain, which they believed was the ascent of the great peak, a theory which was soon disproved. Manitou is at the foot of this great mountain. It was first described at length by an English tourist who visited the Manitou Springs just half a century ago. He traveled alone, and exhibited not only an immense amount of bravery, but also unlimited judgment in evading the attacks of wild beasts and equally savage Indians.

His description of the trip is full of great interest. He describes how a band of mountain sheep advanced to the edge of an overhanging precipice to gaze upon the intruder, and how, a moment later, a herd of black tailed deer ran in front of him, with that contempt of danger seen only in animals which have not come in contact with human beings or modern weapons. The birds, he tells us, were indifferent as to his presence. They sang almost within arm's reach, and their rich plumage completely fascinated him. He continued in his hunter's paradise until he accidentally stumbled upon an Indian camp. No Indians were present, but the smouldering camp-fires warned him that they were not far distant. Later, he saw two Indians, who were evidently Arapahoes, carrying a deer between them, and he knew that the delightful hunting he had promised himself would not be forthcoming.

He was shortly afterwards captured in a prairie fire, in which he was in great danger of being destroyed; nothing but the daring of his horse saved his life. He had heard from the friendly Indians he had met on his march that the Great Spirit had endowed the waters of the Springs of Manitou with miraculous healing powers, and he drank freely from the pure springs. These springs made Manitou a veritable Mecca for Indians of the West and Southwest for many generations before the white men discovered them. Pilgrimages were made across mountains and rivers of great magnitude, and when an Indian chief showed signs of failing health, and was not benefited by the machinations of medicine men, he was generally carried to Manitou, no matter how far the journey might be, or how great were the obstacles to be overcome.

Among the many stories told concerning journeys of weeks' and even months' duration, one is exceptionally vivid, and is evidently founded on fact, although superstition has surrounded the facts with so much coloring that they are hard to discover. The story runs that in days long gone by, a great chief, who had conquered every tribe of whose existence he was aware, fell sick and could not be benefited by the medicine men, who were summoned from every direction. A number of these unfortunate physicians were put to death as a penalty for their failure to restore health to the dying chief. Finally, there were very few medicine men remaining in the vicinity; those who had not been decapitated having proved their strong desire for further life by discreetly retiring to parts unknown.

One day tidings were brought the chief of a young medicine man in a neighboring tribe who had been overlooked by the searchers, but who had been phenomenally successful in wooing back health and prolonging life. The tribe had long since been reduced to a condition of subjection, and the said chief sent a detachment of his braves, with instructions to bring back the medicine man alive or dead.

The young man, who had been expecting a summons of this kind, did not display the alarm anticipated. Even when he was told that the old chief was certainly dying, and that it was impossible to help him in any way, he maintained his stolid indifference and merely smiled.

He carried with him a primitive vessel, filled with some mysterious fluid, upon the virtues of which he had implicit reliance. When he reached the camp in which the sick chief lay, he was summoned immediately before the ailing autocrat. That individual stated his symptoms, and then, instead of asking, as we are apt to ask our physicians, whether there was any medicine available for them, he told the young medicine man that if no improvement was effected within a few days there would be a funeral in the village, and there would be one less medicine man in the vicinity.

This somewhat startling introduction did not disconcert the young man, who poured out a liberal dose of the fluid he had brought with him, and made the old chief drink it. During the night he repeated the doses several times, and on the following day he kept up the treatment. To every one's astonishment the blood began to flow again in the veins of the once invincible chief, and those who had been pitying the young medicine man began to congratulate him on his triumph. When, after a few days, the improvement became more marked, the young doctor explained to the chief that the water he had given him had been brought from springs in the distant mountains, and that if the chief desired to obtain another lease of life, he must visit those springs and remain there for some weeks.

With the enthusiasm of renewed vigor, the old man promptly agreed to the suggestion, and in a few days arrangements were complete for a grand march over the Rocky Mountains to Manitou. Tradition tells of the splendor of the march, and of the way in which obstructions and hindrances were overcome. Finally, the great mountain was seen in the distance, and a few days later a halt was made at the springs. Here the old chief was given a regular treatment, and in a few days he was able to walk as vigorously as ever. Finally, he returned to his tribe, not only renewed in health, but also renewed in youth. The records of his race state that his appearance was entirely changed, and that, instead of looking like an old man, his features were those of a youth in his twenties. The chief lived many years, and finally died in battle.

The fame of his cure naturally spread abroad with great rapidity. The old man was so well known that he became a walking testimonial of the merits of the springs, and expeditions without number were in consequence made to them. White people, as they came in contact with the Indians of the Far West, heard of the springs from time to time and of this wonderful cure. By many the stories were confounded with the legends concerning the search of Ponce de Leon for the fountain of perpetual youth. Later, however, more thorough investigation was made, and for more than a generation the truth, as well as the legends of Manitou, have been generally known.

As a result, a great watering place has sprung up on the site of what was once a mysterious resting place of the Indians, and a retreat which it was dangerous to enter. About 2,000 people live here, and during the season there are often 3,000 or 4,000 health-seekers in addition. There is a grand avenue through the village eighty feet wide and well kept. Instead of being laid out in a mathematically straight line, it follows the meanderings of the River Fontaine-qui-Bouille. This feature gives it a novel as well as a delightful appearance. There is also a little park, which possesses features not to be found in the recreation grounds of large cities, and there is a foot-path known as Lover's Lane, which is so romantic in its appearance that it is obviously well known.

The springs of Manitou are naturally the most interesting feature of the place. The Shoshone Spring, in the center of the village, is, perhaps, the best known. The Navajo Spring is but a few yards distant, and is considerably larger. The Manitou Spring itself is on the other side of the river, and is covered over with a very elegant spring-house. The Iron Ute Spring is in Engelman's Cañon or glen, and is regarded by many as the best of all. Caves and cañons innumerable abound in every direction. The Manitou Grand Cañon is within two miles of the village. It presents the appearance of a natural mansion, with rooms several hundred feet long and high. The natural formations of the peculiar rocks present bewildering combinations of galleries, columns and frescoes. Here is to be seen the wonderful stalactite organ. This, according to many, is one of the wonders of the world. It consists of a number of thin stalactites of varying powers of reverberation, and these play delightful tunes or at least tones.

One of the great objects of a trip to Manitou is to gain a sight of the world-renowned, but singularly named, Garden of the Gods. The most direct road to reach it from the village is by way of Manitou Avenue and Buena Vista Drive, the latter being a well-traveled road, which enters the avenue on the left, about a mile from the town, as one advances towards Colorado City. The entrance to the Garden is past Balanced Rock, an immense boulder which stands directly to the left of the road, poised on such a slender base that it suggests an irregular pyramid standing on its apex. To the right, as one passes this curious formation, is a steep wall of stratified stone, draped with clinging vines, and overgrown with evergreens. Pausing a moment on the brow of the elevation which is reached here, one can look down into the valley below in which the Garden lies. To the west are the mountains; to the east the plains. The road which winds through the valley is a pleasant way. One's eyes and mind are kept busy beholding and recording the interesting views which here abound.

No one knows why this valley was named "The Garden of the Gods." There is nothing especially garden-like in its appearance; but, doubtless through "apt alliteration's artful aid," the name has become greatly popular, and it would be foolish to quarrel with it, or make any attempt to change it. There are, however, ample suggestions that Titanic forces have been at work here, and it requires but little imagination to ascribe these innumerable quaint sculpturings, these magnificent architectural rock works, these grand and imposing temples, not made with hands, to the agencies of the gods. Here are to be found carved in the stone by those cunning instruments of the hands of Nature—the wind, the rain, the sunbeam and the frost—curious, often grotesque, figures irresistibly suggestive of forms of life. Here stands a statue of Liberty, leaning on her shield, with the conventional Phrygian cap on her head;' there is a gigantic frog carved in sandstone; yonder is a pilgrim, staff in hand. Groups of figures in curious attitudes are to be seen on every hand.

Stone figures of the lion, the seal and the elephant are all found; indeed, a lively imagination is not needed to discover in this Garden of the Gods an endless variety of imitative forms of human beings, of birds and beasts and reptiles. These figures possess a curious interest and attract wondering attention; but the notable and majestic objects here are the "Great Gateway" and the "Cathedral Spires." Two lofty tables of carnelian colored sandstone, set directly opposite each other, about fifty feet apart, and rising to a height of 330 feet, form the portals of the far-famed Gateway. They rise from perfectly level ground, and present a strangely impressive spectacle.

The "Cathedral Spires" are of a similar character to the Gateway, but their crests are sharply splintered into spire-like pinnacles. The forms assumed by the rocks here are remarkable indeed, but their color is still more remarkable. No sandstones of the East glow with such a splendor of carnelian hue. The striking contrast formed by these crimson crags outlined against the deep blue sky, and gilded by the high, white light of the unclouded sun of Colorado, cannot be described.

One of the most visited prairie-dog towns is close to the Garden of the Gods. It is interesting to the tourist, and is generally visited on the return from the Garden to Manitou. The town is situated on the road which passes through the great Gateway to Colorado City, and may be seen on a little plateau to the left. There are a great number of little hills of sand and gravel thrown up by the dogs around their burrows. Every fine day they can be seen at work around their dwellings, or sitting on their haunches sunning themselves, and chattering gaily with some neighbor. The burrow has an easy incline for about two feet, then descends perpendicularly for five or six, and after that branches off obliquely; it is often as large as a foot in diameter. It has been claimed that the prairie-dog, the owl and the rattlesnake live harmoniously together.

Concerning this, Mr. William G. Smith, the well-known naturalist, says: "Impossible. The burrowing owl will generally be seen where dogs congregate, and wherever the ground is undermined his snakeship is apt to be found; but rest assured there is some lively 'scattering' to get out of his way if he draws his slimy carcass into their burrows. The dogs have no desire to contest his right to it, and give him all the room he wants." The dogs at home are neat little fellows, and allow no litter to accumulate around their doors. They go to bed early, and never go around disturbing their neighbors before daylight.

Adjoining the Garden is a region of ridges. One ridge leads up to another, and that to a third, and so on. This broken country, covered with pine and cedar, and clothed with bunch grass and grama, makes a capital tramping-ground, especially in winter, when rabbits, mountain grouse and sage-hens are numerous enough to make it worth while to shoulder a gun.

The way to reach the ridges is to take the road to the Garden of the Gods, and follow it till the Quarry Road is reached. Pursuing the latter up a gorge, and then turning to the left on a branch road, which zigzags up the sides of the gorge, one soon finds oneself on the top of a ridge. The rule in ridge-climbing is never to cross a gully, but always to keep on top. All the ridges in this vicinity converge to the main ridge, which overlooks Queen's Cañon. This ridge bends to the northwest, and in two or three miles joins a still higher one, which, strange to say, will be found to overlook the Ute Pass, a thousand feet above the Fontaine qui-Bouille, which flows in the bottom of the cañon below—Eyrie, the site of a private residence—a most interesting glen, but not open to the public. The character of the monoliths in this cañon is more remarkable even than those of the Garden of the Gods.

The Major Domo is a column of red sandstone, rising to a height of 300 feet, with a curious swell near the summit, which far exceeds in diameter the base of the shaft. It looks as though it might fall at any moment in obedience to the laws of gravity, and it is not exceeded in this regard by the Leaning Tower of Pisa. There is another glen of a similar character, about two miles to the northwest, which is known as Blair Athol. It is a beautiful spot, but, lacking water, has never been used as a dwelling place. It abounds in wildly picturesque scenery, and possesses rock formations of strange shapes and brilliant colors. There are groves of magnificent pines; and the view of the distant plains stretching to the eastern horizon is unobstructed, and of great interest.

We have already spoken of the discovery of Pike's Peak. At the summit of this mountain, 14,147 feet above the sea level, there is a little signal service station, which can be reached by railway. When the mountain was first discovered several efforts were made to reach the summit, but without success. Major Pike himself recorded his opinion that it would be impossible for any human being to ascend to the summit. In these days of engineering progress there is, however, no such word as "impossible." Several enthusiasts talked as far back as twenty years ago of the possibility of a railroad to the very summit of the once inaccessible peak, and fifteen years ago a survey was made, with a view to building a railroad up the mountain, by a series of curves and nooks.

It was believed possible by the engineers that a railroad of standard gauge and equipment could be operated without special appliances, and so strongly was this view held that work was commenced on the project. Eight miles of grading was completed, but the project was then abandoned in consequence of adverse reports received from experts, sent out for the purpose. Their statement was that no grade would be able to stand the force of the washouts, though, strange to say, all the grading that was accomplished stands to-day, as firm as ever. Three or four years later another project, destined to be more successful, came into existence. In 1889, grading commenced, and finally the work was completed, and the summit of Pike's Peak can now be reached by railroad.

The road itself is one of the most remarkable ones in the United States, and, indeed, in the world. The road-bed is fifteen feet wide, and there is not a single foot of trestle work in the entire construction. There are three short bridges of iron, and the precautions in the way of cross sections of masonry are very elaborate. The average ascent per mile is 1,320 feet, and the total ascent is nearly 8,000 feet. In the center of the track, between the heavy steel rails, are two cog rails, of great strength. These are provided to insure absolute safety for travelers, one being for general use and the other as a kind of reserve.

Special locomotives are used on the line. These were constructed by the Baldwin Company, of Philadelphia, and include the latest patents in engine building. When standing on a level track they appear to be at a slant of about 8 per cent. When on a mountain road, like that of

HIEROGLYPHIC BOULDERS FOUND IN CLIFF-DWELLERS' HOUSES.

PICTURE BOULDER MARKED BY INFERIOR RACE.

HIEROGLYPHIC BOULDERS FROM GRAVES.

FOUND IN ANCIENT RUINS.

Hieroglyphic Memoirs of Past Ages.

Pike's Peak, they are approximately level. There are three wheels on each side of the engine, but these are not driving wheels, being merely used to help sustain the weight. The driving wheels operate on the cog rails in the center of the track. The cars also slope, or slant, like the engine. No couplings are used, so that one great element of danger, is avoided. The engine and the cars have each independent cog brakes of almost unlimited power. When traveling three or four miles an hour, the little train, with the locomotive pushing instead of pulling it, can be stopped instantly. When the speed reaches eight or nine miles an hour, stoppage can be effected in less than one revolution of a wheel.

Not only is the ride up Pike's Peak a wonderful sensation and a constant reminder of the triumphs of engineering, but it is also a source of continual delight to the lover of the beautiful and awful in nature. About half way up the mountain is a most delightful little hillside retreat, aptly named "The Half-Way House." It is a very comfortable establishment within rustic walls. The pines and firs which surround it add a great charm to the outlook, and the cool mountain breeze is charged with very pleasing odors. Tourists frequently spend a night here and consider the sensation one of the most unique of a long trip.

A tourist describing a ride up Pike's Peak by this singular railroad, says:

"We are now far above timber line. On all sides can be seen strange flowers, of lovely forms and varied hues. Plants which attain considerable proportions on the plains are here reduced to their lowest forms. It is not an unusual thing to find a sunflower stalk in the prairies rising from a height of eight to ten feet; here they grow like dandelions in the grass, yet retaining all their characteristics of form and color. Beyond this mountain meadow are great fields of disintegrated granite, broken cubes of pink rock, so vast in extent that they might well be the ruins of all the ancient cities in the world. Far below flash the waters of Lake Morain, and beyond, to the southward, lie the Seven Lakes. Another turn of the track to the northward, and the shining rails stretch almost straight up what appears to be an inaccessible wall of almost peerless granite. But no physical obstruction is formidable enough to stop the progress of this marvelous railway; and passing the yawning abyss of the 'Crater,' the line proceeds direct to the summit. The grade here is one of 25 per cent., and timid passengers will not escape a thrill of fear as they gaze over the brink of this precipice, although the danger is absolutely nothing. At last the summit is reached, and, disembarking, the tourists can seek refreshments in the hotel, which will cater to their wants, and then spend the time before the train returns in enjoying the view, and in rambling over the seventy acres of broken granite which form the summit.

"The view from the Peak, once beheld, can never be forgotten. The first sensation is that of complete isolation. The silence is profound. The clouds are below us, and noiselessly break in foaming billows against the faces of the beetling cliffs. Occasionally the silence is broken by the deep roll of thunder from the depths beneath, as though the voice of the Creator were uttering a stern edict of destruction. The storm rises, the mists envelop us, there is a rush of wind, a rattle of hail, and we seek refuge in the hotel.

"Pause a moment before entering, and hold up your hands. You can feel the sharp tingle of the electric current as it escapes from your finger-tips. The storm is soon over, and you can see the sunbeams gilding the upper surfaces of the white clouds that sway and swing below you half way down the mountain sides, and completely hide from view the world beneath. The scenery shifts, like a drawn curtain the clouds part; and as from the heights of another sphere we look forth upon the majesty of the mountains and the plains, an ocean of inextricably entangled peaks sweeps into view. Forests dark and vast seem like vague shadows on distant mountain sides. A city is dwarfed into the compass of a single block; water courses are mere threads of silver, laid in graceful curves upon the green velvet mantle of the endless plains. The red granite rocks beneath our feet are starred with tiny flowers, so minute that they are almost microscopic, yet tinted with the most delicate and tender colors.

"The majesty of greatness and the mystery of minuteness are here brought face to face. What wonders of creation exist between these two extremes! The thoughtful mind is awed by the contemplation of this scene, and when the reflection comes that these vast spaces are but grains of sand upon an infinite shore of creation, and that there are worlds of beauty as far and varied between the tiny flowers and the ultimate researches of the microscope as those which exist, on an ascending scale, between the flowers and the great globe itself, the mind is overwhelmed with wonder and admiration. It is in vain that one strives to describe the scene. Only those who have beheld it can realize its grandeur and magnificence."

Lovers of horseback riding regard the vicinity of Pike's

Peak and Manitou almost in the light of a paradise. A ride of a few miles in any direction leads to some specially attractive or historic spot. Crystal Park is one of the popular resorts of this kind. It is enclosed by high mountains on all sides, with an entrance which partakes of the nature of a natural gateway. In summer time this park is a profusion of bloom, with wild flowers and vines seldom seen in any other part of the world in such splendor. There are several elevated spots from which the surrounding country can be seen for miles. Above the park is Cameron's Cone. This is a mountain of much interest, although it can only be reached and climbed by hardy, athletic individuals. All around there are a profusion of cañons. The Red Rock Cañon was at one time a popular resort. It took its name from the profusion of red sandstone on all sides. This natural wealth finally destroyed the beauty of the cañon, which is now a mass of stone quarries. Bear Creek Cañon has less of the practical and more of the picturesque about it. A very charming brook runs down the center, and there are two or three small but very delightful falls.

The Ridge Road is a species of boulevard recently constructed for the use of visitors to Manitou. At places the grade is so abrupt that timid ladies do not care to drive down it. Otherwise it is a very pleasing thoroughfare, with fresh surprises and delights awaiting the tourist every time he passes along it. The view in every direction is most charming and extensive. Pike's Peak can be seen to great advantange, and in the forty miles of the road many different features of this mountain can be observed. The road also leads to William's Cañon.

Cheyenne Mountain, although dwarfed somewhat by

Pike's Peak, is deserving of notice. It is very massive in its form, and its sides are almost covered by cañons, brooklets and waterfalls. Two vast gorges, know as the North and South Cañons, are especially asked for by visitors. The walls of these gorges are of rich granite, and stand perpendicular on each side a thousand feet high. The effect is very wonderful in a variety of ways. In the South Cañon are the celebrated Seven Falls, which were immortalized by Mrs. Helen Hunt Jackson, the well-known poetess, whose remains were interred on Cheyenne Mountain by her own request. The Seven Lakes must also be seen by all visitors to the Manitou region, and there are so many more special features to be examined and treasures to be discovered that, no matter how long one stays in the neighborhood, a pang of regret is felt when the visit is brought to a termination.

There are other spots in America where more awful scenes can be encountered. There are few, however, where the combinations are so delightful or the general views so attractive and varying.

CHAPTER XVIII.

INTO THE BOWELS OF THE EARTH.

The Grand Cañon of the Colorado—Niagara Outdone—The Course of the Colorado River—A Survey Party Through the Cañon—Experiences of a Terrible Night—Wonderful Contrasts of Color in the Massive Rocks—A Natural Wall a Thousand Feet High—Hieroglyphics which have Never been Deciphered—Relics of a Superior Race—Conjecture as to the Origin of the Ancient Bearded White Men.

WE have already spoken of Niagara as one of the wonders of the world, and one of the most sought-after beauty spots of America. We will now devote a few pages to a description of a far more remarkable natural wonder and to a phenomenon which, were it situated nearer the center of population, would have long since outclassed even Niagara as a tourist's Mecca.

Reference is made to the Grand Cañon of the Colorado.

Few people have the slightest conception of the magnitude or awfulness of this cañon. It is clearly one of the wonders of the world, and its vastness is such that to explore it from end to end is a work of the greatest possible difficulty.

Even in area, the cañon is extraordinary. It is large enough to contain more than one Old World country. It is long enough to stretch across some of the largest States in the Union. Some of the smaller New England States would be absolutely swallowed up in the yawning abyss could they, by any means, be removed to it bodily. An express train running at a high rate of speed, without a single stop and on a first-class road-bed, could hardly get from one end of the cañon to the other in less than five hours, and an ordinary train with the usual percentage of stoppage would about make the distance between morning and evening.

Reduced to the record of cold figures, the Grand Cañon is made up of a series of chasms measuring about 220 miles in length, as much as 12 miles in width, and frequently as much as 7,000 feet in depth.

This marvelous feature of American scenery is very fully described in "Our Own Country," published by the National Publishing Company. In describing the cañon, that profusely illustrated work says that the figures quoted "do not readily strike a responsive chord in the human mind, for the simple reason that they involve something utterly different from anything that more than 99 per cent. of the inhabitants of the world have ever seen. The man who gazes upon Niagara for the first time, is astounded at the depth of the gorge as well as at the force of the water; and he who has seen Niagara can appreciate somewhat the marvels of the Grand Cañon, when he bears in mind that the great wonder of the Western World is for miles at a stretch more than fifty times as deep as the falls and the gorge, generally admitted to be the most awful scenic grandeur within reach of the ordinary traveler. Nor is this all. Visitors to Paris who have enjoyed a bird's-eye view of the gay city from the summit of Eifel Tower, have felt terribly impressed with its immense altitude, and have been astounded at the effect on the appearance of living and inanimate objects so far below them. How many of the Americans who have been thus impressed by French enterprise, have realized that in their own country there is a natural gorge, at points of which the distance between the summit and the base is more than five times as great as the height of the Eifel Tower?"

The Colorado River rises in the Rocky Mountains, crosses the Territories of Utah and Arizona, and then running between the last named and the State of California, finally empties its waters into the gulf bearing the name of the Golden State. For more than two hundred miles of its course it runs through the gorge known as the Grand Cañon, and hence it has been a very difficult river to explore. During the Sixteenth Century, some of the Spanish explorers, to whom this country is indebted so much for early records and descriptions, crossed the then undeveloped deserts of the Southwest and discovered the Grand Cañon. Many of the reports they made of the wonders of the New World read so much like fairy tales, and seemed so obviously exaggerated, that little credence was given to them. Hence it was that their estimates concerning the gorge through which the Rio Colorado Grande flows were treated as fables, and laughed at rather than believed.

Major Powell, than whom few men have done more to enlighten the world concerning the wonders of the Far West, describes the cañon very aptly, and speaks in a most attractive manner of the countless cañons and caverns, whirlpools and eddies, brooklets and rivers, fords and waterfalls, that abound on every side. In his first extended description of the cañon, he stated that "every river entering it has cut another cañon; every lateral creek has also cut another cañon; every brook runs in a cañon; every rill born of a shower and living only in the showers, has cut for itself a cañon; so that the whole upper portion of the basin of the Colorado is traversed by a labyrinth of these deep gorges. About the basin are mountains; within the basin are cañon gorges; the stretches of land from brink to brink are of naked rock or of drifting sands, with here and there lines of volcanic cones, and of black scoria and ashes scattered about."

Of late years thousands of people have been attracted to this great cañon, although but very few have succeeded in exploring its entire length. Few, indeed, have been able to pass along the balcony of the cañon, and to gaze up at the countless wonders of nature, piled one above the other, apparently up to the very region of the clouds. The common notion of a cañon, as Captain C. E. Dutton tells us, is that of a deep, narrow gash in the earth, with nearly vertical walls, like a great and neatly cut trench. There are hundreds of chasms in the plateau country which answer very well to this notion. It is, however, unfortunate that the stupendous passway for the Colorado River through the Kaibabs was ever called a cañon, for the name identified it with the baser conception. At places the distance across the chasm to the nearest point on the summit of the opposite wall is about seven miles. A more correct statement of the general width would be from eleven to twelve miles. It is hence somewhat unfortunate that there is a prevalent idea, in some way, that an essential part of the grandeur of the Grand Cañon is the narrowness of its defile.

As Major Powell expresses it, there are rather a series of cañons, than one huge one. Wherever the river has cut its way through the sandstones, marbles and granites of the Kaibab Mountains, beautiful and awe-inspiring pictures are seen, while above there are domes and peaks, some of red sandstone and some of snowy whiteness. Cataract Cañon alone is forty-one miles long, and has seventy-five cataracts and rapids, of which fifty-seven are within a space of nineteen miles. A journey along the bank of a river with a waterfall every twenty feet, on the average, is no joke, and only the hardiest men have been able to accomplish it. In the spring of 1889, the survey party of a projected railroad from Grand Junction to the Gulf of California, made this journey, and from its published description more actual information can be gleaned concerning the cañon itself than almost any mere verbal description.

The surveyors had to carry with them, on their backs, for a great portion of the way, the limited supplies of food they took with them, because it was frequently impossible to get the boats along at all. When the boats were used, several were upset, and everything was uncertainty as to the bill of fare that would be presented at the next meal, even if there was to be a meal at all. Mr. Frank M. Brown, president of the railroad company, lost his life in one of the whirlpools. He was in a boat, a little ahead of the others, and seemed to be cheerful and hopeful. He shouted to his comrades in the rear to come on with their boats, and that he was all right. A moment later, his friends were astonished to see the boat gone, and their leader swimming around and around in a whirlpool, trying hard to reach smooth water.

He was a good swimmer, and a brave man, but his efforts were futile, and finally he sank. The party waited and watched for hours, but were finally compelled to recognize the fact that their friend and leader was gone forever.

It was determined almost immediately to beat a retreat. While the party was hunting for a side cañon leading northward, through which they could make their exit, it became evident that a storm was brewing. Rain commenced to fall in a steady shower, and to increase in quantity. The surveyors had no dry clothing beyond what they stood up in, and there was no shelter of any kind at hand. They were near Vassey's Paradise, in the deepest part of the cañon they had yet reached. A storm in such a location had its awfulness intensified beyond measure, and the frightened men looked in every direction for shelter. Finally, about forty feet up the side of the marble cliff, the opening to a small cavern was seen. Into this Mr. R. B. Stanton, one of the party, climbed. There was not room enough for his body at full length, but he crawled in as best he could, curled himself up, and tried to sleep.

A terrible night followed. At about midnight he was awakened by a terrific peal of thunder, which re-echoed and reverberated through the cañon in a most magnificently awful manner. He had been caught in storms in mountain regions and deep valleys before, but he had never felt so terribly alone or so superstitiously alarmed as on this occasion. Every now and then a vivid flash of lightning would light up the dark recesses of the gorge, casting ghastly shadows upon the cliffs, hill sides, ravines and river. Then again there would be the darkness which, as Milton puts it, could be felt, and the feeling of solitude was almost intolerable.

The river in the meantime had swollen into a torrent, by the drenching rain, which had converted every creek into a river, and every feeder of the Colorado into a magnificent, if raging, river itself. The noise caused by the excited river, as it leaped over the massive rocks along its bed, vied with the thunder, and the echoes seemed to extend hundreds of miles in every direction. What affected the stranded traveler the most was the noise overhead, the reverberation inducing a feeling of alarm that huge masses of rock were being displaced from their lofty eminence thousands of feet above his head, and were rushing down upon him.

The night was passed, finally, and when the storm had spent itself, the survivors of the party succeeded in getting out of the cañon and reaching a plateau, 2,500 feet above. They then took a brief rest, but with that disregard for danger which is characteristic of the true American, they at once organized another expedition, and a few months later resumed the task so tragically interrupted and marred with such a sad fatality.

The trip through Glen Cañon was like a pleasure trip on a smooth river in autumn, with beautiful wild flowers and ferns at every camp. At Lee's Ferry they ate their Christmas dinner, with the table decorated with wild flowers, picked that day.

On December 28th they started to traverse, once more, that portion of Marble Cañon made tragic by the fatality of the summer before. "On the next Tuesday," writes Mr. Stanton, "we reached the spot where President Brown lost his life. What a change in the waters! What was then a roaring torrent, now, with the water some nine feet lower, seemed from the shore like the gentle ripple upon the quiet lake. We found, however, in going through it with our boats, there was the same swift current, the same huge eddy, and between them the same whirlpool, with its ever-changing circles. Marble Cañon seemed destined to give us trouble. On January 1st, our photographer, Mr. Nims, fell from a bench of the cliff, some twenty-two feet, on to the sand beach below, receiving a severe jar, and breaking one of his legs just above the ankle. Having plenty of bandages and medicine, we made Nims as comfortable as possible till the next day, when we loaded one of the boats to make him a level bed, and constructing a stretcher of two oars and a piece of canvas, put him on board and floated down river a couple of miles—running two small rapids—to a side cañon, which led out to the Lee's Ferry road."

The next day, after discovering a way out of the deep ravine, one of the party tramped thirty-five miles back to Lee's Ferry, where a wagon was obtained for the injured surveyor. Eight of the strongest men of the party then undertook the task of carrying the injured man a distance of four miles, and up a hill 1,700 feet high. It is indicative of the extraordinary formation of the Grand Cañon that the last half mile was an angle of 45 degrees, up a loose rock slide. The stretcher had to be attached to ropes and gently lifted over perpendicular cliffs, from ten to twenty feet high. The dangerous and tedious journey was at last accomplished, and the trip continued.

Finally the unexplored portion of the cañon was reached. For thirty miles down Marble Cañon, to the Little Colorado River, the most beautiful scenery was encountered. At Point Retreat, the solid marble walls stand perpendicularly 300 feet high from the river edge. Behind these walls the sandstone lies in benches, and slopes to an aggregate height of 2,500 feet. Above the narrow ravine of marble, the color is mostly rich gray, although the presence of minerals has in places imparted so many tints that quite a rainbow appearance is presented. Caves and caverns relieve the monotony of the solid walls. Here and there a most delightful grotto is seen, while the action of the water rushing down the cliff sides has left little natural bridges in many places. Countless fountains of pure, sparkling water adorn the smooth rocks, and here and there are little oases of ferns and flowers, which seem strangely out of place so far down into the very bowels of the earth.

Below Point Hausbrough, named in honor of Peter M. Hausbrough, who was drowned during the first exploring trip, the cañon widens rapidly. The marble benches are replaced by strata of limestone, and between the river and the rocks green fields and groves of trees become common. The view from the river, looking across this verdure, with sandstone rocks for the immediate background, and snow-capped mountains in the distance, is extraordinary in its magnificence and combinations. Between the grand junction of the Little Colorado with the main cañon and the Granite Gorge, there is about eight hundred miles of a very different section. Evidences of volcanic action abound. Rocks and boulders seem to have been blown out of position and mixed up all in a heap. The rocks are largely charged with mineral, and, as a result, almost every known color is represented, in the most remarkable purity. The river runs through a wide valley, with the top walls several miles apart.

The Granite Gorge itself is entirely different. Here the great walls of granite start from the water's edge. The first few feet are usually vertical. Then, for a thousand feet or more, the rise is at an angle of about 45 degrees, while occasionally masses of rock stand out prominently and overhang the river. Above the granite comes a mass of dark colored sandstone, with a vertical front. In many places it is perfectly black, the color being intensified by the brightness of the red below. If an artist were to paint a cliff deep red, with a jet black border along the top, Old World critics would be apt to declare him insane. Yet this is really the coloring of this section of the most wonderful cañon in the entire world.

Although the cañon at this point varies in width at the top from six to twelve miles, the river really runs through a narrow gorge, and partakes very much of the nature of a long rapid or cataract. For ten miles the fall averages twenty-one feet per mile, sufficient to make the current very dangerous even at low water, and something terrible after heavy rains or much snow melting. In one place the fall is eighty feet in about five hundred yards, and here, of course, navigation is practically out of the question. The explorers, to whom we have referred, were compelled to proceed with great deliberation at this point. Occasionally they ran the rapids, but very often they were compelled to lower their boats by means of lines, and even to lift them over exceptionally dangerous rocks.

At the worst point of all, one of the boats, while being lowered by lines, was struck by an eddy and run tightly in between two rocks. It became necessary for men to go into the water to liberate the boat. With lines tied securely to their bodies, some of the boldest of the explorers ventured into the water and tried to loosen the boat, or at least to secure the invaluable provisions and blankets on board. It was January, and the water was so intensely cold that no man could endure it more than a few minutes at a time, so that the process was a long and tedious one. Finally the boat was got out, but it took five days to repair it, and even then it was a very poor means of navigation. A few days later, a still more powerful and dangerous rapid was encountered. Some idea of the force of the water can be gleaned from the precautions that were necessary. A line 250 feet long was strung out ahead, and the boat was swung into the stream. It went through apparently the most dangerous places without much difficulty. The line was loosened slowly and the boat held under control, but when it reached the main eddy it began to get contrary, and finally swung round, and seemed to have struck a back current. Several hours' work got the boat to shore, but the next one was dashed into a thousand pieces while crossing over some of the sharp-pointed rocks.

The forty miles of the Granite Gorge are replete with wonders. The strangely misnamed section, the Bright Angel Creek, is absolutely dark, even at midday. It has been described as a sentinel of the great cañon, and few people have dared attempt to pass through it. Farther down, the granite walls become less steep, and black granite relieves the monotony of color. Here and there, at side cañons and sudden bends, the vast rear view of the gorge, with its sandstone cliffs, is brought into view. These are benched back several miles from the river, with huge mountains here and there intervening. Above the dark sandstone there are flattened slopes of yellow, brown, red, green and white rock, rich in mineral. Through these the force of water for ages has cut narrow, trench-like waterfalls, most remarkable in appearance and attractive in their variety of coloring.

It is difficult to imagine an upright wall a thousand feet high with red the predominating color, and with brighter hues near the summit. Benches of marble, with tufts of grass and bush, appear here and there, while occasionally

A Fin de Siecle Pleasure Steamer.

there is a little tract of faultless green. Above all this, there is something like two thousand feet of a lighter colored sandstone. This is beautified by spiral turrets and domes, and wherever the slope is gradual enough, pine and cedar trees abound in large numbers. Behind all this there is the background of snow on the summit of the mountains, and when an unexpected view can be obtained from the river below, there is so great a profusion of coloring that the eye rebels, and a feeling not unlike headache is produced.

Further wonders are revealed every few thousand feet. At the mouth of the next creek the coloring is different. The strata dips visibly, and the marble, which has hitherto been exposed to view, is now beneath the surface. The sandstone forms the river boundary, and rises at a sharp angle from the water's edge. The river itself is narrow in consequence, but the great valley is even wider at the top. The walls vary in height from 2,000 to 8,000 feet, and in rainy seasons the water rushes down the side in great profusion. Thousands of little rivulets join the main stream, and add greatly to the volume of water. Sometimes the river will rise four or five feet in a single night, upsetting all calculation, and making navigation risky in the extreme. When, by chance, the sun is able to penetrate into the depths of this cañon, the kaleidoscopic effects are exquisite, and cause the most indifferent to pause and wonder.

The discovery of an extinct volcano explains a great deal of the wonders of the great cañon. The volcano is examined by thousands of tourists, this being one of the spots to reach which scientists are willing to incur countless hardships and risks. No one can tell when the volcano was active, but from the nature of the crater it is perfectly clear that at one time it belched forth volumes of lava, which had a marked effect on the formation of the rock and the lay of the land of the surrounding country. Past the volcano, for many miles, the bright colors already referred to are supplanted by more sombre hues. Occasionally there is a little scarlet, and, as a rule, the sandstone is covered with the mysterious substance brought out of the bowels of the earth by the now silent, but once magnificently awful, mountains.

The exploring party to which we have referred, went through 600 miles of cañons, and found that no two miles were really alike. Finally, after three months of hardship, they emerged into an open country, and became almost frantic with joy. Never did country seem so beautiful, or verdure so attractive, and the panorama of beauty which was presented to their view caused them to shout with delight, and to offer up cries of thankfulness for their ultimate deliverance from a series of hardships and dangers which at one time seemed almost insurmountable.

The region also abounds with archæological curiosities and remarkable hieroglyphics. Many of these are found in close proximity to the Grand Cañon of the Colorado, and on the cliffs in which the far-famed cliff dwellers of old took up their abode. Hieroglyphics, marked upon rocks or other lasting substances, have been used by nearly all ancient races to perpetuate the history of certain events among them. Especially true is this of the ancient people who lived in Arizona. The remarkable picture rocks and boulders, with strange symbols upon them, left by the prehistoric races of Arizona, have been the cause of much discussion among those who have seen them, as to who these ancient hieroglyphic makers were. These rock records may be divided into three different kinds, which it is thought were made by two different races. The first, or very ancient race, left records on rocks, in some instances of symbols only, and in other instances of pictures and symbols combined. The later race, which came after the first race had vanished, made only crude representations of animals, birds or reptiles, not using symbols or combinations of lines.

The age of the most ancient pictographs and hieroglyphics can only be conjectured, but all give certain indications that they are many centuries old, and the difference between the work of the ancient and the later race leads the observer to believe that the older hieroglyphics were made by a people far superior to those who came after them, and who left no record in symbols, as we have said, with the exception of crude representations of animals and reptiles.

In many instances it is quite evident that the same rock or cliff has been used by the two different races to put their markings upon, the later, or inferior, race often making their pictographs over or across the hieroglyphic writings of the first race. Of the superiority of the first people who left their writings on the rocks and boulders found in the ancient mounds, ruins and graves, there can be no doubt, for their writings show order and a well-defined design in symbols, which were evidently intended to convey their history to others; and it is quite probable that those who made the great mounds, houses and canals were the authors of these writings. It may be truthfully asserted that the cliff dwellers of the rock houses in the deep cañons of the mountains were of the same race as the mound builders of the valleys, for exactly the same class of hieroglyphics found on boulders from the ancient ruins of the valleys, are found on the rocks near the houses of the cliff dwellers.

If this superior race were so distinctive from all other ancient races of Arizona—in their work being so far advanced as to solve what would be called, even at the present day, difficult engineering problems; to dig great canals many miles in length, the remains of which can be seen at the present time, and to bring them to such perfection for irrigating purposes; to build such great houses and to live in cities—may it not have been, as many who have studied this subject now contend, that this superior race were white people instead of a copper colored race, as has generally been supposed?

The hieroglyphics of the more ancient race are often found on sheltered rocks on the slopes of the mountains leading up from the valleys. Generally protected from the elements by overhanging cliffs, the dry climate has kept the writings from wearing away, and being in most instances picked into rocks which have a black, glistening surface, but of a lighter color underneath, the contrast is very noticeable, and when in prominent places these hieroglyphics can be seen several hundred feet away.

As no metal tools have ever been found in the mounds, ruins or cliff dwellings, the hieroglyphics were probably picked into the rock with a sharp-pointed stone much harder than the rock upon which the work was done. It is a singular fact that, although iron, copper, gold and silver abound in the mountains in Arizona, no tools, utensils or ornaments of these metals are found in the mounds or ruins. Yet furnace-like structures of ancient origin have been found, which appear to have been used for reducing ores, and in and around which can be found great quantities of an unknown kind of slag.

In many instances the hieroglyphic boulders have been found in great heaps, of several hundred in number, as if many different persons had contributed a piece of this strange writing to the collection. These etched boulders have been found buried in the ground with ollas containing the charred bones of human beings, and could the writings on the boulders be deciphered, we would undoubtedly learn of the virtues of the prehistoric deceased, just as we do of a person who dies in the present day, when we read the epitaph on a tombstone of the one who is buried beneath.

In opening some of the mounds, the investigator finds they are made of the fallen walls of great adobe buildings, and as he digs deeper he finds rooms of various dimensions, and which, in many instances, have cemented walls and floors. In one instance there were found the impressions of a baby's feet and hands, made, presumably, as the child had crawled over the newly laid soft cement. In another mound the cemented walls of a room were found covered with hieroglyphics and rude drawings, which were thought to represent stellar constellations.

To a certain extent, some of the pictured rocks tell us of part of the daily life of this ancient race, for in a number of instances the pictures picked into the rocks, although rudely formed, are self-explanatory, and the ancient artist tells plainly by his work what is meant. On the edge of a little valley in the Superstition Mountains, there was found a great rock on which had been etched many small animals, apparently representing sheep, and at one side was the figure of a man, as if watching them. It may be the ancient herder himself, sitting in the shadow of the great rock, while his sheep were grazing in the valley below, has passed away the time in making this rock picture. The hardy wild sheep still found in the mountains of Arizona may be the remnants of great bands formerly domesticated by these people.

The skeleton of the prehistoric man dug from beneath the stalagmites in the cave of Mentone, France, and which set all the scientific men of the world talking and thinking, gives proof of no greater age than many of the skeletons, relics or bones of some of these ancient mound and canal builders.

An incident illustrating the great antiquity of prehistoric man in Arizona, is the following: In digging a well on the desert north of Phœnix, at the depth of 115 feet from the surface a stone mortar, such as the ancients used, was found standing upright, and in it was found a stone pestle, showing the mortar had not been carried there by any underground current of water, and that it had not been disturbed from the position in which its ancient owner had left it with the pestle in it. There is only one way to account for this mortar and pestle. They had originally been left on what was at that time the surface of the ground, and the slow wash from the mountains had gradually, during unknown ages, raised the surface for miles on every side to the extent of 115 feet.

The question is often asked, Will this hieroglyphic writing ever be deciphered? The authors of the most ancient hieroglyphic writings or markings seem to have had well-defined forms or marks, which were in common use for this class of writing. Is it not most reasonable that a race so far advanced in other ways would have perfected a method of transmitting by marks of some kind their records to those who might come after them? Again, where so much system is shown in the use of symbols, it may be presumed that the same mark, wherever used in the same position, carries with it a fixed meaning, alike at all times. Having such a settled system of marks, there must be a key to the thoughts concealed in writing, and quite likely the key for deciphering these hieroglyphics will sometime be found on one of the yet undiscovered hieroglyphic rocks in the high mountains or in the mounds not yet examined. On the other hand, there can be no key to the inferior class of pictographs made by the people who came after the mound, canal and city builders had disappeared, for the crudely marked forms of reptiles, animals or similar things had a meaning, if any, varying with each individual maker.

Who were these people who formed a great nation here in the obscurity of the remote past? Were they the ancient Phœnicians, who were not only a maritime but a colonizing nation, and who, in their well-manned ships, might have found their way to the southern coast of America ages since, and from thence journeyed north? Or were they some of the followers of Votan or Zamna, who had wandered north and founded a colony of the Aztecs? Whoever these people were, and whichever way they came from, the evidences of the great works they left behind them give ample proof that they were superior and different from other races around them, and these particular people may have been the "bearded white men," whom the Indians had traditions of when Coronado's followers first came through the Gila and Salt River valleys in 1526.

CHAPTER XIX.

OUR GREAT WATERWAYS

Importance of Rivers to Commerce a Generation Ago—The Ideal River Man—The Great Mississippi River and Its Importance to Our Native Land—The Treacherous Missouri—A First Mate Who Found a Cook's Disguise Very Convenient—How a Second Mate Got Over the Inconvenience of Temporary Financial Embarrassment.

DURING the last quarter of the century in which we write the figures "1" and "8" in every date line, the steam railroad has, to a very large extent, put out of joint the nose of the steamboat, just as, at the present time, we are threatened with so complete a revolution in travel and motive power as to warrant a prediction that, long before another quarter of a century has passed, electricity will take the place of steam almost entirely. But even if this is so, old acquaintance should not be forgot, and every citizen of the United States should feel that the prosperity of the country is due, in very large measure, to the country's magnificent waterways, and to the enterprise of the men who equipped river fleets and operated them, with varying degrees of profit.

The true river man is not so conspicuous as he was in the days when St. Louis, Cincinnati, Memphis and other important railroad centers of to-day were exclusively river towns. The river man was a king in those days. The captain walked the streets with as much dignity as he walked his own deck, and he was pointed to by landsmen as a person of dignity and repute. The mate was a great man in the estimation of all who knew him, and of a good many who did not know him. Ruling his crew with a rod of iron, and accustomed to be obeyed with considerable and commendable promptness, he adopted a tone of voice in general conversation considerably louder than the average, and every one acquired a habit of making way for him.

The levee in a river town, before the railroads came snorting and puffing across country and interfering with the monopoly so long enjoyed by the steamboat, was a scene of continuous turmoil and activity. Sometimes, now, one sees on a levee a great deal of hurrying and noise. But the busiest scenes of to-day sink into insignificance compared with those which are rapidly becoming little more than an indistinct memory. The immense cargoes of freight of every description would be ranged along the river front, and little flags could be seen in every direction.

These flags were not, perhaps, exactly evidence of the activity of the schoolmaster, or of the prevalence of superior education. They were, rather, reminders of the fact that a great majority of the rank and file of river workers could read little, and write less. To tell a colored roustabout twenty or thirty years ago to fetch a certain cargo, labeled with the name of a particular boat or consignee, would have been to draw from the individual addressed a genuine old-time plantation grin, with some caustic observation about lack of school facilities in the days when the roustabout ought to have been studying the "three Rs," but was not. It was, however, comparatively easy to locate a cargo by means of a flag, and identification seldom failed, as the flags could be varied in color, shape and size, so as to provide distinction as well as difference.

Those who remember the busy levee scene, with the flag adornment referred to, will agree that there was something picturesque as well as noisy about the old river days, and will be inclined to regret, and almost deplore, the fact that things are not, from a river man's standpoint, what they were.

In no country in the world has railroad building been carried on with so much enterprise as in our native land. Prior to the enormous expenditure on track building and railroad equipment, advantage had to be taken of the extraordinary opportunities for navigation and transportation afforded by the great waterways of the country. As railroads were naturally built in the East before the West, the value of our Middle and Western waterways is naturally best understood by the average reader, because they continued to play an indispensable part in the transaction of business of every character until quite a recent period.

The Eastern rivers are less magnificent in extent and volume than those of the West, though many of them are picturesque and attractive in the extreme. The Hudson has often been spoken of as the "Thames of America," not because there is any resemblance between the length of the two rivers upon which are situated the two greatest cities of modern times. The simile is the result rather of the immense number of costly family residences and summer resorts built along the banks of both rivers.

In another chapter we say something of a trip down the picturesque Hudson, whose banks are lined with historic landmarks and points of pressing interest. We give an illustration of a pleasure boat on the Hudson, which reminds one of many delightful river trips taken at various periods, and also of the events of national importance which centered around the river that is crowded, year after year, with pleasure-seekers from the overcrowded metropolis at its mouth.

The Mississippi River is the largest and grandest in North America. A few miles above St. Louis it is joined by the Missouri River, and if the distance from the source of the latter to the Gulf of Mexico be calculated, the longest river in the world is found. At a considerable distance from the source of the Father of Waters are the Falls of St. Anthony, discovered more than two hundred years ago by enterprising pioneers, who thought they had discovered the headwaters of the great river. The scenery of the river at the falls and beyond them is very attractive, and in many cases so beautiful as to be beyond verbal description. In many other parts of the river the scenery is grand, though occasionally there are long stretches of flat country which are inclined to become monotonous and barren of poetic thought.

Of the entire river, Mr. L. U. Reavis writes enthusiastically:

"The more we consider the subject," says this author, "the more we are compelled to admit that the Mississippi is a wonderful river, and that no man can compute its importance to the American people. What the Nile is to Egypt, what the great Euphrates was to ancient Assyria, what the Danube is to Europe, what the Ganges is to India, what the Amazon is to Brazil—all this, and even more than this, the Mississippi River is to the North American Continent. In an earlier age men would have worshiped the Mississippi, but in this age we can do better, we can improve it. To this all our efforts should be directed, and we should continually bear in mind that no other improvement, ancient or modern, relating to the interests of commerce has ever commanded the attention of men equal in importance to that of the Mississippi River, so as to control its waters and afford ample and free navigation from St. Paul to the Gulf of Mexico."

During the last few years, the agitation in favor of river improvement has assumed very definite shape, and from time to time large appropriations have been made by Congress for the purpose of keeping the river navigable at all periods of the year. As long ago as 1873, the Chairman of the Senate Committee on Transportation Routes censured the Government for neglecting to thoroughly improve the big rivers. A quarter of a century has nearly elapsed since then, and, in the opinion of many competent river men, there is still room for much improvement, not only in the river, but in the method of arrangements for designing and carrying out the improvements.

The Missouri River, the great tributary to the Mississippi, has often been described as one of the most treacherous and aggressive rivers in the universe. It seems to be actuated by a spirit of unrest and a desire for change, so much so that the center of the river bed frequently moves to the right or left so rapidly as to wipe out of existence prosperous farms and homes. Sometimes this erratic procedure threatens the very existence of cities and bridges, and tens of thousands of dollars have been spent from time to time in day and night work to check the aggression of the stream and to compel it to confine itself to its proper limits.

The Mississippi proper brings down from the lakes to its junction with the Missouri River clear water, in which the reflection is so vivid, that the verdure on the banks gives it quite a green appearance. The Missouri, on the other hand, is muddy and turbulent, bringing with it even at low water a large quantity of sand and sediment. At high water it brings with it trees and anything else that happens to come within its reach, but at all periods of the year its water is more or less muddy. At the junction of the two rivers the difference in color of the water is very apparent, and, strange to say, there is not a complete intermingling until several miles have been covered by the current. Under ordinary conditions, the western portion of the current is very much darker in shade than the eastern, even twenty miles from what is generally spoken of as the mouth of the Missouri.

The Muddy Missouri rises in the Rocky Mountains. It is really formed by the junction of three rivers—the Jefferson, the Gallatin and the Madison. By a strange incongruity, the headwaters of the Missouri are within a mile of those of the Columbia, although the two rivers run in opposite directions, the Columbia entering the Pacific Ocean and the Missouri finding an inlet to the Gulf of Mexico via the Mississippi. At a distance of 441 miles from the extreme point of the navigation of the head branches of the Missouri, are what are denominated as the "Gates of the Rocky Mountains," which present an exceedingly grand and picturesque appearance. For a distance of about six miles the rocks rise perpendicularly from the margin of the river to the height of 1,200 feet. The river itself is compressed to the breadth of 150 yards, and for the first three miles there is but one spot, and that only of a few yards, on which a man can stand between the water and the perpendicular ascent of the mountain.

At a distance of 110 miles below this point, and 551

miles from the source, are the "Great Falls," nearly 2,600 miles from the egress of the Missouri into the Mississippi River. At this place the river descends by a succession of rapids, and falls a distance of 351 feet in sixteen and one-half miles. The lower and greater fall has a perpendicular pitch of 98 feet, the second of 19, the third of 47 and the fourth of 26 feet. Between and below these falls there are continuous rapids of from 3 to 18 feet descent. The falls, next to those of Niagara, are the grandest on the continent.

Below the "Great Falls" there is no substantial obstruction to navigation, except that during the midsummer and fall months, after the July rise, there is frequently insufficient water for steamboating. This results from the fact that, although the Missouri River drains a large area of country and receives many tributaries, some of which are navigable for many hundreds of miles, it passes for a great portion of its course through a dry and open country, where the process of evaporation is very rapid. The channel is rendered intricate by the great number of islands and sandbars, and in many cases it is made exceptionally hazardous by reason of countless snags.

Volumes have been written concerning the adventures of pioneers and gold hunters, who went up the Missouri in advance of railroads and even civilization, in order to trade with the Indians or to search for yellow metal in the great hills in the unexplored country, where so much in the way of easily acquired wealth is looked for. Some of the wealthiest men in the West to-day have a vivid recollection of the dangers they encountered on the voyage up this river, and of the enemies they had to either meet or avoid. Sometimes hostile Indians would attack a boat amid-stream from both sides of the river, and when an attempt was made to bring gold or costly merchandise down the river, daring attacks were often made by white robbers, whose ferocity and murderous designs were quite as conspicuous as those of the aboriginal tribes. Many a murder was committed, and the seeds were sown for countless mysteries and unexplained disappearances.

The Ohio River is another of the great tributaries of the Mississippi. In years gone by the importance of this waterway was enormous. The Mississippi itself runs through Minnesota, Wisconsin, Illinois, Iowa, Missouri, Arkansas, Kentucky, Tennessee, Mississippi and Louisiana. The Ohio taps and drains a much older country than many of these States, and hence its importance in the days when Cincinnati was the great gateway of the West and a manufacturing city of first importance.

The Ohio is a great river for more than a thousand miles, and connects Pittsburg with Cairo, running through such important towns as Louisville and Cincinnati. On this river some of the most interesting events in river history have been enacted in the past. Many a tragedy and many a comedy are included in its annals, and even to-day, although paralleled, crossed and recrossed by railroads, it is a most important highway of commerce.

The Tennessee River is a tributary of the Ohio, which it enters so near the Mississippi as to have a very close connection with that great river. Entering the Ohio at Paducah, Kentucky, the Tennessee is one of the largest and most important rivers east of the Mississippi. It is formed by the union of two rivers which rise in the Allegheny Mountains and unite at Kingston, Tennessee. The river then runs southwest through Alabama, and turning northward, passes through portions of Tennessee and Kentucky. In length the Tennessee exceeds 1,200 miles, and, with the exception of very dangerous places here and there, it is strictly a navigable river.

Running as it does, through a country not yet thoroughly supplied with railroad accommodation, the Tennessee forms an important connection between a number of small shipping points, which would otherwise be cut off from commercial intercourse with large centers. Hence the transportation facilities are good, and in many respects remind one of old days when river traffic was general. Boats run almost all the year around up this river as far as Alabama points, and not only is a large and lucrative freight business transacted, but pleasure and health-seekers are also carried in large numbers.

Everything was not prosaic in river life in the old days. All of us have heard of the great races on the Mississippi River between magnificent steamers, and of the excitement on deck as first one and then the other gained a slight advantage. Stories, more or less reliable, have been told again and again of the immense sums of money made and lost by speculators who backed their own boats against all comers. Tricks and jokes also prevailed and continue up to the present time. The passenger on a Tennessee River boat is almost sure to be told how a very popular first mate escaped arrest by disguising himself as a cook. The story is amusing enough to bear repetition, and bereft of corroborative detail, evidently designed to lend artistic verisimilitude to the narrative, it is as follows:

The boat was detained at a landing at a small Kentucky town where the laws against gambling were supposed to be very strict. Some of the officers of the boat were

Whaleback Steamers on the Lakes.

determined to kill time by staking a few dollars at poker, faro or something worse, and inquiries were made in consequence as to where a game could be found. These resulted satisfactorily from the gamblers' standpoint, and the crowd took themselves to the appointed spot, taking with them the very stout, good-natured, but not very speculative first mate. The game was played in a small room at the rear of an almost equally small restaurant. Everything went well for awhile, and those who were winning thought they had everything the heart could possibly desire. All at once one of the colored help came rushing in with a notification that the place was being raided.

It was a case of every man for himself. As is usual in cases of this kind, one or two got under the table, where of course they were promptly found and arrested. Two others jumped out of the window, into the arms of two deputies, who were standing there to receive them. The mate, caught for the first time in his life in a gambling resort, thought of a very good plan of escape. Snatching up his hat and coat he walked into the kitchen, where he found a good-natured colored lady hard at work stirring batter in anticipation of some table luxury for a coming meal. With admirable presence of mind the mate picked up an apron, tied it around him and telling "mammy" to take a few minutes' rest as she was evidently overtired, he seized her wooden spoon and went on stirring the batter as though he had never done anything else in his life.

In the meantime every other member of the party had been caught and taken to the little frame building which answered the purpose of jail and police-court combined. Various conjectures were exchanged as to the fate of the mate, whose ignorance of the events incidental to gambling raids was expected to prove very inconvenient to him in a variety of ways. All anxiety on this score was, however, thrown away. The old man acted his part so well that when the raiders saw him laboriously at work with the wooden spoon they concluded that he was a member of the establishment. In consequence of this they let him alone, and when the raid was over he replaced his hat and coat, with the indifference and nonchalance of an experienced actor, and went quietly back to the boat.

Here he informed friends of the incarcerated individuals of the fix they were in, and advised them to go to their release, preferring himself to keep as far as possible from the representatives of the law. Liberty was obtained by the payment of considerable sums in the way of fines and costs, and although the event took place some years ago, the way in which the inexperienced gambler escaped, while his more hardened and experienced friends were caught, is still a constant source of merriment among officers and passengers.

It was while enjoying a delightful and distinctly sensational trip on the Columbia River that the passengers were enlightened as to a comparatively old trick, which was executed with the utmost promptness and despatch by a young second mate. This young man was never known to have any money. Generous in the extreme, and heartily full of fun, he managed to get rid of his salary as promptly as it was paid him, and his impecuniosity was a standing joke among members of the crew and regular passengers. On one occasion the boat met with an accident, and was tied up at a small town for four or five days. The hero of the story, with a number of other light-hearted individuals, naturally went ashore on pleasure bent. They had what is generally called a good time, but what little funds they had when they started were soon exhausted.

Two or three councils of war were held as to how a supply of liquid refreshments, of a character not included in the temperance man's bill of fare, could be obtained. Finally, the second mate undertook to secure the needful without the expenditure of any money. He borrowed a heavy overcoat belonging to one of the party, and then hunted up two large wine bottles. One of these he filled with water and securely corked. The other he took empty, and with these in his pockets entered the saloon. Producing the empty bottle he asked the bar-keeper how much he would charge for filling it, and on hearing the amount told him to go ahead.

As soon as the bottle was filled and returned to the second mate, he slipped it in his pocket, and in a very matter-of-fact manner began to make arrangments for the liquidation of the debt, at a convenient period. The saloon-man naturally resented any discussion of this character, and told his customer to either pay for the liquor or return it right away. Assuming an air of injured innocence, our friend took out the bottle of water, handed it to the bar-keeper and said he "guessed he'd have to take it back." The unsuspecting purveyor of liquor that both cheers and inebriates, grumbled considerably, emptied the bottle of water into the demijohn of whisky, handed back the bottle to the apparently disconsolate seeker after credit, and told him to "get out."

Naturally, no second order was necessary. Five minutes later, the entire party could have been seen sharing the contents of the bottle which had not been emptied, but which they lost no time in emptying. The trick answered its purpose admirably. When, about two weeks later, the man who had played it was again in the town, he called at the saloon to pay for the whisky. He was treated very kindly, but hints were freely given as to the necessity of a keeper accompanying him on his travels. In other words, the bar-keeper declined distinctly to believe that he had been hoodwinked as stated. This feature of the joke was, in the opinion of its perpetrators, the most amusing feature of all, and it need hardly be said that very little effort was made to disabuse the unbelieving but somewhat over-credulous bar-keeper.

The Columbia River is one of the most interesting and remarkable on the continent. Rising, as it does, quite near the source of the Missouri River, it runs, by a very circuitous route, to the Pacific Ocean, being in places very narrow, and in others abnormally wide. The Dalles of the Columbia are known the world over. They are situated some sixty or seventy miles west of the city of Portland, and are within easy distance of the American Mount Blanc. They extend from Dalles Station, a small town on the Union Pacific Railroad, to Celilo, another station about fifteen miles farther east. Between these two points the bed of the Columbia is greatly reduced in width, and its boundaries are two huge walls of rock, which rise almost perpendicularly from the water level. The width of the chasm, through which the water rushes wildly, varies considerably, but at no point in the western section does it exceed 130 feet, although on either side of the Dalles the width of the river itself ranged from about 2,000 to much more than 2,500 feet.

As the volume of water is enormous at this point, especially after rain and much melting of snow, there is often a rise of fifty feet in a few hours in the narrow channel of the Dalles. Sometimes the rise exceeds seventy feet, and an effect most extraordinary in character results. From many points along the river banks, Mount Hood can be seen towering away up into the clouds. The bluffs themselves are marvels of formation, very difficult to explain or account for. When the water is low, there is an exposure of almost vertical cliffs. The bluffs vary in height to a remarkable extent, and the lower the water, the more grotesque the appearance of the figures along them. When the water is very low, there is a cascade, or waterfall, every few feet, presenting an appearance of continuous uproar and froth, very attractive to the sightseer, but very objectionable from the standpoint of navigation.

When the water is high, these cascades are lost sight of, and the rocks which form them are covered with one raging torrent, which seems inclined to dash everything to one side in its headlong course towards the Pacific Ocean. Logging is a most important use to which the Columbia River is put, and when immense masses of timber come thundering down the Dalles, at a speed sometimes as great as fifty miles an hour, all preconceived notions of order and safety are set at naught. There is one timber shoot, more than 3,000 feet long, down which the logs rush so rapidly that scarcely twenty seconds is occupied in the entire trip. The Dalles generally may be described as a marvelous trough, and the name is a French word, which well signifies this feature.

Farther down the river, and near the city of Portland, there are some very delightful falls, not exceptionally large or high, but very delightful in character, and full of contradictions and peculiarities. Steamboating on the Columbia River, in its navigable sections, is exceedingly pleasant and instructive. The river is the largest in America which empties into the Pacific Ocean. For more than 140 miles it is navigable by steamers of the largest kind, while other vessels can get up very much higher, and nearer the picturesque source. On some sections of it, glaciers of great magnitude can be seen, and there are also many points concerning which legend and tradition have been very busy. According to one of these traditions, the Indians who formerly lived on the banks of the river were as brave as the ancient Spartans and Greeks, though if this is approximately correct, the law and argument of descent must be entirely erroneous, for the Indians of this section to-day rank among the meanest and most objectionable of the entire country.

An artistic illustration is given of the "whaleback" steamer, used principally on our Northern lakes. The whaleback varies from a somewhat clumsy looking craft, resembling in appearance very much the back of a whale, to the much more attractive and navigable craft shown in the illustration. These whalebacks have a very important part to play in internal navigation. It seems able to withstand, readily, bad weather and rough water. Unlike most vessels which are safe under these conditions, it requires very little water to be safely navigated, and it can carry heavy loads in six or eight feet of water.

The revival of the steamboat trade on our great rivers, and the recovering from the railroads of at least a portion of the trade stolen away, is a pet hobby among river men generally, and especially among those whose parents taught them from the cradle up the true importance of the magnificent internal waterways bountifully provided for **our native land by** an all-wise Providence. It is **seriously** proposed to attempt this revival **by** aid of whaleback steamers, and **if the** project is carried out, the success which will attend the effort is likely to agreeably surprise even the most enthusiastic among those who are now advocating it.

CHAPTER XX.

THROUGH THE GREAT NORTHWEST.

The Importance of Some of our Newest States—Romantic History of Montana—The Bad Lands and their Exact Opposite—Civilization Away Up in the Mountains—Indians who have Never Quarreled with White Men—Traditions Concerning Mount Tacoma—Wonderful Towns of the Extreme Northwest—A State Shaped like a Large Chair—The Falls of Shoshone.

WITHIN the last few years new States have been admitted into the Union which, in themselves, form a magnificent empire. We allude to the great Northwestern Territories which have become States within the last decade, and which have added so much luster to the escutcheon of our native land. The utmost ignorance prevails as to these States, and as to the northwestern corner of the United States proper, a term generally applied to this great Republic, with the exception of Alaska.

Every now and again the report comes of a great forest fire in the Northwest, and occasionally the world is horrified by reports of a terrible calamity of this character, involving great loss of life and property. Owing to this fact there is a tendency to look on the northwestern tier of States as one huge forest, ever offering a temptation to that terrible destructive agency—fire. People who profess to have made tours through the country, add to the complication by enlarging on this one characteristic, and omitting all reference to the other features, in which the great Northwest towers head and shoulders above competitors, and teaches the entire world a lesson in productiveness, fertility, and, we may add, industry.

The World's Fair served to very largely disabuse the public mind concerning what is destined to become one of the wealthiest sections of the United States. The elegant State buildings that were erected on the shores of Lake Michigan, and the gorgeous displays of fruits, grain, ore, and different products, must have convinced the average visitor that there was a great deal more in the far West and Northwest than he had dreamt of. Many were induced in consequence of the information they received, to blend their fortunes with the young States, and although the financial condition of the country has not been calculated to expedite the fulfillment of their Aladdin-like hopes, most of them have done well enough to be able to congratulate themselves on the change in the location and occupation.

We can only speak of some of the most remarkable features of this great section, greater, indeed, than several Old World nations combined. Helena is the capital of one of these new States, to which is given the euphonic name of Montana. The name is very appropriate, as it signifies "belonging to the mountains." The Indians had a very similar name for the territory now included in the State, and Judge Eddy called it the "Bonanza State" because of its mining sensations, a name which has clung to it with much fidelity ever since. The arms of the State are significant and almost allegorical. The present is linked with the past by means of a retreating buffalo, significant of the extermination of this interesting and valuable species. The great mining resources of Montana are shown by a miner's pick and shovel, and in the rearground the sun is setting behind eminences of the Rocky Mountains. Montana was first discovered by Canadians, some two hundred years ago. The first permanent settlement was early in the present century, and, until within the last fifty years, all goods and utensils used in it were dragged up the Missouri River from St. Louis, a distance of nearly 2,000 miles. When the war broke out, the Territory was occupied almost entirely by Indians, with a few daring fur traders and a number of missionaries, who, in exercise of their duty, had no fear at all. The discovery of gold which took place almost simultaneously with the firing of the first shot in the conflict between the North and the South, brought thousands of adventurers from all parts of the Union and introduced millions of capital. Some of the mines turned out phenomenally successful, and although there were the usual heart-burnings on account of failures, the average of success was very great. The State's gold mines have yielded fabulous sums, and more recently steps have been taken to extract from the quartz and rock a full measure of wealth that is to be found there.

Montana is a Northwestern State in fact as well as name. It is situated on the high plateau between the Continental Divide and the Bitter Root Range. Fully one-fifth of its area lies beyond the Rocky Mountains, and its northern boundary is the snow-covered region of Canada and British Columbia. The eastern portion of the State, bordering upon the Dakotas, is for the most part prairie land, rising rapidly in the direction of the west, and forming the approach to the mighty Rockies. The western portion, bordering upon Idaho, is much more mountainous in character. Some 50,000 square miles of hilly country are to be seen here, many of the peaks rising to heights exceeding 10,000 feet. The State alone is larger in area than the entire British Islands, and it is infinitely larger than the whole of New England. That it is a country of magnificent distances, is shown from the fact that the northern frontier equals in length the distance between the great seat of learning and culture in Massachusetts and the capital city of the short-lived Confederacy.

Although most of Montana is rich in either agriculture or mineral, a considerable area is occupied by the notorious Bad Lands. General Sully described these lands very accurately, or at least aptly, when he said that they reminded him of "the other place with the fires out." So many descriptions of the Bad Lands have been given, that we need scarcely refer to them at great length. The clay, rock and peculiar dust which lies all around this territory becomes, on the slightest provocation, the nastiest kind of quicksand. Nothing can thrive or prosper in the Bad Lands which, however, are full of evidences of prehistoric life and which, perhaps, at one time were the scenes of activity and even prosperity.

In exact contrast to the Bad Lands is the Gallatin Valley, about four hundred square miles in extent. It is stated to be one of the most fertile spots in the world, and by common consent it has been called the Egypt of Montana. A portion of it has been cultivated, and its yield per acre has been found to be prodigious. At no great distance from this fertile spot, two of America's most remarkable rivers have their rise. The greatest of these is the Missouri, which, measured from its source to final entrance into the Gulf of Mexico along the bed of the Mississippi River, is really the longest river in the world. Away up here in the mountains, the Missouri, which subsequently becomes one of the most treacherous and destructive rivers in the universe, runs through picturesque cañons and over great gorges of rock, finally leaving the State a great river, though still insignificant in comparison with the volume it is to assume, and the drainage work it is to accomplish farther away from the mighty hills among which it had its source.

The Northern Pacific Railroad runs through this wonderful State, with so great a future before it. Helena, the capital city of Montana, was originally a mining camp, and early prophecies were that it would not outlive the mining enthusiasm. These prophecies, however, have proved entirely mistaken. It is no longer a mere mining town, with rough, busy, uncultured men rushing hither and thither in the eager pursuit of their daily avocation. It is now not only the judicial capital of Montana, but it is also the great center of educational advance. It has a number of very handsome public buildings, and is the home of many men, who, having made their fortunes in the mines of the new Northwest, have been so impressed with the beauties of scenery and climate, that they have decided to abide where at first they merely intended to sojourn. Helena is more than 4,000 feet above the sea level, and its 20,000 inhabitants are reputed to be worth more than $100,-000,000. The apostle of socialism or communism who suggested an equal division among the 60,000,000 of our people of all the wealth of the nation, would find little encouragement in this great mountain city, where poverty, if not unknown, is very scarce.

Much more typical as a mining city is Butte. This is situated upon a hill quite peculiarly located, and is reached by a ride along the Silver Bow Valley. Close here is the wonderful Anaconda mine. The mines in the neighborhood have a reputation for immense yield, the annual extracts of gold, silver and copper being valued at more than $33,000,000. The Anaconda smelter, built some twelve years ago, is said to be the largest in the world, and the town itself seems to literally talk mining by its streets, its houses, its business, its habits and its people.

Missoula is the third largest city of Montana. Its site is a splendid one for a city. The Hell Gate Cañon and River merge into a magnificent plain, the foot of the noted Bitter Root Valley. The Hell Gate River breaks out from the cañon and mountains into the wide plain and sweeps majestically across the extreme northern limit of it, hugging closely the Mission Range to the north. At the western side of the valley the Bitter Root River combines with the Hell Gate, and together, and now under the name of the Missoula River, they flow westward between high mountains. The northern end of the valley is perhaps six miles or more wide. The great opening in the mountain is rather triangular in shape, with the apex of the triangle many miles up the valley to the south. Here is a city laid out and built up in perfect harmony with its location, as is evidenced by the tasteful manner in which the place is planned and the character of its business blocks and residences. Telephones, electric lights, and water supply are found even in the remote suburbs of Missoula.

The mountains literally hem them in. Immediately to the northeast is a bare hill that is startling in its resemblance to an animal. It is like a huge, recumbent elephant, the hind quarters of which form the northern end of Hell Gate Cañon, around which the railroad curves as it issues from the cañon. The "Mammoth Jumbo," as it is appropriately known, reclines with head to the north and trunk stretched out behind him. One eye is plainly seen, and one huge shoulder is visible. Down in the south, sharp, decisive, with a steep, rocky escarpment facing us, and a long ridge descending from it, is Lolo Peak, of the Bitter Root Range, a noted landmark. This overhangs Lolo Pass, through which Chief Joseph came in his famous retreat from General Howard in 1877, which terminated in the battle of the Bear Paw Mountains, October 5th, where the brave and able chieftain was captured with the rest of his tribe, when almost within reach of freedom just across the Canadian border.

At the southern extremity of the valley on the banks of the Bitter Root River, and with the range serving as an effective background, is Fort Missoula, a pleasantly located military post. Several interpretations of the meaning of the word "Missoula" are given. Father Guidi, a priest of long residence in the country, gave me what he considers the true one, which also indicates the manner in which the Hell Gate Cañon and River were christened. The spot where Missoula is located was once the scene of conflict between the various tribes of Indians. The "Flatheads" and "Blackfeet" were deadly enemies, and, presumably, may have fought over this lovely spot. At any rate, the ground just at the mouth of the Hell Gate Cañon was covered long ago with skulls and human bones.

These Flathead Indians are noted for the fact that they have never adopted a hostile attitude towards white people. They are advanced in civilization, as readers of Chapter IX and its accompanying illustration will have noted. Tradition states that their religion demands that the head of every infant must be flattened by means of a board before the bones harden sufficiently to assume a shape. However this may be, none of the surviving members of the tribe have particularly flat heads, and all deny emphatically the statement that nature is ever interfered with in the manner stated. These Indians call themselves "Selish," a name apparently without reason or derivation. The Flathead Reservation was formed about forty years ago. On three sides it is walled in by high mountains, and it consists of about 2,240 square miles of territory. The railway station, Arlee, is so named after the last war chief of the Flatheads. Passengers are often amused by the gaudily decked Indians who are seen at this station, which is quite near the reservation.

An interesting story attaches to the Jocko River and Reservation. It is stated that an Irishman named Jacob Finley established a ranch on the river early in the present century. The French Canadians who settled in the neighborhood and intermarried with the Indians, called Finley by his Christian name with a peculiar French pronunciation, which made it sound very like much Jaco or Jocko—the latter name gradually becoming generally adopted. It was quite natural to call the river and the valley after the ranch owner, and the name finally became generally accepted as correct. This man Finley left behind him a family of seventeen, and before he had been dead many years his direct descendants numbered within three or four of an even century.

The Indians called the stream the Nlka, an unpronounceable combination of letters, resulting from a most interesting though variously described event.

Mrs. Ronan, the well-known writer, tells an interesting story of how names are given by Indians. Thus, her own daughter's name was Isabel, but the Indians called her "Sunshine." In February, 1887, the little girl was born. For some days prior to her birth the weather had been gloomy in the extreme. Almost simultaneously with the child's birth the sun, so long hidden under the clouds, burst forth to gladden the heart of man. With one accord, the Indians declared that the little one had brought sunshine with her, and hence the name, which, as subsequent events have proved, was exceptionally appropriate.

Accompanying this chapter is an illustration of Mount Tacoma. This mountain is one of the most attractive, as well as lofty, in the Northwest. As can easily be supposed, traditions without number are connected with it. No greater mistake can be made than to imagine that the Indians who are found in this region are naturally atheistic, as well as ignorant. To the student of religion there is rather an inherent belief in the Supreme Being among these people, with very strong proofs of the truth of the divine revelation. One of the traditions, told with much fervor and earnestness about Tacoma, involves in it a Savior of mankind. With great reverence and awe the good listener among the band of tourists is told that at one period—legends are seldom very specific in the matter of time or space—a Savior arrived in a copper canoe, his mission being to save the Siwash Indians, who were spoken of as the chosen people of the Great Unseen. That some prophet or missionary certainly came to this region and preached appears to be evident from the very definite survival of the doctrines taught by him. His creed seems to have been a very apt blending of all that is best in the teachings of Buddha, with many of the precepts of the "Sermon on the Mount" added.

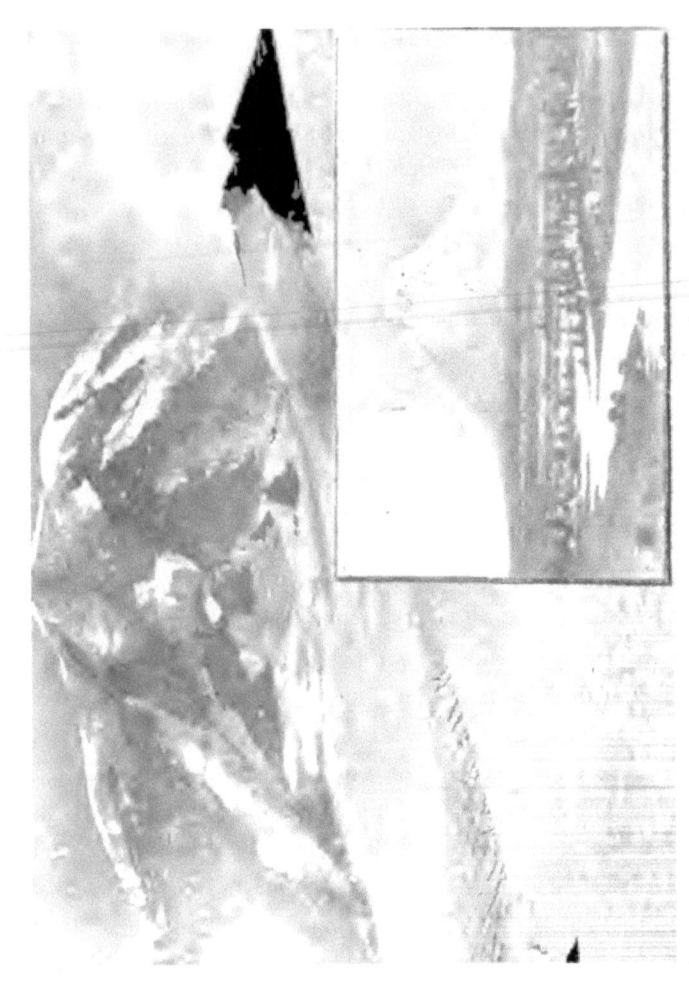

Love to mankind, the evil of revenge, and the glories of forgiveness form the principal features of the doctrine. The legend, or tradition, goes on to say that so violent was the opposition to this crusader, who attacked local institutions so bitterly, that finally he was seized and nailed to a tree. This act of crucifixion resulted from a final sermon, in which the wanton destruction of human beings was denounced in terms of great vehemence. As nine, instead of seven or three, is the general number talked of in this section, it is not surprising that the story should go on to state that after nine days the "Mysterious One" was reanimated, and once more commenced his work of reformation and tuition.

Nothing in connection with the story can be objected to. By some it is supposed to be the result of casual immigration from the regions of Palestine, to which also is attributed the story of the flood.

Among nearly all the Indians of the Northwest there is a flood story, or legend, and there must be hundreds of Noahs in the minds of the story-tellers. We are told, for example, that when the Great Spirit flooded the entire earth, there was not quite enough water to cover the summit of Mount Tacoma. The man chosen to prevent the human race from being entirely obliterated was warned in a dream, or by some other means, to climb to the summit of this great mountain, where he remained until the wicked ones below him were annihilated, without a man, woman or child escaping. After the flood was over and the waters began to recede, the Great Spirit hypnotized or mesmerized this solitary human being, and created for him a wife of exceptional beauty. Together these two recommenced the battle of life, and, as the legend runs, every human being in existence can trace his lineage to them.

The mountain is surely worth all that has been said about it. Its great height has already been commented upon. Standing, as it does, with its summit 14,444 feet above the sea level, it is actually a sentinel for almost the entire State. Hazard Stevens, the first man to climb Tacoma, reported that it was so called by the Indians because the word means, in their vocabulary, "mountain," and was given to Tacoma because it was a veritable prince among hills. It was at one time called Rainier, after a British lord, but the Indian name has generally prevailed.

Tacoma has been described by many tourists as a rival to the most vaunted peaks of the Swiss Alps. As will be seen from the illustrations, which are remarkably good ones, there is a dim mistiness about the mountain. When the light is poor, there is a peculiar, almost unnatural, look about the cloud-topped peak. When the clouds are very white, the line of demarcation becomes faint in the extreme, and it is very hard to distinguish one from the other. Sometimes, for days together, the mountain is literally cloud-capped, and its peak hidden from view. Those who are fortunate enough to be able to appreciate the awful and unique in history, never tire of gazing upon Tacoma. They are glad to inspect it from every side. Some call it a whited sepulchre. There was a time when it was anything but the calm, peaceful eminence of to-day. Every indication points to the fact that it was once among the most active volcanoes in existence.

There is a town, or rather city, of the same name as the mountain. This is situated on Commencement Bay. It is under the very shadow of the great mountain of which we have spoken, and which seems to guard it against foes from inland. Fifteen years ago it was a mere village, of scarcely any importance. It has rapidly grown into a town of great importance. In 1873 the Northern Pacific Railroad Company decided to make it the western terminus of their important system. This resulted in renewed life, or rather in a genuine birth to the place, which now has a population of 40,000 people, and is an exceedingly wealthy and prosperous city. The Tacoma Land Company, ably seconded by the railroad, has fostered enterprise in this place in the most hearty manner, and now some of the large buildings of the town, of the very existence of which many Eastern people affected ignorance, are more than magnificent—they are majestic.

Seattle is another and even more brilliant diamond in Washington's crown. It is a great city, with a magnificent harbor, its name being that of a powerful Indian chief who, when the town was founded forty years ago, had things practically his own way. It grew in importance very rapidly, but in 1889 one of the largest fires of modern times destroyed $10,000,000 worth of property, including the best blocks and commercial structures of the city. People who had never seen Seattle at once assumed that the city was dead, and speculation was rife as to what place would secure its magnificent trade. Those who thus talked were entirely ignorant as to the nature of the men who had made Seattle what it was. Within a very few days the work of reconstruction commenced. The fire hampered the city somewhat, and checked its progress. But Seattle is better for the disaster, and stands to-day a monument to the "nil desperandum" policy of its leaders.

Spokane Falls is another wonderful instance of Northwestern push and energy. It is a very young city, the earliest records of its founding not going back farther than 1878. When the census of 1880 was taken, the place was of no importance, and received very little attention at the hands of the enumerators. In 1890 it had a population of some 20,000, and attracted the admiration of the entire country by the progress it had made in the matter of electricity. Its water power is tremendous, and taking full advantage of this, electricity is produced at low cost and used for every available and possible purpose.

The State of Washington, in which these three cities are situated, borders upon the Pacific Ocean, and is one of the greatest of our new States. The first modern explorer of the territory was a Spaniard, followed a few years later by English sailors. Just at the end of the last century, some Boston capitalists, for there were capitalists even in those days, although they reckoned their wealth by thousands rather than millions, sent two ships to this section to trade with the Indians for furs. One of these ships was the "Columbia," which gave the name to the region, part of which still retains it, although the section we are now discussing now owns and boasts of the name of the "Father" of his and our country.

Washington became a State five years ago. It is a great mining country, but is still more noted for its wonderful lumber resources. The trade from Puget Sound is tremendous. One company alone employs 1,250 men in saw mills and logging, and it is responsible for having introduced improved machinery of every type into the section. The early history of the great lumber business is full of interest, and this is one point alone in which the advance has been tremendous. Another great company cut up 63,000,000 feet of lumber in one year, and shipped more than half of it out of the country. White cedar of the most costly grade is very common in Washington, and it is used for the manufacture of shingles, which sell for very high prices, and are regarded as unusually and, indeed, abnormally good. White pine of immense quantity and size is also found. Some of the logs are so large that they are only excelled by the phenomenal big trees of abnormal growth which are found some hundreds of miles farther south on the great Pacific Slope.

Idaho is another of the great States of the great Northwest. It lies largely between the two States just described so briefly, and its shape is so peculiar that it has been spoken of as resembling a chair, with the Rocky Mountains and the Bitter Root Range as its front seat and back. Another simile likens it to a right-angled triangle, with the Bitter Root Range as its base. It is a vast table-land, wedge shape in character, and may be said to consist of a mass of mountain ranges packed up fold upon fold, one on top of the other.

Three names were submitted to Congress when the Territory was first named. They were Shoshone, Montana and Idaho. The last name was chosen, finally, because it is supposed to mean "The sight on the mountain." The more exact derivation of the name seems to be an old Shoshone legend, involving the fall of some mysterious object from the heavens upon one of the mountains. The scenery in this State is varied in everything save in beauty, which is almost monotonous. Bear Lake, one of its great attractions, is a fisherman's paradise. Its waters extend twenty miles in one direction and eight or nine miles in the other. This vast expanse of water is one of the best trout fishing resorts in the world. Although in a valley, Bear Lake is so high up in the mountains that its waters are frozen up for many months in the year, the ice seldom breaking up until well into April. At all times the water is cold, and hence especially favorable for trout culture. Lake Pen d'Oreilles is about thirty miles long and varies in width from an insignificant three miles to more than fifteen. It is studded with islands of great beauty and much verdure. Close by it is the Granite Mountain, with other hills and peaks averaging, perhaps, 10,000 feet in height. The lake has an immense shore line, extending as much as 250 miles. For fully a tenth of this distance the Northern Pacific tracks are close to the lake, affording passengers a very delightful view of this inland scene, which has been likened to the world-renowned Bavarian lake, Königs See.

The State is also well known on account of the reputation for weird grandeur won by the Snake River, also known as the Shoshone. This is a very rapid stream of water. By means of its winding course it measures fully a thousand miles in Idaho alone, and drains about two-thirds of the State. Near the headwaters of the Snake River, in the proximity of Yellowstone Park, there are very fertile bottoms, with long stretches of valley lands. The American Falls plunge over a mass of lava about forty feet high, with a railroad bridge so close that the roar of the water drowns the noise of the locomotive. For seventy miles the Shoshone River runs through a deep, gloomy cañon, with a mass of cascades and many volcanic islands intervening. Then comes the great Shoshone Falls themselves, rivaling in many respects Niagara, and having at times even a greater volume of water. The falls are nearly a thousand feet in width, and the descent exceeds two hundred feet. Many writers have claimed that these falls have features of beauty not equaled in any part of the world. According to one description, they resemble a cataract of snow, with an avalanche of jewels amidst solid portals of lava.

Bancroft, in summing up the great features of this State, says very concisely that: "It was the common judgment of the first explorers that there was more of the strange and awful in the scenery and topography of Idaho than of the pleasing and attractive. A more intimate acquaintance with the less conspicuous features of the country revealed many beauties. The climate of the valleys was found to be far milder than, from their elevation, could have been expected. Picturesque lakes were discovered among the mountains, furnishing in some instances navigable waters. Fish and game abound. Fine forests of pine and firs cover the mountain slopes, except in the lava region; and nature, even in this phenomenal part of her domain, has not forgotten to prepare the earth for the occupation of man, nor neglected to give him a wondrously warm and fertile soil to compensate for the labor of subduing the savagery of her apparently waste places."

CHAPTER XXI.

IN THE WARM SOUTHEAST.

Florida and its Appropriate Name—The First Portions of North America Discovered by White Men—Early Vicissitudes of its Explorers—An Enormous Coast Line—How Key West came to be a great Cigar Town—The Suwanee River—St. Augustine and its World-Renowned Hotel—Old Fort Marion.

FLORIDA is the name given to one of the least known States in the Union. Ponce de Leon was the godfather of this southeastern corner of our native land. Its baptism took place in a remote period. The day of the event was Easter Sunday, which in the Spanish language is called Pascua Floria, which is literally interpreted "The Flowery Festival." Almost by accident, therefore, Florida received a name which is singularly appropriate and well chosen. From end to end, in either direction, there is a profusion of semi-tropical beauty and of flowers, some of them entirely peculiar to the immediate vicinity. There is an abundance of fruit as well, and frequently the blossoms on the fruit trees make a lovely flower show in themselves.

The State arms are very peculiar and appropriate. The main figure is that of an Indian lying upon a bank, scattering flowers around him. In the distance the sun is setting amid beautiful hills. In the center there is a river with a steamboat upon it, and with a large cocoanut tree growing by the side. The State's motto is one which has been adopted by many communities, but which is ever welcome for the purpose—"In God We Trust."

A Tropical Scene.

In regard to its climate, Florida can offer a great deal of variety. Consumptives by the tens of thousand have sought a renewed lease of life in the warmest sections of the State, and many have come back greatly benefited. The winters are of the Indian summer order, being singularly dry, healthy and free from dust. The Gulf Stream adds from five to ten degrees to the temperature in cold weather, and in the southern section the temperature rarely gets below freezing point. The exceptionally cold spell of 1894-95 may be quoted as quite an exception to the general rule, and the heavy loss to growing fruits was as great a surprise as it was a loss.

Florida has the honor of being the first portion of North America to be discovered by white people. Ponce de Leon, whose very name is suggestive of romance and poetry, explored a section of the country in the year 1513, when he proclaimed the sovereignty of Spain over it. In 1527, a Spanish company of soldiers attempted to drive out the native inhabitants. The attempt failed, but another one some fourteen years later was more successful. Spain was not given a clear title to the peninsula without protest. French Huguenots built Fort Caroline on St. John's River at about the middle of the century. Shortly after this enterprise, a Spanish fleet surprised and annihilated the pioneers, upon whose graves they placed the inscription, "Not as Frenchmen, but as Lutherans." This brutal attempt to give a religious aspect to the murder was resented very soon after. A French expedition captured the fort, hung the garrison one after the other, announcing that they did so, and hanged the ruffians "Not as Spaniards, but as traitors, thieves and murderers."

West Florida was settled at the close of the Seventeenth

Century, and in 1763 the territory now included in the State was ceded to Great Britain in return for Cuba. Colonization followed, and a very large number of British Tories settled in the country. In 1814, the United States seized portions of the country, and four years later it became evident that European rule must cease in it. When in 1821 Spain ceded this territory to the United States, the number of white inhabitants was barely 600, although there were fully 4,000 Seminoles residing in it.

The Seminole War commenced in 1835, and continued for seven years. The war cost some $20,000,000, and over 1,500 American soldiers lost their lives during the campaign. Over 30,000 troops were engaged in the conflict, and the Indians by taking advantage of their knowledge of the country, held out against superior force for an extraordinary length of time. Gradually the savages were driven south, and at last the Seminoles were overpowered. Those who survived were for the most part sent west of the Mississippi River. A few are still found, however, on a reservation some fifteen miles from Fort Pierce on Indian River.

When the Southern States seceded, Florida went with them. In 1864, General Seymour led 7,000 troops nearly as far as Lake City. Jacksonville remained under Federal control, but the State fortunately escaped being made a battle-ground to any extent between the opposing forces.

Florida has a very interesting geological record. It was evidently founded on coral reefs, and the formations are so recent that few minerals are found. Phosphate rock is one of the most remarkable natural productions of the State, and the actual value of this has not yet been thoroughly ascertained. The State itself is naturally divided into two sections, the East and the West. East Florida includes a long peninsula, and extends westward to the Suwanee River, concerning which the negro melodist delights to sing. Western Florida is more inland in character. The measurements of the State are peculiar. Thus it is 700 miles from the Perdido River to Cape Sable. From the Atlantic to the extreme west the distance is about 400 miles, and from north to south the distance is slightly greater. The peninsula itself averages rather less than 100 miles in width throughout. Florida naturally possesses an enormous coast line. Of this nearly 500 miles is on the Atlantic seaboard, with some 700 miles on the Gulf of Mexico. Harbors abound on every side, and when Florida becomes a manufacturing State as well as a fruit-growing one, its resources for exporting will be an immense advantage to it in overcoming competition and opposition.

This coast line makes sea fishing one of the most profitable occupations in the State. About 10,000 men are kept constantly employed in this work. Some of the fish found here are choice and costly delicacies, and include red snapper, pompano, Spanish mackerel and sea trout. Of turtle there is an abundance, and tarpon fishing provides amusement to those who are more strictly sportsmanlike in disposition. Fishing for sponges is also a fairly remunerative occupation, which always excites much interest when watched by visitors from other States. Key West alone sends away sponges worth $500,000 every year, two great capitals of Europe being the best customers.

Key West is, however, better noted for its cigars. It is situated on what was originally called Bone Reef by the

Spaniards, on account of great quantities of human bones being found on it by the early explorers. Eighty years ago, a number of New England fishermen located at Key West, which is about sixty miles from Florida proper and about ninety miles from Havana. The great revolution in the nature of the town's business and habits was brought about by the settlement in it, less than a quarter century ago, of a large band of Cuban exiles. These brought with them the secrets of the manufacture of cigars of the highest grade. They at once set about establishing factories as large as their means allowed, and the business has grown so rapidly that there are now facilities for manufacturing nearly 150,000,000 cigars every year. To the man who appreciates the difference between good and bad cigars it is hardly necessary to say that in quality, as well as quantity, the product of this Spanish-American island has progressed.

The harbor of Key West is the ninth port of entry in the country. It is so naturally impregnable that it escaped capture during the Civil War, when the Gulf Coast ports were a special source of attack and envy. Legend and history twine around the harbor stories of thrilling interest, many of which have formed the plots for successful and celebrated novels. The town has peculiar but attractive streets, with tropical trees on both sides. Seven miles distant is Key West, the most extreme southern point of United States territory. From the immense light-house pier the distance to the island of Cuba is less than eighteen miles.

Returning to the inland, we may spend a few minutes

> 'Way down 'pon de Suwanee Ribber,
> Far, far away—
> Dare's wha' my heart is turnin' ebber—
> Dare's wha' de ole folks stay.

This river, as we have seen, forms the western boundary of Eastern Florida. It is a very romantic stream, running through a country of surpassing beauty, with tropical trees and undergrowth coming right to the water's edge. It enters Florida from Southern Georgia, and runs through a country which varies from forest to plain and from upland to valley. Along its banks there are a number of little Southern homes, few of them boasting of the magnificence of which we often read, but all of them peaceful and attractive. Of one of these we give an illustration. At first glance they may not appear to be anything very remarkable about the little house and its surroundings, but on second thoughts and glances something more than poetical will be discovered. The old negro ballad from which we have quoted above gives in its lines a charming idea of the river and of the memories and thoughts which cling to it. Excursion parties are very frequent along the river. Some indulge in hunting, and take advantage of the profusion of game on every hand. Others prefer to indulge in peaceful reverie and to think only of the quaint old folks, who, as we are told in the song, still stay in the vicinity.

The Ocklawaha River resembles the Suwanee in many respects. Steamboats run along it for a considerable distance, and there is seldom difficulty in securing passengers. It is said that there are more alligators to a hundred square feet of water, in sections of this river, than can be found in any other water in the world. From the deck of a passenger steamer it is quite interesting to watch the peculiar proceedings of these dangerous creatures, and many conjectures are exchanged as to what would happen in the event of any one of the watchers falling overboard. On the banks of the river, cedar groves are frequently seen. Florida supplies the world with the wood required for lead pencils, and the inroads made into her cedar forests for this purpose threaten to eventually rob the State of one of its most unique features. Cypress, a wood which is just beginning to be appreciated at its true worth, is also abundant in this vicinity, and many of the much talked-of cypress swamps are passed. Pineapples are also seen growing vigorously, and also the vanilla plant, which resembles tobacco in its leaf. Vanilla leaf is gathered very largely, and sold for some purpose not very clearly defined or explained.

The banyan tree has to be seen to be understood. It is really an exclusive product of Florida and is found in the Key West country, where sea island cotton will grow all the year around, indifferent to changes of season. The banyan is almost a colony of trees in itself, having, apparently, a dozen trunks in one. All the upper boughs are more or less united, and the old proverb of "In union there is strength," seems to have in it a unique illustration and confirmation.

Lake Worth is one of the prettiest lakes in the South. It is a very beautiful sheet of water, broken only by Pitts' Island, which is located near its northern end. The most useful and desirable products of the North have here a congenial home, alongside those most loved in the region of the equator. A New Englander may find his potatoes, sweet corn, tomatoes and other garden favorites, and can pluck, with scarcely a change in his position, products that are usually claimed as Brazilian. He finds in his surroundings, as plentiful and as free as the water sprinkling before him, such strange neighbors as coffee, the tamarind.

mango, pawpa, guava, banana, sapadillo, almond, custard apple, maumee apple, grape fruit, shaddock, Avadaco pear, and other equally new acquaintances.

And these are all neighbors, actual residents, natives of the soil, not imported immigrants or exacting visitors to be tenderly treated. Giant relatives, equally at home, are the rubber tree, mahogany, eucalyptus, cork tree and mimosa. All these, within forty hours' travel of New York, to be reached in winter by an all-rail trip, and to be enjoyed in a climate that is a perpetual May. It was but a few years ago (less than a dozen) that the beauties of Lake Worth were at first dimly reported by venturesome sportsmen, who had gazed upon its unspeakable loveliness.

To-day the taste and labor of wealthy capitalists from East and from West, have lined its fair shores with elegant homes. One of these, the McCormick Place, has for the past two years been famous for its wondrous beauty. It is situated at Palm Beach, on the eastern shore of the lake, and faces westward or inland. It thus receives the cool air from the lake and the breezes from the Atlantic, which is but a stroll distant. The entire estate comprises 100 acres, all under high cultivation. It has a water front on both lake and ocean of 1,200 feet. In this lovely spot Mr. McCormick built a castle, so handsomely finished, inside and out, so tastefully designed and so elegantly furnished, that one would imagine he expected to entertain royalty within its walls.

It is said that nowhere on the continent is so great a variety of vegetable growth presented in one locality, as is here to be seen in the full perfection of lusty growth. The cacti at this point are marvels of variety and beauty. One's idea of what a cactus is can never be complete until one has witnessed a scene such as this, and a collection of this magnitude. The fruit trees form a mass of groves. In some of these, huge cocoanuts tower away above all other growth, while alongside of these monarchs of arbory culture there are groves of dwarf trees, less tremendous but quite as interesting.

This region has been described as a mental quicksand. There is something in the atmosphere which makes the most industrious man contentedly idle. Here the nervous, irritable, fussy individual, who for years has never known what rest meant, and who has fidgeted when he could not work, finds himself relaxing, against his will, into a condition of what a celebrated statesman described as "innocuous desuetude." The balminess of the air, which is at once warm and invigorating and bracing, without being severe, brings about a natural feeling of rest. The fascination which this creates soon becomes overpowering. The longer the visitor remains the more completely and hopelessly does he give away to his feelings, until at last he only tears himself away by a painful effort.

Biscayne Bay stands at the terminus of the peninsula of Florida, and at the extreme southeastern end of the United States. The visitor who stands here is on what is frequently called the great projecting toe of the Union. South of him there are a number of islands, but of the main land there is no more. The bay is almost a lake. It sets well into the coast, but is not quite enclosed by land. It is between five and ten miles wide and is forty miles long. A score of little inlets feed it from the ocean. The water is blue and clear and of no great depth, making the lake one of the finest cruising places in the world. All along the shores there are picturesque little settle-

A Restful Southern Home.

ments, all of them distinctly Southern in their appearance, and concerning each of which the traveler can hear legend without number.

St. Augustine is perhaps the most talked-about city in Florida. It is a quaint old Spanish city with a great history. The evidences of the past seem to be disappearing rapidly, the retreat being forced by the introduction of modern ideas and immense sums of modern capital. Memorial Church is one of the features of the town, and behind it the traveler sees, as he approaches, turrets and towers of every shape and size. The pavements are almost uniformly good, and as one is driven along the streets for the first time, every turning seems to bring to light some new wonder and some unexpected beauty. Hedges formed of oleanders, arbor vitæ, larches and cedars, to say nothing of masses of roses of all kinds, upset all his preconceived notions of tree, shrub and flower growth, and convince him that he has come to a land flowing indeed with milk and honey, where winters are practically unknown.

The Hotel Ponce de Leon is naturally the great object of his search, and if his purse affords it the tourist certainly stops here, if only for the sake of saying that he has slept, for one night at least, in this extraordinary and marvelously magnificent hostelry. If the Ponce de Leon were in New York, Philadelphia, St. Louis or Chicago, it would excite murmurs of admiration on every hand. But its existence would not be regarded as something extraordinary, as it certainly is in a town of the size of St. Augustine. The enterprise which led to its construction has been commented on again and again, and the liberal methods of management have also been the subject of much comment. As the carriage passes through the arched gateway into the enclosed court, blooming all the year round with fragrance and beauty, the tourist begins to apologize mentally for the skepticism in which he has indulged, concerning this wonder of the age. After mounting several successive terraces of broad stone steps, he finds himself at last before the magnificent front of the great hotel. Before him there is the grand doorway, surmounted by the oft-described arch of Spanish shields in terra cotta. All around there are broad galleries and wide windows, with very costly, artistic cappings. The galleries are supported by massive but neat pillars, and the shaded nooks and quiet corners are full of romantic influence.

Everything is reminiscent of old Spain, although the magnificence and architecture is often that of the extreme East. There are five elegantly decorated salons, in which there are tables of costly onyx, and on whose walls there are paintings of great splendor. On the ceiling above him exquisite frescoes tell the story of the old cavalier after whom the hotel is named, and of his patient and faithful search for the fabled fountain of youth which no one has yet found. At dinner the visitor is almost appalled by the magnificence of the service, and his appetite is apt to be injured by his reflections as to the cost of the silver and porcelain set before him. Sometimes as many as a thousand guests sit down together, and the service seems to be perfect for an unlimited number of visitors.

This great hotel was erected like the great temple described in scripture, practically without hammer or nails. Being molded from concrete, it is practically proof against weather and time, and it is fireproof in a sense of the term

An Afternoon in June.

far more literal than that generally adopted in large cities. There is no sham work, from basement to tower. Italian marble, terra cotta and Mexican onyx are the principal materials used, and nothing "equally as good" is tolerated.

The view from St. Augustine can hardly be excelled in any part of the world. The old city gates remind the tourist of Spanish stories and Oriental fables. Not far distant he sees Fort Marion, described as the oldest fortification in the United States. It was built by one of the Spanish Kings at great expense, and, according to the opinion of experts, is likely to survive many generations to come. It is constructed of cocquina cement, found only in Florida, and which seems to be everlasting in character.

Fort Marion has been the scene in years gone by of countless events of thrilling interest, and the student of history, who sees it for the first time, delights to conjure up reminiscences concerning it. In the old Indian war days there were several massacres at this point, in which the Indians occasionally outdid themselves in deeds of blood. About twenty years ago, the old fort was turned into an Indian prison, and to it were taken some of the worst and apparently most irreclaimable members of Indian tribes. This included Mochi, the Indian squaw who seemed to regard murder as a high art and a great virtue, "Rising Bull," "Medicine Water," "Big Mocassin" and other red ruffians who had proved themselves beyond all hope of reformation. The watch-tower of the fort stands high above surrounding buildings, and is probably one of the oldest watch-towers and light-houses in the world.

The old sea-wall runs from the fort past the historical old slave-market and the plaza, where cool breezes can be obtained on the hottest days. There is the cathedral, the oldest place of worship in the country, if the local historians are to be believed, with its chime of bells which first called the faithful to worship more than 200 years ago. On the east the smooth waters of the attractive bay rivet the attention of every visitor who has in him a particle of poetry, or appreciation of the beautiful. Not far away is Anastasia Island. At the north of Mananzas Bay is the spot where Sir Francis Drake, one of England's first admirals, landed, and close by is the oft-described lighthouse, with its old Spanish predecessor just north of it.

Not far from St. Augustine is the Carmonna vineyard. Here there are seventy-five acres of land covered with grape vines. The second year these vines yielded two and a half tons of grapes per acre. The sea of leaves, responding to the gentle breeze which generally blows up, presents an appearance of green very restful to the eye, and opens up new ideas as to color and expanse. All around Moultrie there are acres and acres of white Niagara grapes, and in a few years Florida shipments of this fruit will be enormous.

www.ingramcontent.com/pod-product-compliance
Lightning Source LLC
Chambersburg PA
CBHW051742300426
44115CB00007B/672